The Other

A Restructuring of the Islamic Concept

The Other

A Restructuring of the Islamic Concept

by

Fathi Osman

CONTENTS

Acknowledgements

This book has been published under the care of *"Pharos Foundation"* in Los Angeles, California. Many thanks go to the Pharos Board: Dr. Abdelmageed Ahmed, Dr. Samy Adham, Mr. Sadik Alloo, Dr. Sami Hakim, and Mr. Tarek Sheikhi for their enthusiasm, efforts, and care about this project. Thanks to Ozman Trad for his wonderful, artistic cover design. The help that I usually receive in all my writings from my wife Dr. Aida Osman is really beyond any expression of gratitude, and can only be rewarded by the bountiful almightiness of God. No words can begin to capture Aida's heartfelt dedication to and tireless efforts for this project. My daughter, Dr. Ghada Osman's scholarship, painstaking accuracy, sincere devotion, deep understanding, and creativity in editing this book, were really invaluable. Last and not least, thanks to Ms. Rasha Dakhil for her great effort in turning this book initially from my disorganized, and in some cases unreadable, handwriting to the typed form, and to Mr. Riaz Ahmad Qureshi for his untiring and efficient effort in typing the second rendering of this manuscript. God's reward is the best for all who have helped in making this book available to the readers today.

INTRODUCTION

Why Such a Restructuring?

God has created humankind with a disposition towards *diversity*. Individuals and societies are distinct based on the given objective environmental circumstances of the time and place in which they live, their own subjective motivations, and the interaction between the two elements. Such diversity is obvious in terms of human beings' inborn qualities, and is naturally more strongly manifested in their acquired traits and characteristics. Humankind has been favored by God with *free human will* and *dynamic human intellect*, both of which stimulate and galvanize human diversity.

The Quran stresses the range of human beings' inborn qualities: "And among His wonders is the creation of the heavens and earth, and the diversity of your tongues and colors, and in this there are signs and messages for all who can appreciate and learn" (30:22), "and We have made you into nations and tribes so that you might come to know one another [and complement one another in each's distinctive qualities]" (49:13). As for acquired diversity, which is energized by the invaluable divine gifts of human free will and human intellect, the Quran clearly states: "And had your Lord so willed, He could surely have made all humankind one single community, but [He willed it otherwise, and so] they continue to hold divergent views – [all of them –] save those on whom your Lord has bestowed His grace [through His guidance about dealing methodically and ethically with the divergences]" (11:118-9), "And [know that] all humanity were once but one single community, and only later did they begin to hold divergent views. And had it not been for a [divine] decree that had already gone forth from your Lord [through letting each follow his(/her) free will and intellect], all their differences would have been settled [initially in their creation, or by God's judgment in this world's life]" (10:19), "And had We so willed, We could indeed have imposed Our guidance upon every human being, but [We have not willed it thus, since following one's free will and intellect establishes his(/her) accountability for judgment. . .]" (32:13).

However, such diversity should never give way to any group's claim of superiority, since human beings – with all their diversity – are equal in their human origin: "O human beings! We have created you *all* out of one male and one female" (49:13), "O human beings! Be conscious of your Lord, who has created you out of one living entity, and out of it has created its mate, and out of the two He has spread all over a multitude of men and women. . ." (4:1).

Religion has its inherited roots in the individual. But at the same time, the religious message continuously acquires and accumulates conception, interpretation, and implementation through varying circumstances in different times and places. The "*other's*" inherited or acquired situation has to be appreciated and tolerated through the Islamic perspective. Religious faith cannot mean exclusive and permanent rightness for a certain individual or group, and the opposite for all "*others*," since all human beings have free will and intellect, and no human is errorless, except those individuals who were entrusted by God to convey His message to people and were protected by Him against making any error in delivering that divine message. All humans without exception enjoy "the favors" that the Creator has bestowed on *"all" the children of Adam* (Quran 17:70), including "the spirit," the nature of which is only known by the Creator (17:85), but the existence of which

6

is common in all human beings (7:172-3). The believers are required to listen to whatever is said and follow the best of it (39:18), and they have been taught by the Prophet to search for wisdom and acquire it wherever it may be found [reported in al-Tirmidhi].

The very act of thinking and rethinking, and the variety of ways in thinking among different people and in different circumstances, all represent an essential characteristic of human nature. Such differences of approach are certainly reflected in the understanding and interpretation of the religious source. God's messages followed one another, all emphasizing the belief in the One God and the role of human accountability that will be judged and requited in the eternal life to come, but all, nonetheless, differing in their guidance for reforming human practices according to the given circumstances. A goal of the message of Jesus was "to confirm the truth of the Torah [which had been revealed] before and to make lawful unto you some of what [aforetime] was forbidden to you" (3:49).

As for Islam, God's final message according to the Quran (33:40), the potential in its laws for meeting the changing circumstances of human life has been secured from within its very sources. The Quran mainly indicates general principles of justice in human affairs, and their permanent relevance in any society is obvious. The relatively detailed rules in the Quran are mostly related to family affairs, and their formulation has also allowed different interpretations. Otherwise, we find Quranic verses pointing to general rules such as: "*God enjoins justice, and the doing of good, and generosity toward one's kinsfolk; and He forbids all that is shameful and all that runs counter to reason, as well as aggression*" (16:90), a verse urging the securing of all that is beneficial and restraining of all that is harmful and corruptive,

7

and considered by the distinguished jurist 'Izz al-Din ibn Abd al-Salam (d. 660H./1261) as the most comprehensive verse in the Quran [1].

Among such verses emphasizing general principles one reads: *"God wills that you shall have ease and does not will you to suffer hardship"* (2:185), *"God does not want to impose any hardship on you"* (5:6), *"God does not command any human being with more than what he[/she] is able to bear"* (2:286), *"and forget not [that you are to act with] grace towards one another"* (2:237), *"and if one is driven by necessity – neither coveting it nor exceeding his[/her] immediate need – no wrong-doing shall be upon him[/her]"* (2:173), *"and let not your own hands throw you into destruction"* (2:195), *"and neither scribe nor witness must suffer harm"* (2:282), *"and do not conceal what you have witnessed"* (2:283), *"Do not devour one another's possessions wrongfully..., and do not destroy one another"* (4:29), *"keep up your bonds"* (5:1) etc. Along the same lines, a very concise and comprehensive tradition of the Prophet states: "There should be no harm initially or reciprocally inflicted" [reported in Ibn Hanbal and Ibn Majah].

Such a construction of the main Islamic sources, the Quran and the Sunna of the Prophet, allows enormous range for the human mind to understand, interpret and implement their rules in light of given circumstances of time and place. This process in Arabic is called *"ijtihad"*, a word that means the practice of the greatest possible intellectual effort to interpret and implement the divine guidance. This includes considering the sources in their entirety and recognizing their structure and their inter-relations. The message of Islam spoke to the particular Arabian society in the 7th century C.E.

8

with its given circumstances and the needs of its time, while simultaneously including principles that addressed humanity in its entirety in all times and places.

It is essential to differentiate between the universal permanent and the local transient in the Quran and the Sunna. Hundreds of years ago, the jurists undertook a similar process, as they characterized the different levels of command in the sources, discerning if each represented an obligation, merely an encouragement or even simply a piece of advice, and the different levels of forbiddance, determining whether each represented a strict prohibition or just a discouragement. In general, in their practice of *ijtihad*, jurists applied the general principles of the sources to the particular realities of a given situation at different times and places. Thus they continuously developed new rules in order to respond to emerging and changing situations.

Juristic heritage has discussed in great depth "the goals" of Shari'a and its general maxims as derived from the numerous Quranic verses and the Prophet's traditions. Furthermore, most juristic schools accepted "*the common benefit*" (al-maslaha al-mursala) as a legitimate generator of new rules. Analogy to a particular rule in the Quran or Sunna has been widely applied by jurists through time in their different environments, and preference (*istihsan*) of what may be more beneficial to most people has been used when different analogies can be made for a certain problem. Moreover, everything is considered allowed in Shari'a unless it is specifically restricted or prohibited in the divine text.

It has been wisely stated that variations in jurisprudential rulings are basically differences in the given circumstances of a case at a certain time and place, rather than differences in arguments about the texts themselves.

In his book *I'lam al-Muwaqqi'in* (*Informing Providers of Legal Opinions*), the distinguished jurist Ibn al-Qayyim (d. 751H /1350) wrote a chapter on "The change of the juristic opinion, *fatwa*, according to the change in time, place, conditions, intentions, and customs," wherein he emphasized how ignorance of this matter has led to serious errors about Shari'a. Those, in turn, have caused unnecessary pressures, hardships and requirements of the impossible, all circumstances that the superb Shari'a in its culminated observance of human interests would never bring about. The structure and foundation of Shari'a represent the observance of human interests in this worldly life and in the eternal life to come. Shari'a is entirely justice, mercy, and observance of human interest; thus "whatever means injustice not justice, mercilessness not mercy, and impairment not benefit cannot be related to Shari'a, even if a relation may be forged through a certain interpretation" [2]. A well-known historical precedent is the discontinuation of giving Zakat to "those whose hearts to be won over" (al-mu'alafat qulubuhum) [Quran 9:60], as Islam became strongly held, according to the opinion of caliph Umar ibn al-khatab [3].

A contemporary Azharite jurist, Muhammad Mustafa Shalabi, quoted in his doctoral dissertation many precedents from Muslim history after the death of the Prophet, in which the Prophet's Companions tried to recognize the *"reasons"* for the rules of Shari'a, and to deduce their reasons if they were not explicitly mentioned in the texts. Such deductions relied on what should be the benefit or the purpose of the legal rule, namely achieving the good and avoiding the harm. Based on this process, the Companions could change a legal rule if what had been meant by it had changed [4]. Abu Hanifa (d.150H. /767) and Muhammad ibn al-Hasan (d. 189H. /806), a pillar of the Hanafi juristic school, used to walk around in the markets to recognize how the dealings were conducted [5].

The prominent jurist 'Izz al-Din ibn 'Abd al-Salam states, "Any action that fails to achieve the purpose for which the action is meant becomes null" [6]. Thus, Shalabi believes that the Prophet's Companions *"perceived Shari'a in its entirety, observing its general principles and comprehensive rules at the same time, while others may look at particular texts in isolation from the others, as if each one has brought about a permanent law that cannot be changed."*

In the field of *mu'amalat*, or human practices in worldly matters, the Quran succinctly highlighted the general principles, such as fairness and mutual consent. The Prophet's traditions in this field are also concise, especially as compared with what they include regarding faith, worship and moral values. Thus, according to the general principles of Shari'a, *the human intellect through the practice of ijtihad is allowed enormous room to respond to the human ever-changing needs and interests.* Emerging transactions ought to be thoroughly studied, not hastily considered forbidden on the grounds that they are chancy, speculative or ambiguous [7]. Furthermore, a particular view of a Prophet's Companion or a specific decision of one of the early Four Caliphs that responded to a certain interest in the given circumstances of time and place should not be considered a permanent general law for the entire Muslim umma until the Day of Resurrection. Such particular views or decisions, as Ibn al-Qayyim stressed, "were based on the Quran and Sunna in one way or another, but could they be considered permanent and universal laws that should never be changed throughout time, or mere particular responses to certain needs that observe the people's interest in a given time and place and have to be restricted to those circumstances?" [8] The eminent Maliki jurist al-Qarafi (d. 684 AH/1285 CE), brilliantly categorized the Prophet's traditions in worldly affairs into what were mentioned by him in his capacity as an *imam*, a leader and head of the Muslim state, a context in which *ijtihad* might preponderate, versus what was directed by him as a *mufti*, a judge or a deliverer of legal opinion, based on God's law, Shari'a. The due Muslim consideration of each category is not the same [9].

The Other
In the Contemporary World

In the perspective of a Muslim – as a believer in the One God and Creator – the *"other"* is represented in humankind through its extensive diversity, be it based on gender, race and ethnicity, or religious faith. According to the Quran, all human beings are equal and enjoy equal dignity determined for the entire human species through its successive generations by the Creator Himself: *"We have conferred dignity on the children of Adam, and have borne them over land and sea, and have provided for them sustenance out of the good things of life, and have favored them far above most of Our creation"* (17:70). The Quranic reference to bearing the children of Adam *"over land and sea"* emphasizes the universality of the human species, and indicates that all places in this world are open to humans for their residence and activities, and that all humans are equal in enjoying these qualities granted to them by their Creator.

Such an open universal perspective needs to be well-represented through the Muslim intellectual heritage and political-military history. But instead, expansion into others' lands by force and subjugation of their peoples has occurred at the hands of Muslims throughout the centuries. The use of force entailed ceaseless attacks and counterattacks from both sides of the conflict. Such a climate influenced the jurisprudence of *"jihad"* and affected its dealing with "the other." Thus war was considered a permanent obligation for Muslims. It might be an obligation for *every individual* in case of a defense against aggression, *fard 'ayn,* or a *collective* obligation for the entire Muslim people wherever any group of them may enjoy the power to bring more land and people under the Muslim authority.

Accordingly, an idea developed that beside "the land of Islam" (*dar al-Islam*) where Muslims live, all the *other* world is a "land of disbelief" (*kufr*), and of potential war if its authorities may obstruct by force the propagation of Islam in their land. The Shafi'i school added a third division for the land that accepts the sovereignty of Muslims through a peaceful agreement and has not been annexed by force, calling it a "land of treaty" (*'ahd*). Within this system arose the idea that the "others" in the "land of disbelief" all over the world cannot be taken as allies, *awliya'*. Similarly, the belief spread that "the others" under Muslim authority could not be considered equal to the Muslims, who had annexed their country in which they and their ancestors had been living for centuries.

Today, such a political-military practice and a condescending view are not conceived by Muslims as mere history. Rather, such a human Weltanschauung, or world view, that was related to a particular time and is therefore alterable as circumstances change, became a permanent Islamic standpoint. Even when Muslims became weak and lacked any political or military superiority, but on the contrary came under "the other's" political and military domination during the colonial period, such views about "others" were revived to motivate and mobilize the Muslim peoples for survival and struggle. When Muslims encountered the democratic trend in modern times, some reservations were raised against equal citizenship and equal political rights with regard to non-Muslims, as well as to women. International relations with non-Muslim world powers always raise questions, suspicion, and even resentment, which might be justified because of neo-imperial and exploitative global plans, but should not be based on religious grounds.

Such feelings and concepts might not have greatly affected Muslims in their relations with others in a pre-globalization era, but now advanced technology – with its network of mass communications and transportation – means that universal interrelations are inevitable and crucial for all parties throughout the entire world. A split with an "other" hurts both parties, as well as humanity as a whole. Advanced technology may be used or abused in spreading violence through hidden or open hostilities, which have accumulated through history and may have been fuelled by certain mistaken views about "the other" that are improperly attributed to Islam. As the concept of "sacrifice" for the common benefit or for the cause of God is deeply rooted in the heart and mind of the believer, it may hurt the different parties and the entire world if it is abused and wrongfully directed to certain others. Contemporary globalization is a concrete reality that cannot be ignored or obstructed by any party. It has its practical positives and negatives, and all of humankind has to cooperate in order to benefit from the positives and avoid the negatives. Thus, a restructuring of certain Muslim essential concepts about "the other" that have accrued throughout history, have now become urgently required.

It is of great importance to keep in mind that understanding "the other," accepting and dealing with him/her as an equal human being who has the full right to have differences from us, does not mean that we want to *imitate* the other or to repeat the other's model of thinking or living. We also have full rights to choose our way of thinking and living, but this should not signify any feeling of our superiority or others' inferiority. Holding different views is necessitated by human nature itself, according to individual difference in thinking and free choice: "*And had your Lord so willed, He could surely have made all humankind one single community, but [He willed it otherwise, through allowing individual thinking and free will and choice, and so] they continue to hold divergent views, [all of them] save those upon whom your Lord has bestowed His grace*" (11:118-119). Those who are blessed with the Lord's grace are those who realize how to tackle the natural and legitimate human differences, thoughtfully, ethically, and behaviorally, not those who ignore or deny them. <u>Understanding "the other," means the acceptance of human nature, and equal human rights for all humans</u>. It removes the assumption that human difference denotes antagonism and confrontation, but never means implying any need to lose the individual and communal identity, or change one's own self for the sake of the other.

An essential and legitimate question has to be raised: What does "*identity*" really mean for Muslims? Does it mean the faith and the moral values nurtured by it, to which the Muslims are committed and by which they should be characterized? Or has it been taken to mean something else?

Prophet Muhammad, before receiving the divine revelation at the age of forty, had been known among his people for his honesty, and that moral identity provided a solid base for his message when he received God's revelation. His patience, firmness, care and compassion for his Companions and others presented the Islamic human model to the Arabs and to humanity in its entirety. The Prophet's genuine and obvious identity was in his morale and morality. However, he was like any reasonable and respectable Arab in his dress, food and living, except in what was prohibited in his message such as alcohol, pork, or any extravagance. The Quran characterizes Prophet Muhammad as: "a Conveyor of [God's] message *from among yourselves,* heavily weighs upon himself *what you might suffer, full of concern* for you, and full of *compassion and mercy* towards the believers" (9:128); "And it was by God's grace that you *deal gently with them* [the believers], and if you had been harsh and hard of heart they would have broken away from you. *Pardon them* [when they act wrongfully], and *pray that they be forgiven*, and *take counsel with them* in matters of common concern, then when you reach a decision about an action place your trust in God" (3:159), "And surely you are *of tremendous character and morality*" (68:4).

It is essential in characterizing the Muslim identity to distinguish between the *Arab physical, outward and external way of life* at the time of the Prophet, in which the Muslim men and women were relatively similar to their Arab fellow residents in Mecca or Medina at that time, and the essential and significant distinction in the faith and the morale, moral values and behavior. This was what was nurtured by the faith in God and the ensuing belief in the accountability of the human being. It is also essential to differentiate between the *history* of the message of Islam and *the teachings* of the message itself.

The message of Islam was the same message of all prophets and conveyors of God's message before it in its basics of faith in the One God, the accountability of the human being, and his/her requital in the eternal life to come. Through faith, moral values are taught and observed, with emphasis and specifics about certain practices according to the particular circumstances of the addressed people of a given time and place. Prophet Muhammad addressed by his message a tribal people, so he presented his message first to the leading persons in his Meccan tribe "*Quraysh*," among whom some believed, some did not follow but did not act in a hostile way, and others showed enmity and declared

17

war against the message and its Conveyor and the believers. Because of this war and its accompanying oppression, some Muslims migrated to Abyssinia looking for safety and justice. The Prophet then went on to present his message to leading persons in other tribes, either in their home areas or when they came to Mecca for pilgrimage. In a few cases he asked for mere protection (*jiwar*), from those in a position to offer it.

After many years, the Prophet found believers from Yathrib who offered him their support if he moved to their city. The Muslims began to migrate to Yathrib, and the Prophet himself migrated in the year 622 C.E. There, in addition to his mission as a Conveyor of God's message, he became the political leader of the City that was renamed "*al-Madina,*" or Medina. The believers from Yathrib/ Medina came to be called "*the Supporters,*" (*Ansar*) because of their support for the Prophet's message, while the Muslim immigrants from Mecca were known as "*the Immigrants*" (*Muhajirin*); the two groups formed the Muslim community living under the Prophet's leadership. The hostile leaders of Quraysh continued their contentions, striving against Muhammad and the Muslims in Medina, confronting them directly. They also encouraged other potential opponents within Medina itself, and among the bedouins around the city and throughout the desert who were used to living on raiding settled Arabs and traveling caravans.

Muslims in Medina had to <u>defend themselves, and thus the earliest battles in the history of Islam (*ghazawat/ maghazi*) emerged</u>. *Jihad* or war was defensive and due to historical circumstances, not a part of the religion of Islam. The divine revelation in the Quran was related to the nature of the circumstances, not the essence of the religion itself; it urged the Muslims to face steadfastly and courageously the challenge that had been inflicted upon them and that they had never wished upon themselves. Self-defense was, and continues to be, the only legitimate reason and justification for war in Islam. However, within the historical circumstances of Prophet Muhammad and the message of Islam, many Quranic verses were revealed to *hearten and convince* the early Muslim Arabs of the legitimacy of the just and noble cause they were defending, as early Muslim Arabs were not by nature or by faith war- seekers or lovers. When a ten-year truce was agreed upon by the Prophet and the hostile leaders of Quraysh in the agreement of Hudaybiya at the end of the year 6 AH/627 CE, allowing Muhammad and the Muslims as well as his opponents in Quraysh to seek peacefully the support and alliance of Arab tribes in the peninsula, it was described by the Quran as "*a manifest victory*" (48:1).

Thus, Islam in its essentials does not look for confrontation. Rather, the early Muslims were merely forced to defend themselves when war was imposed on them. The Prophet, supported by God's revelation, welcomed peace between the Muslims and their enemies when it could be reached, even at the expense of hindering the Prophet and Muslims from going to the Inviolable House of Worship (*al-Masjid al-Haram*) in Mecca, a purpose for which they had initially come to the city, even at the expense of Quraysh's insistence to make the agreement with Muhammad as a person not as a Prophet, and despite the presence of some other unfair terms in the treaty. As a result of the peace that followed the agreement, Islam was able to acquire a large number of believers through its peaceful existence among the Arabs. However, some allies of Quraysh broke the agreement after a few years and attacked the allies of the Prophet, and thus Muslims had to go to war. Consequently, the Prophet and the Muslims were able to return victoriously to Mecca with a huge army in the year 9 AH/ 630 CE, and the Prophet granted Quraysh a general amnesty.

Therefore, the migration to Abyssinia, and then to Medina, the circumstantial clashes and the victorious return to Mecca were all simply historical events, and the related verses in the Quran represent the mere history of the message, not its teachings. The message gained believers mainly from dissemination and exhortation, *da'wa*, not from war. Migration is not a religious obligation as long as one is able to stay in one's own domicile, even under bearable pressure, as the Prophet did in Mecca for 13 years until his enemies plotted to kill him. Many contemporary Islamists repeatedly mention the Prophet's battles, *ghazawat*, but ignore or neglect the agreement of Hudaybiya for peace, the "manifest victory" according to the Quran. The Prophet and the early Muslims acted under certain historical circumstances, and the Quran records those circumstances. Those confrontations were fully justifiable within their historical context, but they can never conceptually or practically be a part of the universal permanent message of Islam.

The Prophet returned to Mecca when the opportunity arose, but this was because of the special religious place of Mecca within Arabia, not simply because it was his hometown. Mecca was, and is, home to the Inviolable House of Worship, *al-Masjid al-Haram*, established by Prophet Ibrahim and his son Isma'il to worship the One God, which all the Arabs revered and used to visit yearly as pilgrims. The return of the Prophet to Mecca should not imply that every immigrant from a Muslim land has a religious obligation to return to that land at the first available opportunity.

The Quran indicates that moving around the earth by sea or land or whatever means is one of God's favors for human beings (17:70; 45:12-13), and that the earth is commodious for human movement (4:100, 29:56, 39:10). When the Ottoman *mufti* issued a religious opinion *(fatwa)* that Muslims in Bosnia had to migrate to a Muslim land after their land was annexed to the Austro-Hungarian Empire in 1909, he was rightfully refuted by Muhammad Rashid Rida in his monthly magazine *al-Manar*. The Mufti's view was that the Muslim Bosnians' marriages and other dealings that were required to be held under the *Shari'a* and carried out by Muslim authorities, would be void as long as the Muslims lived under the rule and laws of non-Muslims. But that *fatwa* contradicts the principles of *Shari'a*, the practices of the early Muslims who lived under dominant non-Muslim power, and the successive generations of Muslims who lived as minorities all over the world.

The Quran does not by any means forbid Muslims from living anywhere outside the land in which they have power, but rather states that the Muslim authorities in such a land would not be responsible for defending those Muslims who live outside the bounds of their power in the same way as those who live under their power: *"And as for those who have attained to faith and have not immigrated [to the land which is under your power], you are not in charge of them [or responsible for securing their protection and needs] until they migrate [to your land]. Yet, if they ask you for support against oppression that occurs due to their faith, it is your duty to give [them] this support, except against a people with whom you have a covenant."* (8:72). In the same light, the Quranic verse that dealt specifically with certain hypocrites can be understood: *"Do not take them as associates to you, awliya, until they migrate to your land"* (4:89).

21

The Islamic permanent and universal principles demonstrate justice and magnanimity in all their dimensions in dealing with others, and teach the dissemination of the message with wisdom, and good, impressive exhortation. Furthermore, these principles emphasize the importance of a fair, objective and ethical discussion in case of argument [16:125]. The message urges the believers to meet the wrongdoing of others with good deeds, and thus "*the one between whom and yourself was enmity, [may then become] as though he [/she] had [always] been a close true friend. Yet, [achieving] this is not given to any but those who are used to be patient, it is not given to any but those who get the great share*" [41:34-5, also 23:96]. This is what happened when the Prophet and the Muslims returned to Mecca and gave their former enemies a general amnesty, and thus they gained them to their side.

The history of the early believers represents past events that happened under given circumstances of time and place. However, since circumstances undergo continuous change, the believers in the universal permanent message of Islam must act according to their own circumstances during their given time and place. Muslims, as all human beings, should benefit from the lessons of history in any contemporary moment and any existing place. Moral virtues such as commitment to the cause, steadfastness, self-denial, group solidarity and compassion, courage and sacrifice can be educational and impressive through any human experience in history. The earliest examples in the history of Islam – while illuminating and inspiring – are surely no exception: they should never trap Muslims in the pathways of the past. Such ossification is neither the teaching of their religion nor the natural way of dealing with the normal laws of material and social change and dynamism.

This discussion by no means aims to dilute Islam, or to foreground our own given circumstances of time and place at the risk of losing Islam's genuine authenticity or misleading Muslims about their essential identity. The discussion rather aims to keep Islam active in the frontline in our time – as well as at all times – as God's guidance to humankind under all circumstances through its dynamism. We should stand firmly against all attempts of those who advocate that religion was merely for the past, not for our scientific dynamic age that can only be directed by the human intellect. After all, the Lord Creator would never benefit from our worshiping Him or following His guidance, since He is in no need of such recognition. It is the human being that retains the need for the harmonious and dynamic interaction between, and combination of, His divine guidance and His blessing of the human intellect according to the natural change and dynamism of this life.

I

THE MISTAKEN AND AMBIGUOUS "JIHAD"

Does Jihad Mean a Permanent War against the Entire non-Muslim World?

Particular Circumstances of Arabia in the 7ᵗʰ Century C.E.

Islam is a <u>universal message</u>, but it initially addressed a <u>particular people that had been living under given circumstances</u> of time and place. In order to reach subsequent generations, decades, centuries and millennia after its revelation in the seventh century, the message had *to address the specific circumstances of its immediate audience, to respond to their existing needs, and to provide the reform specifically required.* Thus, Islam had to deliver its *interim local* message to the Arabs in Mecca, then in Medina, then all of Arabia, while at the same time, through the same divine revelation, disbursing a *permanent universal* message to all of humankind. It is essential for any serious reading of this revelation to *characterize and distinguish each address and group of addressees,* not to take the Quran as a monolithic block with indistinct components. Such a simplistic understanding ignores the fact that the Quran was revealed during a period of 23 years, throughout which the constituting requirements and the addressees changed.

Just as jurists capably distinguished between the different levels of requirement, obligation (*wujub*), encouragement (*nadb*) and even advice (*irshad*), and between levels of interdiction from strict prohibition (*tahrim*) to discouragement at various levels (*karaha*), it should be equally essential to distinguish the addressees of a certain text, and whether the text was meant to be interim and local, or permanent and universal. This can be gleaned from the textual structure and its linguistic, logical, and historical context and connotations.

There are about 375 verses in the Quran that are related to *"jihad"* in the context of struggling against an aggressor. Most of them deal with particular historical confrontations between the Prophet joined by his followers on the one side, and the assaulting polytheists on the other. Only about 60 verses may be related to the permanent universal laws of war when it becomes inevitable for self-defense, after the failure of all efforts to maintain peace, which is emphasized as the general permanent universal rule for Muslims.

Events related to the confrontations have been addressed in the following suras:

- the Battle of *Badr* (2 AH/ 623 CE) in sura *"al-Anfal"* (no. 8);
- the Battle of *Uhud* (3 AH/ 624 CE) in sura *"Āl-Imran"* (no. 3);
- the Battle of *Bani al-Nadir* (3 AH/ 624 CE) in sura *"al-Hashr"* (no. 59);
- the Battle of *Al-Ahzab* and the Battle of *Bani Qurayza* (5 AH/ 626 CE) in sura *"al-Ahzab"* (no. 33);
- the confrontation and subsequent treaty of *al-Hudaybiya* (6 AH/ 627 CE), in sura *"al-Fath"* (no. 48);
- the campaign to *Mecca* and the Battle of *Hunayn* (8 AH/ 629 CE), and the campaign to *Tabuk* (9 AH/ 630 CE) in sura al-Tawba (no. 9).

Such particular events had certainly their moral lessons, but they may not necessarily provide permanent laws of war. Side by side with such historical accounts in these suras, we find permanent universal rules of war such as:

"And fight in God's cause *against those who have initially waged war against you, and do not commit aggression*, for God does not love aggressors" (2:190),

28

"Hence, fight against them [the aggressors] until there is no more oppression and all matters of faith would be left absolutely [to the person's conviction with regard] to God [free from any obstruction], and when they desist, all hostility should cease, and no use of force is allowed except against those who commit transgression" (2:193),

"And if you need good reason to fear treachery from people, act against them openly and fairly" (8:58),

"And if they [the enemies] incline to peace, incline you to it as well, and place your trust in God [...] And should they seek but to deceive you [by their show of peace], God is [protector] enough for you" (8:61-62),

"And whenever any of those who associate others with God [who have initially waged war against you in Arabia] seeks your protection, grant him protection, so that he might [be able to] hear the word of God [from you], and arrange to let him reach the place where he can feel secure, for they might not know [the truth of your message and the circumstances of such a war]" (9:6),

"O you who have attained to faith! Be true to your agreements and promises" [5:1],

"It may well be that God will bring about [mutual] affection between you [O believers] and those from among them [the unbelievers] whom you [now] face as enemies, and God is all-powerful and God is much-forgiving, mercy-giving. As for such [of the unbelievers] as do not fight against you on account of [your] faith, and do not drive you forth from your homes, God does not forbid you from being kind to them and from behaving towards them with full equity, and God loves those who act equitably" (60:8).

Muslim Wars during the Time of the Prophet (1-11 AH/ 622-632 CE)

The Quran has urged patience in approximately 65 verses, and forgiveness and pardoning in about 17 verses. Even when self-defense is legitimate, self-control, endurance, and pardoning are still urged and encouraged:

"A requital for an offence should be the same as it without any excessiveness, and *whoever pardons [the offender] and makes peace, his [/her] reward rests with God* [...] Yet, as for any who only defend themselves after having been wronged, no blame whatever attaches to them; blame attaches but to those who oppress [other] people and behave outrageously on earth, offending against all right [...] *But withal, if one is patient [and has self-control] and forgives – this is the best that requires a strong will"* (42:39-43).

Meeting an offence with a similar one may develop a vicious circle of offences that may continue to escalate intentionally or unintentionally. Hence, the ideal is to meet wrongdoing with what is better than it:

"And good cannot be equal to evil; *repel [evil] with what is better; thus one between whom and yourself was enmity, [may then become] as though he [/she] had been a close and true friend.* Yet, [to achieve] this is not given to any but those who have patience; it is not given to any but those endowed with the greatest good fortune" (41:34-35), "Repel the evil [which any may commit against you] with what is better" (21:96).

However, some commentators and jurists saw in the verse 9:5, referred to as "the verse of the sword," an abrogation of all verses that urge self-control, patience and forgiveness. This verse made a general declaration of war against the assaulting polytheists in Arabia who had previously waged war against the Muslims on several previous occasions. The verse reads: "And when *the sacred months are over,* fight against those who associate others with God wherever you may come upon them, and take them captive, and besiege them, and lie in wait for them at every possible place. Yet, if they repent and take to prayer and render the purifying welfare dues, let them go their way, for God is much-forgiving, mercy-giving" (9:5). The Andalusian commentator Abd al-Haqq ibn Ghalib ibn 'Atiyya (d. 546 AH/ 1247 CE) for example wrote, "This verse has *abrogated all reconciliations and truces* and whatever may be similar in the Quran, and those were mentioned to be 114 verses" [(10)].

Such a view isolates the verse from its textual and historical context, ignoring the numerous preceding assaults that had been waged against the Muslims by the polytheists from Mecca, from around Medina, and from other areas in Arabia. Yet these numerous preceding assaults are apparent, having been referred to in a following verse in the same sura: "Wouldn't you fight *against people who on several occasions before have broken their solemn pledges* [of keeping up peace and refraining from attacking you], *and have done all that they could to drive the Conveyor of God's message away, and had initially attacked you*" (9:13).

Meanwhile, the sura stresses maintaining peace and observing the previous agreements with whomever among the Arab polytheists had been faithful to the Muslims: "But excepted [from that declaration of war] shall be – from among those who associate others with God – *[people] with whom you [O believers] have made an agreement and*

31

who thereafter have never failed to fulfill their obligations towards you, and neither have aided anyone against you: observe, then, your agreement with them until the end of the term agreed with them" (9:4), "[. . .] *except those [among those who associate others with God] with whom you [O believers] have made an agreement in the vicinity of the Inviolable House of Worship: so long as they remain true to you, be true to them,* for verily God loves those who are conscious of Him" (9:7).

Furthermore, "And whenever any of those who associate others with God [who have initially waged war against you] *seeks your protection, grant him protection,* so that he might [be able to] hear the word of God [from you]; and thereupon arrange to let him reach the place wherever he can feel secure; for they might not know [the truth of your message and the circumstances of such a war]" (9:6). As the prominent commentator and jurist Ibn Jarir al-Tabari (d. 310 AH/ 922 CE) astutely noted in his outstanding commentary on the Quran about the verse: *"And fight against them wherever you may come upon them, and drive them away from wherever they drove you away,* for oppression is even worse than killing" (2:191), " the verse is addressing the *Immigrants* [from Mecca to Medina], and the pronoun [they, of the third person plural] refers to the infidels of Quraysh" [(11)]. Indeed, the verse explicitly refers to those who *"drove you away",* as well as specifically the Inviolable House of Worship (*al-Masjid al-Haram*): *"and fight not against them near the Inviolable House of Worship until they fight against you there first."*

In addition, one has to keep in mind that the early Muslims were not only confronted by the hostilities of Quraysh in Mecca and the Jews in Medina, but by the raids of the bedouin tribes that lived in the desert neighboring

Medina. These bedouins used to earn their living through raids on caravans or settled communities, among which Medina became well known after the migration of the Prophet and the Muslims to it, and its subsequent development as a Muslim city-state [12]. With such a way of life, the bedouins were easily tempted to support any Arab party against its enemies, thus leading to an alliance of convenience between the polytheist leaders of Quraysh and the tribe of Ghatafan at one point, and the Jews in Medina at another, both alliances that were used against the Prophet and the Muslims [13].

The Muslims unceasingly suffered from perpetual assaults from bedouin tribes such as Adhurh, al-Qarra, Ra'l, 'Usayya and Dhakwan at sites such as Bi'r Ma'una in 3 AH/ 624 CE and 'Urayna in 6 AH/ 627 CE, and from Bani Tamim in the year 9 AH/ 630 CE. Many bedouin tribes such as Bani Sulaym, Bani Asad, Faraza, Ashja', Bani Murra, and others attacked Medina with Quraysh in the year 5 AH/ 626 CE; that attack was therefore called "the battle of the Confederates/al-Ahzab". The Prophet thought of offering Ghatafan one third of the fruits of Medina for their withdrawal, but he abandoned the idea when the Medinese Muslims (the Supporters/ al-Ansar) were unhappy with this potential agreement [14]. The clan of Huwazin fought against the Muslims in the battle of Hunayn in the year 8 AH/ 629 CE. In general, some bedouin clans that had adopted Islam were sometimes reluctant to obey the Prophet [15]. The Prophet had to fight Ghatafan and Bani Sulaym early in the year 3 AH/ 624 CE, and later in 7 AH/ 628 CE. He confronted Bani Tha'laba, Anmar, and Bani Sulaym in the year 6 AH/ 627 CE, and sent a campaign against Bani Tamim in the year 9 AH/ 630 CE shortly before his death [16]. Such frequent attacks of the bedouins against the Muslims brought about another serious front for the

Muslim war in Arabia, and represented a grave danger even after the Muslims' prevalence over Quraysh in Mecca and the Jews in Medina.

Although the constant bedouin attacks against Muslims were encouraged by Quraysh and the Jewish tribes, their roots lay deep in the bedouins' own way of life and their interests. Thus their assaults continued even after the prevalence of Muslims in Medina and Mecca. *The bedouin factor* in the war that was waged against the early Muslims in Arabia, and their pressing need to defend themselves against those raids, would explain why Sura al-Tawba (no. 9) declared such a <u>"general" war against those belligerent polytheists in Arabia</u> in the year 9 AH/ 630 CE. A clear exception was granted for those who kept their agreements and promises with the Muslims *"and have never failed to fulfill their obligations towards you, nor have aided anyone against you"* (9:4). In this sura, the bedouin way of life and their material opportunism are well described: *"The bedouins are more tenacious in [their stubborn] refusal of the truth, and in their hypocrisy, and more liable to ignore the ordinances which God has brought down to the Conveyor of His message [. . .] And among the bedouins there are such as regard all what they might spend [in God's cause] as a loss, and wait for a mishap to encompass you"* (9:97-98).

However, a Muslim should never lose hope in any human being's potential for a change for the better. Furthermore, he/ she should never generalize a condemning judgment about an entire human group, since the potential for good – whatever its proportion – exists in every human being. Thus, this Quranic verse follows: *"However, among the bedouins, there are [also] such as believe in God and the Last Day, and regard all they spend [in God's cause] as a means of drawing them nearer to God and of [their being*

34

remembered in] the prayers of the Conveyor of His message. Verily, it shall [indeed] be a means of [God's] nearness to them; God will admit them into His grace" (9:99).

The Arabian tribal structure, with its rivalries between different tribes and clans, and between settled and nomadic groups, was what brought about the bedouin attacks against Medina and the Muslims. These were the historical circumstances behind the "general" war declared against the bedouin polytheists in the year 9 AH/ 630 CE and described by Sura al-Tawba (no. 9), just two years before the Prophet's death. The revelation was merely a part of Arabian history, and should never establish a general rule.

It was this very tribal structure that led to the apostasy movement all over the peninsula at the end of the Prophet's life and just after his death. The movement was a symptom of tribal disobedience and rebellion against the supremacy of one group and the establishment of one organized state authority, rather than a religious stand against a certain faith. Those who claimed prophethood were only supported by their tribes that wanted to evade the superiority of Mecca and Quraysh, and to assure their own tribal command. Thus, tribalism stood behind the pretenders of prophethood: Musaylima was supported by Bani Hanifa and others in the Yamama region, Tulayha al-Asadi was supported by Bani Asad, Tayyi', and Ghatafan, and al-Aswad al-'Ansi was supported by Mudhaj and others in Yemen. Sajah, who had forged an alliance with Musaylama and who was related to Bani Taghlib in Upper Mesopotamia (al-Jazira), was supported by Bani Tamim, and a descendant of the former dynasty of Hira called "*al-Maghrur,*" (the Conceited One) was supported by Rabi'a. Medina was attacked by the bedouins around it such as Bani 'Abs, Bani Murra, and Dhubian. The renouncement of Islam reached 'Uman and al-Bahrayn.

As the known biographer of the Prophet Muhammad ibn Is-haq (d. 151 AH/ 768 CE) explicated: "All Arabs renounced (Islam) at the Prophet's death, except the people of the Two (cities of the Sacred) Mosques: Mecca and Medina." Al-Aswad in Yemen and Musaylima in Yamama asserted their rights to their land and its revenues. Others including the bedouins around Medina suggested a stop to the payment of *zakat*, which they saw as a humiliating tribute. Their suggestion was rejected by Caliph Abu Bakr, who was chosen after the death of the Prophet as the Muslim state leader (11-13 AH/ 632-4 CE) and who rightfully considered *zakat* a fundamental obligation in Islam, representing the right of the poor to the wealth of the rich. The Caliph had to send 11 armies to different areas of Arabia to restore order and secure the authority of the Muslim state in that tribal land [17].

Thus, the *"general"* war was a *historical- particular* matter for Arabia with its tribal structure at the time of the Prophet, waged against particular people there with whom *"the Prophet had made an agreement [several times] and they thereupon break their agreement on every occasion"* (8:51), *"they broke their solemn pledges, and did all they could to drive the Conveyor of God's message away, and had initially attacked you"* (9:13), *"and if they were to overcome you, they would not respect any bond, nor any obligation toward you; they seek to please you with their tongues [words], while their hearts remain averse [to you...] They traded away God's messages for a trifling gain, and thus turned away [people] from His path [...] and it is they who transgress the bounds of what is right"* (9:8-10).

Muslims in Medina, therefore, had to fight on three fronts:

- the *first* was against the polytheists of Mecca who initially oppressed them and expelled them out of their homes,
- the *second* front was against the Jews in Medina who were hostile to the Prophet and sided with the Meccan polytheists, in spite of all the Prophet's efforts to remind them of the monotheistic and Abrahamic bonds that related them to the Muslims and to secure their rights in his document following his immigration to Medina,[18]
- the *third* front was against the bedouins, possibly the worst of all enemies since they were scattered across Arabia, were known to be mercurial and opportunistic, and were open to being used by the enemies of Islam in Mecca and the Jews in Medina against the Muslims[19].

It should be noted that the forced flight of the Jews from Medina followed an Arab custom of evacuating the defeated enemy. For example, the tribe *Khuza'a* had been evacuated from around the Ka'ba before Islam by the tribe of *Quraysh,* and the tribes of *Iyad* and *al-Azd* had been evacuated from al-Bahrayn by *'Abd al-Qays* who were related to *Rabi'a.* Similarly, in the long wars between *Bani Taghlib* and *Bakr* in pre-Islamic times, the defeated had to evacuate [20].

Muslim Wars beyond the Arabian Peninsula under the Two Early Caliphs: Abu Bakr and Umar (11-23 AH/ 632-644 CE)

The first Caliph after the death of the Prophet, Abu Bakr (11-13 AH/ 632-4 CE), was highly occupied with the internal tribal rebellions against the newly-established Muslim state. However, he could not overlook the necessity of securing the borders of the new Muslim Arabian state, especially those borders with the neighboring Byzantine and Sassanian empires. Each of those empires had established at its borders a buffer between it and the Arab tribes: a client princedom ruled by an Arab dynasty that was entirely subject to a great power, and dependent on its support. Thus, the Ghassanids in the southern part of Syria neighboring Arabia were the clients of the Byzantines, while the Lakhmids in al-Hira on the Persian Gulf eastward of the Arabian Peninsula were the clients of the Sassanian Persians. Christianity had found its way to the Grasslands as well as to some tribes on the Arabian-Syrian borders who were called "*al-Arab al-Mutanissara,*" (the Christianized Arabs), or "*Rum al-Arab,*" (the Romanized Arabs). Christianity reached al-Hira as well.

Inter-Arab strife was manifest from the days of the Prophet. The Prophet's envoy to the Ghassanid prince in the year 8 AH/ 629 CE was killed, and Arabs related to the tribes of Bahra', Bakr, Lakhm and Judham were mobilized in a huge army against the Muslims at Mu'ta on the Arabian borders with Syria. The Muslim army was barely able to survive, and it had to withdraw after a serious loss. Later, the Prophet's campaign to Tabuk in the year 9 AH/ 630 CE was set in motion as a result of a rumor that the Byzantines were planning a great assault against the Muslims, which proved to be untrue [21]. But significant treaties were also made by the Prophet with Jewish and Christian tribes in Northern Arabia [22]. However, after the Prophet's death, some efforts had to be made to secure the Arabian frontiers with the two neighboring great powers that did not easily accept the growth of a unified Muslim Arabian state on their borders. The early campaigns during the time of the Prophet had not been decisive in that regard, and danger from the Byzantines and their Arab allies loomed on the horizon.

The first Caliph, Abu Bakr, was strongly determined to carry out a campaign that had been planned by the Prophet to the northern borders, where the Mu'ta battle had taken place. At the same time, a disturbing internal insurgence was breaking out in the east, near the Sassanian Persian borders: renunciation of Islam was building in al-Bahrayn and Oman [23]. As Montgomery Watt summarized:

"On the Persian Gulf and the south coast, a faction in each place was in alliance with Muhammad, but this may have been less than half the population. The tribes towards Iraq [...] may not have been Muslims, while those on the Syrian frontier still professed allegiance to the Byzantine Empire. The reason for the position on the east and south coasts was that in the various towns there, Persian influence had kept a pro-Persian faction in power. About the year 614, Persia had overrun Syria, Egypt and other parts of the Byzantine Empire, but Heraclius [610-641] had fought back with grim determination and recovered much ground. In February 628, the Persian emperor died, and succession difficulties led in a few years to the complete collapse of the Persian Empire" [24].

Abu Bakr benefited from "the warlike spirit of a tribe living on the margins of [Iraq], the Bakr ibn Wa'il, whose chieftain was the valorous al-Muthama [...]. It was then that a remarkable thing happened, which the Muslims consider to be a great credit to Islam. For centuries, bedouin tribes had been fighting one another all over the peninsula, carrying on feuds to which only exhaustion or the intervention of certain chieftains could put a stop, but now they placed themselves obediently under the orders of Hijazi commanders, and their advance beyond the frontiers was irresistible. It was undoubtedly favored by the fact that previously, owing to the rapid increase of the population in Arabia, there had been a *steady infiltration of Arabs into Syria, Palestine, and Iraq.* Here they had partially assimilated with the local inhabitants of Semitic origin, for which reason they were known as *musta'riba.* Such people, even if they were of mixed origin, certainly felt themselves bound to the 'pure Arabs' by ties of language and customs, and either because they hated their rulers, or else because they hoped to share the spoils of victory, they received the invaders with enthusiasm, and later strengthened their forces with contingents of their own. [Besides, there was] the lack, during the first phase, of any effective resistance, since the buffer states of the Lakhmids and Ghassanids had actually disappeared [as a real power . . .]. Nevertheless, despite all these concomitant circumstances, the decisive factor in this success was Islam [...]. The armies were not hordes, as those of their invaders were; often they consisted only of a few thousand men who from time to time were reinforced, and they became numerous and formidable only when decisive battles had to be fought" [25].

Thus, the Prophet's campaigns to Mu'ta and Tabuk on the borders between northern Arabia and Byzantine-controlled southern Syria and Palestine aimed merely to secure the northern borders of the emerging Muslim Arabian state, especially in light of the threatening signs of hostility from the Ghassanid tribe and the Byzantine forces. In the end, the Prophet did not meet a military confrontation at Tabuk as he had been led to expect, but instead he seized the opportunity of being in the area to make peaceful agreements with Ayla, Adhurh, al-Jarba', and the Jews of Maqna.

Subsequently, the first Caliph Abu Bakr began his rule by carrying out the campaign to the area that had been planned during the last days of the Prophet's life under the leadership of Usama ibn Zayd. Securing the borders with Syria and Iraq greatly alarmed the Byzantines, who mobilized a big army consisting of their soldiers and their Arab clients such as the tribes of Tanukh, Bani Kulayb, Sulayh, Lakhm, Gudham, and Ghassan. That army was met by the Muslims led by Khalid ibn Sa'id ibn al-'As, who had been sent by Abu Bakr *with strict orders not to go beyond the borders of Tayma' without the Caliph's order*. However, many of the Arab tribes mobilized by the Byzantines defected from them, preferring to side with their Arab blood brethren.

In addition to the blood relations with the Arab and Arabized tribes on the borders between northern Arabia and southern Syria, the Arab commercial caravans between Hijaz – especially Mecca – and Syria had established contacts in pre-Islamic time between the two groups. For example, the notable Meccan Abu Sufyan ibn Harb owned an estate at al-Balqa' on the southern edge of Syria [26]. Thus, revitalizing relations between the Arabs and Arabized tribes near the northern Arabian borders was not difficult. But the defection of the Arab tribes from Byzantine control brought the Muslims in direct contact with the Byzantine forces in Syria. The principal Byzantine vassals, the Ghassanid princedom, had been swept away by the Persian invasion of Syria in the year 613 CE, and it is unclear whether its full power had been restored after the Byzantine victory over the Persians under Emperor Heraclius in 628 [27]. Therefore, the Muslims found themselves directly confronting the Byzantines on main Syrian land, rather than merely at the borders of the Arabian Peninsula as they had expected [28]. A couple of years later, in the decisive Yarmuk battle in the late days of Caliph Abu Bakr in 13 AH/ 634 CE, the inclination of the Arabs within the Byzantine army to support the Muslims re-appeared [29].

To secure the borders with Iraq, Caliph Abu Bakr instructed the leader Khalid ibn al-Walid not to recruit in his army any person against his will. He avoided fighting with the peaceful peasants, and was able to reach a peaceful agreement with al-Hira and some other towns on the Gulf [30]. Arabs feared any confrontations with the Persians, and Caliph Umar, who had succeeded Abu Bakr after his death (13-23 AH/ 634-44 CE), expressed his wish to have a barrier of fire between the Persian empire and the Muslims in Arabia, so that each party might feel safe on its side, and no overstepping of the barrier might occur.

Thus, Caliph Umar strictly forbade the Muslim army from any penetration into the lands of the Persian Empire [31]. However, internal troubles brewed within the imperial house itself. When Yazdigird III was placed on the throne (632-51 CE), the Muslims began to face dangerous counterattacks. The Persian administrative and military bodies were re-organized, and those who had previously signed peaceful agreements with the Muslims broke those agreements and displayed their hostility. As the Muslim situation became more and more critical, the military leadership asked Caliph Umar to change his previous instructions against Muslim penetration through the Persian lands, as it deprived the Muslim army from making military initiatives to acquire better strategic footholds. The Caliph agreed, and in 636-637 another decisive confrontation with a great medieval empire took place [32].

Thus, securing the borders for the Muslim state in Arabia developed in the context of a confrontation with the two powerful neighboring empires: the Byzantine and the Sassanian. The Muslim Arabs were able to secure their foothold in Syria without excessive costs, because of the area's historical, geographic and blood relations with Arabia and the Arabs. Caliph Umar reluctantly agreed to send a Muslim army to Egypt when he was informed that the Byzantines were gathering their forces for a counterattack against the Muslims in Syria. The Caliph tried to send a special emissary to bring back the Muslim army before reaching the Egyptian borders with Syria in the year 19 AH/ 640 CE, but his attempt was unsuccessful [33]. Muslims stopped at the geographic mountainous barriers between Syria and Asia Minor where the heart of the Byzantine Empire existed.

On the Sassanian side, the Muslims were satisfied with simply securing their borders in Iraq. Caliph Umar instructed his leader who was fighting in the Sassanian lands to stop after the Muslim victory in the battle of Jalula' in 16 AH/ 637 CE and to establish a Muslim city – Kufa – as a base for the Muslims in these lands [34]. However, internal developments within the Sassanian Empire resulted in a full confrontation with the Muslim Arabs, ending in a most unexpected collapse of the empire. This came after successive losses over several years, and the submission of the Sassanian lands and population to the Muslim Arabs. In June 637, Muslims entered triumphantly the Sassanian capital Ctesiphon, whose garrison, together with the emperor, had deserted it. Phillip Hitti presented the picture vividly:

43

"The feat was accomplished without loss of life to the army and was hailed as a miracle by Muslim chronicles [... who gave] extravagant descriptions of the booty and treasures captured therein. Their estimate is nine billion dirhams [...] In the meantime, the Sassanid Yazdigird III and his imperial court were fleeing northward [...] In 641, the last great battle that of Nihawand (near ancient Ectabana) was fought [...] and resulted in a disastrous defeat of the last remnant of Yazdigird's army. Khuzestan (ancient Elam, later Susiana, modern Arabistan) was occupied in 640 from al-Basrah and al-Kufah. In the meantime, an attempt was made on the adjoining province of Pars (Faris, Persia proper), on the eastern shore of the Persian Gulf, from al-Bahrayn [...] After Faris, the turn of the great and distant province of Khurasan in the northeast came, and the path then lay open to Oxus. The subjection of Mukran, the coastal region of Baluchistan, shortly after 643 brought the Arabs to the very borders of India [...] The military camp al-Kufah became the capital of the newly conquered territories [...] In 651, the young and ill-starred Yazdagird, fleeing with his crown, treasures, and a few followers, fell victim to the greed of one of his people in a miller's hut near Marw [Persian Marv]. With his death there came to an ignoble end the last ruler of an empire that had flourished with one interruption for some twelve centuries, an empire that was not fully to rise again for 800 years or more [... although] the Moslem arms met with much more stubborn resistance than in Syria [...] Some of the most brilliant stars in the intellectual firmament of Islam during its first 3 centuries were Islamized Iranians"[(35)].

Burdens of Expansion

Whatever the circumstances that led to the early military campaigns on the borders of Arabia under the first two caliphs, and whatever their justifiability at that time might have been, the resulting expansion placed various burdens on the Muslims. In several areas, especially eastward, the expansion was sometimes shaken and had to be restored or reinforced [36]. Perhaps more significantly, the young Muslim caliphate – with its previous limited governing experience – had to now face the unanticipated heavy military and administrative responsibilities of defending and governing those extensive lands, with their wide variety of peoples, languages, cultures, faiths, and governmental traditions through limited expensive and fast expansion.

Deficiency in Leading Officials

High organizational and administrative capabilities combined with impressive morality and leadership merits were essential requirements for governing those lands under the Islamic banner. Presenting models of justice and care for the people, and a creative, observant, and competent central leadership was essential to the organization and supervision of such an extensive area of land and such a diverse population. Caliph Umar led invaluable institutional initiatives by establishing the central administration (*diwan*s), the provinces and their bases (*amsar*), and the land-tax (*kharaj*) to finance the huge state and its administration. He impressively guided and checked on his administration and those in charge. However, finding individuals with both the essential managerial and moral requirements to lead the young state with its escalating responsibilities was a difficult task. Courageous or efficient military leaders might lack the skills to govern and deal with the people, and might be harsh or incompetent as governors. Pious persons might be capable of leading the prayers and preaching to the people but might lack the flair to run the administration.

After the assassination of Caliph Umar in 23 AH/ 644 CE, his successor Caliph Uthman (ruled 23-35 AH/ 644-56 CE) lacked some of his predecessor's essential merits of leadership during a critical, formative period of the Muslim state. The shortcomings in capability and character became more serious and even detrimental under the Umayyads, when the attitude of extension intensified to become expansion for the sake of expansion. Meanwhile, the management of public affairs and the service of the people as a whole continuously deteriorated owing to partiality, favoritism, and corruption [37]. Such a fate might befall any empire after the initial glorious efforts of its mighty conquerors, but the situation of the Muslim universal state was far more serious since it had been essentially founded to represent Islam and its values in governing. Contradictions with the values of Islam and the historical precedents of the Muslim character during the early decades became more persistently obvious and damaging. A serious liability that had led to such contradictions was the burdensome expansion that had exposed the human, structural, and managerial impotence of the expansionist state.

□ *Domination of the Expansionist Attitude*

The clear and limited purpose of securing the borders of Arabia initially began to be infiltrated and later followed by ambitions of conquest for the sake of conquest. This became the overt motivation for extension of the Muslim lands: gaining more people for Islam. The unanticipated collapse of the Sassanian Empire – never the goal of Caliph Umar who had repeatedly instructed his army against deep penetration into Sassanian lands – stimulated the Muslim appetite for more expansion eastward and westward, on the grounds of developing opportunities to spread Islam among the peoples of the annexed lands, without imposing any infringement on religious freedom. Muslims now aspired to topple the Byzantine Empire and annex its lands, as had happened with the Sassanians. The third Caliph Uthman explicitly spelled out the idea of targeting Constantinople from the west through the Mediterranean Sea. A conquest of Andalusia (southern Spain) following that of North Africa would be considered an initial step to secure a later conquest of Constantinople, and thus the conquerors of Andalusia would be actually partners of the future conquerors of Constantinople [38].

Such an aspiration was stressed by Musa ibn Nusayr (d. 97 AH/715 CE), the Umayyad leader who conquered Andalusia in 92-93 AH/ 711-712 CE at the time of the Umayyad sovereign al-Walid ibn 'Abd al-Malik (86-96 AH/ 705-715 CE) [39]. It seems that in this case also internal troubles and conflicts provided another practical merit for expansion wars, as they kept the attention of the Muslim public and the force of the army focused on the external fronts [40]. In this way, campaigns conducted under Caliph

Uthman to Armenia, Tabaristan, Jurjan, and Adherbijan, reached Transoxiana eastward, Nubia southward, and North Africa westward [41].

Under such a climate of expansion, the jurists developed their view of "jihad" as a collective obligation (*fard kifaya*) on the Muslim umma as a whole to spread Islam whenever this is possible. This is different from the case when Muslim land is attacked and jihad then becomes an obligation for every individual (*fard 'ayn*). Such a climate continued under the Abbasids, even after it became obvious that Muslims would not be able to bring down the Byzantine Empire, and that on the contrary the Byzantines had begun to attack the Muslim lands near their frontiers. Harun al-Rashid (170-193 AH/ 786-809 CE) reportedly used to go for pilgrimage one year and for jihad the other, obtaining headgear (*qulunsuwa*) on which was stitched "Conqueror Pilgrim" (*Ghazi Hajj*) [42]. The spoils of war became a considerable lure in the preceding mobilization for battle, and in the subsequent reporting of victories [43].

☐ *The Expansion Tendency Flares Up Among the Converted Population*

The tendency for conquest and expansion – on the pretext of giving opportunities for the spread of Islam –found a favorable climate among the Asian warring communities when they accepted Islam, which they blended with their communal combative culture and traditions. The introduction of *The Cambridge History of Islam* refers to "the two of the principal institutions of Islam: *Shari'a and Jihad*," which were seen as strongly connected and not wholly distinct, since jihad is fought in defense of the Shari'a

"against its external and internal enemies. In political matters as in others, Islam adopted and incorporated contributions from many sources. The successors of the Prophet as heads of his community drew on the customs of Arab tribal leadership, as well as the usage of the Meccan trading oligarchy. They inherited the legacy of the Byzantine administration, as well as the traditions of the Sassanian monarchy. Later, rulers were influenced by other political concepts; those brought into the medieval Islamic world by *Turkish and Mongol* immigrants from the steppes [. . .] " [44].

The rising Iranian and Turkish elements went on dominating the political life of the Muslim countries east of the Syro-Mesopotamian steppes [45].

As an example of the practice of an aggressive expansionist concept of jihad in Asia, B. Spuler pointed to the efforts of the Samanids, whose reign was established in Transoxiana and Persia (261-390 AH/ 874-990 CE).

With this, "the Turks were won over to Islam, which in the following centuries was to become the religion of practically all the Turkish peoples [...] However, in spite of all their religious merits, *the Samanids dug their own grave by Islamizing the Turks.* The Qarluqs were soon pressing on upon Samanid Transoxiana. The *ulama* [...] declared that the advancing Turks were also good Muslims and that holy war *jihad* against them was out of question. Thus the Samanid state was unable to put up any sustained resistance and collapsed in the year 389-394/999-1004 [...]. The lands north of the Oxus came under the dominion of the Kara-Khanids. South of the river their inheritance was taken over by the Ghaznavids who were descended from a Turkish mercenary leader [...]" [46].

In the second half of the 7th century AH/ 13th century CE, as the Seljuk state fell apart, a new kind of principality, the *ghazi state*, emerged in the western marches of Anatolia. This represented

"a territory conquered as a result of the holy wars (sing. *ghaza*) waged against Byzantium and hence [...] known as *ghazi* states. The Ottoman principality was one of these. It was destined within a century to unite Anatolia and the Balkans under its sovereignty and to develop into an Islamic empire [...]. The principalities of the marches had a distinct way of life, which could be described as a *frontier culture*, and this distinguished them clearly from the hinterland. This culture was dominated by the Islamic conception of *holy war or "ghaza"*. By God's command *the ghaza had to be fought against the infidels' dominion, dar al-harb/* the abode of war, ceaselessly and relentlessly until they are submitted. According to the Shari'a, "the property of the infidels, captured in these raids, could be legally kept as booty, their country could be destroyed, and the population taken into captivity

51

or killed. The actions of the *ghazis* were regulated by the Shari'a to which they pay heed. Ceaseless warfare led to the formation of groups commanded by *ghazi* leaders specially blessed by *shaykhs*. The *ghazi* groups were often named after their leaders. Successful leaders naturally attracted the greatest number of *ghazis*. In the Seljuk marches which were dominated by *Turcoman nomads*, these leaders were also often chiefs of tribal clans [. . .] Usually these *ghazi-beyes* paid no taxes to the central government, or they sent only nominal taxes as a token of loyalty. Life in the marches was dangerous and required great personal initiative. *At the other side of the border, there was a similar Christian frontier organization, moved by the same spirit, the Byzantine Akritai.* Ethnically, frontier society was very mixed. It included highly mobile *nomads, refugees from central authority, heterodox elements and adventurers.* In contrast, with the highly developed conservative civilization of the hinterland, with its theology, palace literature, and the Shari'a, *the marches had a mystical and eclectic popular culture*, which had not yet frozen into a final form. *They sheltered heterodox sects, bred a mystical and an epic literature and obeyed customary or tribal law. Their ethos was chivalrous and romantic* [. . .] According to Oruj, the historian in his work *Tawarikh 'i 'Ali 'Osman*, the Ottomans were 'Ghazis and champions striving in the way of truth and the path of Allah, gathering the fruits of *ghaza* and expending them in the way of Allah, choosing truth, striving for religion, lacking pride in the world, following the way of the Shari'a, taking revenge on polytheists, friends of strangers, *blazing forth the way of Islam from the East to the West'* [. . .] The holy war or *ghaza* was the foundation stone of the Ottoman state. The tradition of the *ghazis* of the marches, which lay at its origin, dominated all its history and constituted the fundamental principle of its policies and its organization. The concept of the *ghaza* stimulated great initiatives and endeavors and later attempts at renewal; it inspired both individuals and society. The Ottomans took in all seriousness the duty of *protecting and extending Islam, and even tried to justify their claim to sovereignty over the whole Islamic world, by the argument that they alone were carrying out that duty.* For *ghazis* in the marches, it was a *religious duty to ravage the countries of the infidels who resisted Islam, and to force them into subjection.* The only way of avoiding the onslaughts of the *ghazis* was to become subjects of the Islamic state. Non-Muslims could then enjoy the status of *dhimmis*, living under its protection [...] The concepts of the *ghaza* and the marches were applied by the Ottomans not *only to conquests of infidel territory, but also to expansion within the confines of the Islamic world* [...] The reputation of the Ottomans as *ghazis* was vulnerable to criticism in the case of wars waged against other Muslims. The Ottomans therefore tried to pass off as licit acts annexations achieved through pressure and threats."

At the meeting at which it was decided to proceed with the conquest of Constantinople in 857 AH/ 1453 CE, Mehmed II pointed out, '*The ghaza is our basic duty, as it was in the case of our fathers.* Constantinople, situated as it is in the middle of our dominions, protects the enemies of our state and incites them against us. The conquest of this city is therefore essential to the future and safety of the Ottoman state'" [47].

In such a pattern of thinking and acting, the aggressive expansionist view of jihad developed throughout time to be an obsession for the Asian belligerent communities, and was significantly represented in the wars east of the Sassanian lands and in India.

□ *Constant Rebelliousness and Ethnic Animosity in the Annexed Lands*

The expansionist tendency led to troubles and difficulties familiar in growing empires. Bitter animosity had been planted and inherited in the hearts of the indigenous peoples of these lands against those who had conquered them, even when those indigenous people became Muslims. A conquered land in such an expansion became a liability for the Muslim state rather than an advantage. It was often ready to rebel for any reason, or to host any group or idea that might be hostile to the central authority. Such inherited ethnic splits even continue until now in some areas, such as between the Berbers and the Arabs in North Africa, a chasm that was fueled through colonialism and imperialism, but the original blaze of which had been born centuries before. Another significant example is in Darfur, where the Arabized tribes have been the constant oppressors of the African indigenous people, even though both are Muslims.

In the Eastern lands, a shelter and a front for confronting the state were perpetually provided for its enemies, including the ceaseless rebels, al-Khawarij, in al-Ahwaz and other Persian areas, or the mutineer Abd al-Rahman ibn Muhammad ibn al-Asha'ath the governor of Sijistan in 80-83 AH/ 700-704 CE. Later the Abbasid movement against the Umayyads was able to grow and flourish in Khurasan from 120 AH/ 740(s) CE. North Africa revolted against the Arab conquerors for decades under tribal leaders such as Kusayla and al-Kahina (the vaticinatoress) in 50-83 AH/ 671-702 CE. The Khawarij found among the Berbers in North Africa fertile land for a long-lasting revolution against the Umayyad rule (102-124 AH/ 720-741 CE). The Berber-Arab conflict extended to Andalusia, although both shared fighting as Muslims in the conquest war. In Transoxiana (*ma wara' al-Nahr*), the Muslim state authority was renounced during the rule of Yazid ibn 'Abd al-Malik (101-105 AH/ 720-724 CE). The revolting tendency extended to India, and even to Egypt. The Muslim authority was seriously shaken in the lands around the Caspian Sea (*al-Khazar*) and in Central Asia [48]. Attempts for further expansion in the Byzantine lands and Armenia and for the siege of Constantinople failed, and Byzantine counterattacks followed against the Muslim authority on Mediterranean Islands such as Cyprus, Rhodes, and Crete, and even against the Muslim land frontier with the Byzantines [49].

Furthermore, the ethnic animosity between the Arabs and the non-Arab conquered peoples was crystallized in the *"mawali"* conflict under the Umayyads, who looked to those non-Arab conquered peoples as inferior subjects, although they had become Muslims and fought with the Arabs in their wars. The word *mawali* (singular: *mawla*) in Arabic refers to both the allies and the liberated slaves, [50] and its use for non-Arabs was probably to denote inferiority. Non-Arabs were exploited and oppressed in peace and in war by the Umayyad rulers: working in state forced labor, paying the head tax (*jizya*) although they had become Muslims, and being charged with heavy civil and military burdens [51]. The Umayyads' injustice towards the non-Arabs led to an ethnic protest tendency against the Arabs that was called *"al-shu'ubiyya"* – related to *shu'ub*, (peoples) and aimed to demand equality for the Islamized peoples [52].

Meanwhile, mobilizing the Muslim Arabs towards expansion did not always secure their unity. The gains of conquest created power splits among them, and the incessant tribal conflicts throughout the state lands brought about the end of the Umayyad dynasty [53].

The Impact of the State Expansionist Policy on Jurisprudence

Domination of the Expansionist Tendency

The Umayyad practice of securing power and overcoming any opposition – as carried out by state instruments such as al-Mughira ibn Shuba, Ziyad ibn Abi Sufyan, 'Ubayd Allah ibn Ziyad, Muslim ibn 'Uqba, al-Husayn ibn Numayr al-Sukuni, and al-Hajjaj ibn Yusuf al-Thaqafi – was very oppressive and fierce. When Al-Husayn ibn Ali ibn Abi Talib was killed in the battle of Karbala' in 61 AH/ 680 CE after a rejection of his offer for peace and retreat, his head was cut off and paraded in a military procession in the streets of Kufa. The men and women who were with him were sent as captives to the Umayyad palace in Damascus. Medina was fiercely attacked in 63 AH/ 683 CE when it renounced Umayyad authority after the murder of al-Husayn, and the Umayyad army was fully permitted to kill, rape, and seize belongings there. In the next year, 64 AH/ 683 CE, Mecca was attacked by catapults and the Ka'ba walls were cracked [54].

As such appalling blood baths took place, the Umayyad authorities tried to turn public attention to the external front, a practice often pursued by despots in similar situations. The Mediterranean Islands of Cyprus, Crete, and Sicily, and places in Armenia and Asia Minor were attacked by the Umayyad forces, and the Byzantine capital Constantinople was put under siege twice in 44 AH/ 664 CE and in 98-99 AH/ 716-17 CE. But all these expansionist attempts ended in failure [55]. The conquest of North Africa (al-Maghrib) extended for more than 60 years starting from

26-27 AH/ 646-647 CE [56], and evolved into a conquest of Southern Spain (*al-Andalus*), in 92 AH/ 711 CE, in addition to unsuccessful campaigns beyond the Pyrenees mountains in Frankish lands through 102-114 AH/ 721-734 CE [57]. The expansionist tendency under the Umayyads pushed the Muslim armies eastward to Transoxiana, the Sind valley, the Caspian Sea basin, and Central Asia.

The Abbasids followed the Umayyads in their expansionist tendency, especially in the eastern lands. They also had their suppressive practices against internal rebels, and were no less eager than the Umayyads to demonstrate their external victories and glories. It might be said that Islam in the end benefited from that expansionist tendency, since it is as a result of it that today Muslims exist in most of those conquered areas. Such Muslims are maintaining now their faith through conviction or as an inherited tradition throughout generations, as there has not been a Muslim political or military power that would have forced them to be Muslims throughout the centuries. However, Islam *in the first place* does not allow in any way a spread of its faith by force, as the Quran sharply declares: "*No coercion should ever be in matters of faith*" (2:256).

Umar ibn Abd al-Aziz (99-101 AH/ 717-720 CE) the eighth of the Umayyad dynasty, significantly gained for Islam great numbers of Asian rulers and peoples through peaceful messages and efforts. At the same time, he stopped the siege of Constantinople and ordered back its campaign that had been sent by his predecessor Sulayman in 98 AH/ 716 CE [59]. Islam spread among huge numbers in South Eastern and Eastern Asia peacefully through traders, teachers, and sufis.

But it should never be ignored that the image of Islam has always been stained by the expansionist attempts under successive ruling dynasties, from the Umayyads to the Abbasids and then the Ottomans. Modern Muslim authors have had to continuously argue against the claim that Islam was spread by the sword. The distinguished modern jurists Shaykh Muhammad Abduh (d. 1905), followed by and quoted by Shaykh Abd al-Wahhab Khallaf (d. 1956), had to clearly delineate that "later conquest that occurred (after the early four caliphs) was a result of the *monarchial attitude* of supremacy and domination and did not comply with the rules of the religion" [60]. A saying attributed to al-Rashid (d. 193 AH/ 808 CE), the fifth of the Abbasid ruling dynasty, precisely represented and manifested that monarchial expansionist tendency: he addressed one day a passing cloud, "Move as you like, wherever your rain may come down, its revenue and taxes will be collected and brought back to me" [61].

The aggressive and expansionist view of *jihad* among Muslims met a parallel aggressive and expansionist tendency of "crusading" among Christians. As Ira M. Lapidus rightfully noted,

"The Crusades had origin in a general European counter-attack against Muslim powers in the Mediterranean. Italian towns were pushing back Muslim pirates. The *Reconquesta* had begun in Spain, by 1085, Toledo was in Christian hands. In 1087, *Piza and Genoa destroyed Mahdiya,* the political and commercial capital of Muslim North Africa. The *Normans conquered Sicily* between 1061 and 1091 and moved on to attack the Byzantine Empire [originally "the other" for universal Catholic Christendom]. [Meanwhile] the papacy was eager to reconcile the Greek and Western churches and to support the Byzantine Empire against the Seljuk Turks.

It was eager to establish new states under its auspices in the eastern Mediterranean, to speed the influence of the Latin church among eastern Christian peoples. Alongside the political currents ran a strong passion for pilgrimage [to Jerusalem]" [62].

The confrontations between the two zealous groups were deplorable in deepening the roots of hostilities between the Muslim world and Christendom through history. They were not limited to the states and their organized armed forces, but extended to the self-appointed naval raiders who exchanged surprising attacks on the ships or coastal towns of the other side [63].

□ *Juristic Amalgamation of the General Universal Principles and the Historical Particularities*

The Quran includes *general principles of the law of war*, such as:

– "O you have attained to faith! Submit yourselves wholly to peace, and follow not Satan's footsteps" (1:209),

– "[...] and rather help one another in furthering goodness and virtue and God-consciousness, and do not help one another in furthering evil and enmity, and remain conscious of God" (5:2),

– "Permission [to fight] is given to those against whom oppression and war is initially being wrongfully waged [...] *those who have been driven from their homelands against all right for no other reason than their saying, 'Our Lord is God',* for if God had not enabled people to defend themselves against one another, monasteries and churches, and synagogues, and mosques – in [all of] which God's name is abundantly extolled – would surely have been destroyed' (22:39-40),

– "And fight in God's cause against those *who have initially waged war against you, but do not commit aggression* – for, verily, God does not love aggressors" (2:190),

– "And it may well be that God *will bring about [mutual] affection between you [O believers] and those from among* whom you [now] face as enemies; and God is all-powerful and God is much-forgiving, mercy-giving. *As for such [of the*

60

unbelievers] as do not fight against you on account of [your] faith, and neither drive you forth from your homelands, God does not forbid you to show them kindness and to behave towards them with full equity, and verily, God loves those who act equitably. *God only forbids you to side with such as fight against you because of [your] faith; and drive you forth from your homelands,* or aid [others] in driving you forth; and as for those [from among you] who side with them; it is they who are truly wrongdoers" (60:7-9),

—   "O you who have attained to faith! *Be true to your agreements and promises"* (5:1),

—   "And be true to your bond with God whenever you bind yourself by a pledge, and do not break your oath after having [deliberately] confirmed them and calling upon God to be your witness and guarantor of your good will, behold, God knows all what you do" (16:9),

—   "And if you have reason to fear treachery from people [with whom you have made an agreement], cast it back out then *openly and without any confusion*; for verily, God does not love the treacherous" (8:58), "And make ready against them [your enemies] whatever force and war mounts you are able to muster, so that you might deter thereby the enemies of God who are your enemies as well, and others besides them of whom you may be unaware, [but] God is aware of" (8:60),

—   *"But if they incline to peace, incline you to it, and place your trust in God;* verily, He alone is all-hearing, all-knowing. And should they seek but to deceive you [by their show of peace], behold, God is enough for you [as a supporter against their deception]..." (8:61-62).

On the other hand, there are verses in the Quran that addressed *the particular circumstances of Arabia at the time of the Prophet,* where Muslims had been already oppressed, tortured, and driven out of their homes by the polytheistic leaders of Quraysh and their allies. Such verses are clear in referring *to those particular enemies* and their continuing hostilities and offensives, which made Muslim self-defense in that tribal setting necessary for survival. That particular war in its given circumstances had to be persistent and multi-faceted, and the *relevant verses should not be taken out of context to infer a general and permanent war* declared against *all* polytheists or disbelievers in the entire world. The Quran is very specific in indicating those who were fought against, and the circumstances – limited to the particular time and place – justifying such a war. As examples, the Quran reads:

– "And kill them wherever you come upon them, *and drive them away from wherever they drove you away, for oppression is even worse than killing;* and fight not against them near the *Inviolable House of Worship* unless they first fight against you there [. . .] But if they desist, behold, God is much-forgiving, mercy-giving. Fight *during the sacred months* if you are attacked during them [. . .] Thus, if any one initially commits aggression against you, fight against him as he has initially fought against you, but remain conscious of God, and know that God is with those who are conscious of Him" (2:191-194),

– "Disavowal by God and the Conveyor of His Message to those who associate others with God, and with whom you [O believers] have made an agreement. [Announce to them]: 'Go, then, [freely] about the earth for four months and know that you can never elude God [. . .] And a proclamation from God and the Conveyor of His Message [is made]

62

unto the people on the *greatest day of pilgrimage* that God disavows all who associate others with Him, and [so does] the Conveyor of His Message. Hence, if you repent it shall be for your own good, and if you turn away, then know that you can never elude God [. . .] *But excepted shall be – from among those who associate others with God – [people] with whom you [O believers] have made an agreement and who thereafter have never failed to fulfill their obligations towards you, and neither have aided anyone against you, observe, then, your agreement with them* until the end of the term agreed with them; verily, God loves those who are conscious of Him. And so, *when the sacred months are over,* fight against and [do not hesitate to] kill those who associate others with God wherever you may come upon them, and take them captive, and besiege them, and lie in wait for them at every conceivable place; yet, if they repent and take to prayer and render the purifying social welfare [*zakat*], leave them and let them go their way [. . .] *And if any of those who associate others with God seek your protection, grant him protection* so that he might [be able] to hear the word of God [from you], and thereupon bring him to the place where he can feel secure; because they may be people who [do not follow the truth because they] do not know. How could they who associate others with God be granted promise by God and the Conveyor of His Message, except those with whom you [O believers] have made an agreement in the vicinity of the Inviolable House of Worship; [as for those] so long as they remain true to you, be true to them, for verily, God loves those who are conscious of Him [. . .]" (9:1-7),

– "[Those who had always been hostile to you], *have never respected any tie nor any obligation towards a believer* and it is they who *are aggressors*" (9:10), "Would you, perchance, fail to fight against *people who have broken their solemn pledges, and have done all that they could to*

63

drive the Conveyor of God's Message away, and have been first to attack you? [...] " (8:13),

– "[...] And fight against those who associate others with God *all together just as they have been fighting against you [O believers] all together* [...] " (9:36).

It is very obvious that the above verses are addressing *specific people, in a particular place, under precise circumstances for distinct reasons*, because they repeatedly *broke their agreements and promises* with the Prophet and the believers. The time had come *to confront them once and for all as a group just as they had confronted the believers as a group*. The polytheists in Arabia were given an *appointed period of four months* to reflect on their situation with regard to the message of Islam and the Muslim community. The polytheists of Quraysh in Mecca had oppressed, tortured, and driven out the Muslims from their homes in Mecca, and continued their hostilities against Muslims after the latter's migration to Medina. They ceaselessly worked to manipulate and galvanize any potential for hostilities against the Muslims in their new home, whether it came from the bedouin tribes around the city, or from the Jewish tribes within it. *The polytheist nomads around Medina presented a constant enemy*, following the bedouin custom in raiding the settled areas and the traveling caravans for plunder, and encouraged by the other enemies of Muslims [(64)].

The above verses therefore specifically refer to previous agreements with Muslims that had been broken, exempting those who kept their agreements and promises from the general disavowal. In addition, references such as the Inviolable House of Worship (*al-Masjid al-Haram/ al-Ka'ba*), the sacred months (*al-ashhur al-hurum*), and driving the Prophet out of his home, clearly indicate the particular *circumstances and addressees* of these verses.

The very mention of such specific circumstances closes the door on and cannot allow any generalization and formation of a permanent comprehensive law.

As the sources of a message addressing the Arabs in Arabia with their particular circumstances during the time of Prophet Muhammad, as well as all of humanity as the final divine message, the Quran and the authentic traditions of the Prophet (the Sunna) *require a thorough textual study*. In order *to determine to which of the two categories a text should be related*, the structural, historical, and content indications must be fully examined. Among the 6,236 verses of the Quran, there are about 375 verses that speak of jihad. But only about 60 of these refer to permanent legal rules of war, while the others are descriptive narratives of important battles between the Muslims and their enemies. The verses are distributed throughout the Quran, especially in Sura 2: *al-Baqara*, 3: *al-Imran*, 4: *al-Nisa*, 5: *al-Ma'ida*, 8: *al-Anfal*, 9: *al-Tawba*, 33: *al-Ahzab*, 47: *Muhammad*, 48: *al-Fath*, 57: *al-Hadid*, and 59: *al-Hashr*. Historical information is reported in these suras about the battle of Badr in 2 AH/ 623 CE, Uhud in 3 AH/ 624 CE, Bani al-Nadir in 4 AH/ 625 CE, al-Ahzab in 5 AH/ 626 CE, Bani Qurayza in 5 AH/ 626 CE, al-Hudaybiya in 6 AH/ 627 CE, al-Fath (entering Mecca) in 8 AH/ 629 CE, Hunayn in 8 AH/ 629 CE, and Tabuk in 9 AH/ 630 CE.

These historical narratives have their permanent value as history with regard to information and moral education, but this is distinctive and should always be differentiated from any sort of declaration of a permanent law of war. Belief in the Quran as the permanent and final guidance of God should not obscure the fact that the message of Islam addressed the circumstances and needs of particular people in a given time and place. This exists side by side with the Quran's universal permanent guidance to all of humanity in every time and place. *Unless Islam responded to the particular* circumstances and needs of the Arabs in Arabia at the time of the revelation, it would not have established its roots there and thus reached all humanity at other times and places. Conversely, if the *message had limited itself to the local and interim needs*, the final divine message would be irrelevant due to the changing circumstances and needs of different human communities in different times and places.

Therefore, it is essential for an accurate conception of the Islamic revealed sources to discern the permanent universal on one side, and the interim particular on the other. This would be achieved based on the linguistic, structural, historical and content indications of the text and the context. As for the Sunna of the Prophet, a distinction has to be made between what was said or done by the Prophet as a leader of the Muslim community in his time based on his human judgment on one side, and what was said or done by him as the Prophet and Conveyor of the final message of God to humanity in its entirety on the other [65].

Not a few commentators and jurists viewed the verses at the beginning of the 9th Quranic sura (*al-Tawba*) as a final termination of Muslims' relations with others: "Disavowal by God and the Conveyor of His Message [is herewith announced] unto those who associate others with God and with whom you [O believers] have made agreements [. . .] And when the sacred months are over, fight against and kill those who associate others with God wherever you may come upon them, and take them captive, and besiege them and lie in wait for them [. . .] " (9:1-5). This verse has been called by some "*the verse of the sword.*" Others believe that the title also applies to verse 9:36, "[. . .] and fight against those who associate others with God all together, just as they

66

fight against you all together." In his commentary on the verse 9:5, Ibn Atiyya mentioned that this verse abrogated **all** the Quranic verses that had referred to reconciliation or truce; these are usually reported to be 114 verses, although al-Suyuti (d. 911 AH/ 1505 CE) quoting Muhammad ibn Abd Allah ibn al-Arabi (d. 543 AH/ 1148 CE), gave their number as 114 or 124 [66]. Furthermore, Ibn Atiyya believed that verse 2:191 "And fight against and kill them wherever you may come upon them and drive them away wherever they drove you away, for oppression is even worse than killing" addressed all believers, not only the immigrants from Mecca to Medina who had been driven away from their homes, as had been understood by the prominent commentator al-Tabari [67].

These verses of Sura al-Tawba obviously address a situation in Arabia at the time of the Prophet, in which the Muslims were facing a war. This war, as explicated above, was initially waged by the polytheists of Quraysh in Mecca, and later joined by the bedouins around Medina who were motivated mainly by their own desire of plunder. It was sometimes further encouraged by the other enemies of the Muslims, be they the Qurayshi polytheist leaders in Mecca – especially before the Prophet victoriously reentered the city – or the Jews in Medina first and Khaybar later. Such particular circumstances are obvious in the Quranic context and the historical development. However, such a narrow *literal understanding of the verses, and a view of the Prophet's traditions (Sunna) as one mass that interprets every single text in the Quran or the Sunna as equally and permanently binding, was a product of the historical expansionist practices of the Muslim state that had raised the banner of jihad.*

A jurisprudential definition of jihad was developed *as a permanent collective obligation* on the entire community of believers or *umma* (*fard kifaya*), against any power in any land that obstructed the preaching of Islam. Based on this categorization, whenever some of the *umma* are able to fulfill this obligation, then the whole *umma* would be cleared from its collective responsibility in this matter. According to such a view, jihad, that at the time of the Prophet had been determined to be *fard 'ayn* on the person to whom the Prophet had assigned it, now came to be seen *as a permanent collective obligation for the entire umma, to be fulfilled according to an individual's ability*. The obligation generally rested with the leadership of the Muslim state and their designees, and thus the *umma* was cleared of this responsibility. However, wherever Muslims in any area are attacked, the obligation of jihad shifts to every individual who is able to fight in that area (*fard 'ayn*) to defend the Muslim land and its people.

□ *Jihad in the Scholarly Delineation*

From their early writings, Muslims devoted special care to the wars of the Prophet (*al-maghazi*). In the generation following the Prophet's Companions, that of the Successors (*al-tabi'in*), 'Urwa ibn al-Zubayr (d. 94 AH/ 712 CE), the son of the eminent Companion al-Zubayr ibn al-'Awwam, was one of the early important sources for the Prophet's life. This category of books on the Prophet's life initially became known as the Prophet's wars (*al-maghazi*), before acquiring the more comprehensive name of biography, or *sira*. It seems that alongside key events such as the Muslims' migration to Abyssinia and the Prophet's migration to Medina, those wars were considered a significant part of the Prophet's life.

Urwa's narration was reported by his son Hisham, then later by Muhammad ibn Muslim ibn 'Abd Allah ibn Shihab al-Zuhri (d. 124 AH/ 741 CE), the well-known scholar of the Prophet's traditions (*sunna*) and jurisprudence. 'Urwa was a distinguished jurist in Medina in his time, and his narration was seen in the works of the later writers of *maghazi* such as Muhammad ibn Is-haq (d. 152 AH/ 769 CE) and Muhammad ibn 'Umar al-Waqidi (d. 207 AH/ 822 CE), as well as in the general history of al-Tabari (d. 310 AH/ 922 CE). Another early source of maghazi was 'Aban, the son of the Prophet's Companion Caliph Othman ibn 'Affan (d. 105 AH/ 723 CE), but his name did not appear in the narratives of the later writers on *sira* such as Muhammad ibn Sa'd (d. 230 AH/ 844 CE), the disciple and scribe of al-Waqidi [68].

The conduct of the Muslim state towards the non-Muslims in case of peace or war, *al-siyar*, was identified as a distinctive part in the Islamic law *"Shari'a"* [69]. An early work was dictated by Abu Hanifa (d. 150 AH/ 767 CE), then narrated and added to by such of his disciples as Abu Yusuf,

Zufar, al-Hasan ibn Ziyad al-Lu'lui'i, and Muhammad ibn al-Hasan al-Shaybani. Muhammad ibn al-Hasan (d. 189 AH/ 804 CE) wrote a concise book with the title *al-Siyar*, to which al-Awza'i (d. 157 AH/ 773 CE), responded with a book on the same topic, and this was reacted to in turn by Abu Yusuf (d. 182 AH/ 798 CE). Later on, Muhammad ibn al-Hasan wrote a detailed work on the same topic, *Al-Siyar al-Kabir*, in several volumes [70]. As the prominent scholar Dr. Muhammad Hamid-Ullah rightfully observed, such concern about the Islamic legal rules in dealing with non-Muslim entities during peace or war, and with non-Muslim individuals who live on Muslim land permanently or as visitors, underscores a significant Islamic perspective that was radically different from previous traditions such as those of the Greeks and the Romans. [71] The Muslims considered "non-Muslims" as having "rights" that should be protected by the general divine law, and they even wrote some specific treatises on the topic. Many juristic books also appeared on *"al-jihad,"* and *"al-jihad* and *al-siyar"* had a specific part in any comprehensive collection of the authentic Prophet's traditions (*hadith* or *sunna*), or any comprehensive work on jurisprudence.

Al-Zuhri, followed by al-Awza'i in Syria, supported the view of a permanent collective obligation of jihad on the entire Muslim umma (*fard kifaya*), which if fulfilled by any group of it, absolved the rest of the umma from its responsibility. They supported the war against the Byzantines during the time of the Umayyads, and saw it as a legitimate fulfillment of the collective obligation of jihad. However, it seems that as early as the time of the Caliphs Umar (13-23 AH/ 634-644 CE) and Uthman (23-35 AH/ 644-656 CE), the Muslims in Mecca and in Medina were reluctant to join the armies sent outside Arabia, as the Muslim state had become considerably secure. Both Caliphs had reportedly to motivate the Muslims of Arabia to join the conquest armies. It seemed also that the religious Meccans were more inclined to worship in the Inviolable Mosque (*al-Masjid al-Haram*), for Caliph Umar was reported to assure the people that joining those mobilized armies of conquest would be far more rewarded by God in the eternal life to come [72].

As has been mentioned before, securing the borders of Arabia developed into a full confrontation with the Sassanian Persian Empire that Umar did not anticipate, and which he did his best to avoid. Under Uthman, conquests continued into Azerbaijan, Armenia, several Mediterranean islands, and North Africa. However, it appears that although the view of jihad as a permanent collective obligation against those who obstructed spreading the message of Islam had begun to crystallize, such an understanding was not adopted by all Muslims. Under the Umayyads, such external conquests became more unacceptable, especially in light of the internal state of oppression with its horrible bloody practices in Karabala', Medina, and Mecca.

□ *The View of Jihad as an Obligation Only in the Case of Self-Defense*

Muhammad ibn al-Hasan mentioned a view of the prominent jurist from Kufa *Sufyan ibn Sa'id al Thawri* (d. 161 AH/ 778 CE), distinguished for his piety, wonderful memory, and breadth and depth of knowledge of what is lawful and what is forbidden [73], that *jihad is only an obligation in case of self-defense* when Muslims are attacked. This was, he reasoned, obvious as the Quran clearly states "but if they fight against you, respond and kill them" (2:191), "and fight against those who associate others with God all together, just as they fight against you [O believers] all together" (9:36) [74].

In turn, Ibn Atiyya quoted al-Thawri's view that jihad was voluntary for Muslims who are not subjected directly to an attack, but pointed out that al-Thawri meant that this was the case when a group of Muslims fulfilled the collective duty of jihad, so that it became voluntary for other Muslims. Ibn Atiyya went on to elaborate on his own view indicated above, explaining that, "The consensus continued that jihad is *fard kifaya* (a collective obligation) on the entire umma of Muhammad, and so if it is fulfilled by those from among the Muslims who may have carried it out then the other Muslims would be cleared of the obligation. This is unless the enemy strikes at the Muslim land, then jihad becomes an obligation for every Muslim individual" [75].

Moreover, Ibn Ahmad (d. 595 AH/ 1198 CE) mentioned that Abd Allah ibn al-Hasan had been of the same view as Sufyan al-Thawri in seeing that jihad is voluntary [76]. He most likely meant Abd Allah ibn al-Hasan ibn al-Hasan ibn Ali ibn Abi Talib (d. 145 AH/ 762 CE), who was related to the generation of the Successors (*al-tabi'in*) that had followed that of the Prophet's Companions. He was eminent in his time and was respected by Umar ibn Abd al-Aziz, but was imprisoned in Kufa by the Abbasid sovereign al-Mansur (136-158 AH/ 754-775 CE) when Abd-Allah's sons Muhammad and Ibrahim revolted against the Abbasids, and he died in prison [77].

Furthermore, it is noticeable that *Imam Malik ibn Anas* in Medina (d. 179 AH/ 795 CE) in the version of his book *al-Muwatta'*, which was compiled by Muhammad ibn al-Hasan al-Shaybani, did not categorize the military activities of his time at the Muslim Byzantine frontiers or beyond them as jihad. In *al-Mudawwana*, compiled from Malik's teachings and responses by Sahnun (d. 240 AH/ 854 CE), Malik seemed hesitant or even reluctant to claim those border wars led by the Umayyads legitimately as jihad. Asked about participating in such campaigns, Malik's answer was merely that "there was *no harm* in doing so," pointing to the Byzantine attack on Muslims at Mar'ash (Germanikeia), presumably when it was destroyed by the Byzantine emperor Constantine V in 129 AH/ 746 CE. Roy Parviz Mottahedeh and Radwan al-Sayyid analyzed in *al-Musannaf* by Abd al-Razzaq al-San'ani (d. 211 AH/ 826 CE),

"how jihad as obligatory aggressive war came to be the prevalent opinion in the second half of the 2nd century H./8th century. Abd al-Razzaq mentions a group of highly respected Hijazi jurists in the circle of Ibn Jurayj (d. 150 H./ 762) who rejected the idea that the jihad was obligatory for all, and they seem moreover to have given primacy to other religious acts. Yet the Syrian jurists quoted by Abd al-Razzaq, perhaps *reflecting the determination to make progress on the Byzantine frontier in the first half of the 2nd Islamic century, were quite naturally attracted to the idea*

that aggressive war was obligatory. So in the 'Musannaf', we see that in Syrian circles pious stories circulated about the importance of being a frontier warrior in Syria by sea as well as by land [...] *The more general acceptance of the Syrian school reached its peak in the thought of al-Shafi'i* (d. 204 H./820) who elevates the *destruction of unbelief to be the primary justification of jihad.* Nevertheless [...] , the *opinions of the pre-Shafi'i jurists continued at least up to the seventies of the 2nd Islamic century* [...] "

As jihad became an inseparable part of Shari'a that was continuously treated in comprehensive juristic works, the authors believe that *"the transitions to a formal legal theory of war changed jihad from a theory primarily based on historical memories of the battles fought in the time of the Prophet and the early Islamic period to a more precisely defined and normative theory rooted in very specific events in the life of the Prophet and very specific interpretation of Quranic verses.* In the theory based on Quranic verses, an attempt was made to organize the relevant verses in chronological order, so that the *so-called verse* (or verses according to some) *of the sword,* which made war perpetual and a permanent obligation of the Islamic community, *came last and thus abrogated* verses that could clearly have allowed a different development of the law. Incidentally, Tabari who opens his work on 'The Divergence of the Jurists' [*'Ikhtilaf al-Fuqaha'*] with a careful list of which Quranic verses supersede which others, when it comes to the so called 'verse of the sword' in this Quranic commentary, gives no indication that it supersedes other verses" [78]. However, this verse may also be quoted to support a permanent universal obligation of jihad, "And fight against them until there is no more oppression and all [that is related to] faith would be [straight forward] with God alone [free from any pressure]" (8:39, also 2:193).

□ The View of Jihad as a Permanent Obligation for the Entire Umma

In his voluminous work "al-Siyar al-Kabir," Muhammad ibn al-Hasan al-Shaybani, one of the pillars of the Hanafi school, endorses *"jihad"* and its permanent and essential role as an Islamic obligation, and emphasizes its reward in the eternal life to come. This is very obvious in the extensive first chapter of his work entitled "The Virtue of Ribat" (being on guard of the security of Islam and Muslim land). In a chapter on "Jihad according to its Range of Imperativeness," the author briefly mentions the view of al-Thawri that jihad is legitimate and imperative only in the case of self-defense against an attack initiated by an enemy. At the same time, he elaborated on the opinion of Abu Hanifa (d. 150 H./767), which established that jihad *is an obligation for Muslims, but only when they are needed* and called upon. Al-Shaybani supported the Hanafi view by such Quranic verses:

"O you who have attained to faith! Fight against those who are near you from among the deniers of truth" (9:123),

"Fight against those who do not believe in God" (9:29),

"And strive hard in God's cause with all the striving that is due to Him" (22:78).

Al-Shaybani indicated that the command of jihad was revealed *gradually* in the Quran. At first, the Prophet was merely commanded to *spread the message and to leave alone* all those who associate others with God (15:94), and to *forgive* (15:85). Then followed a command of *arguing with the unbelievers in the best way* (16:125). At a later step, *permission for fighting back for self-defense* was given to the

75

believers, since they had been initially fought against unjustly (22:39), and so Muslims were commanded just to respond when war was initiated against them. Then a condition was made that fighting back should not occur during the Sacred Months (9:5). The last step was the *general command of fighting:* "And fight, then, in God's cause, and know that God is all-hearing, all-knowing" (2:244). Al-Shaybani concluded:

"And the *matter was settled in the end at this,* and the general command indicates *permanent imperativeness,* but the obligation of fighting is *for the purpose of enhancing the faith and overcoming those who associate others with God.* Thus, if the *purpose is achieved by some of the Muslims, the obligation becomes no more binding for the remainder of them [. . .]* But if all the Muslims together abandoned the obligation, they all share the guilt [. . .] The imam should look after the Muslims' interest, for he is appointed for this as a representative of their entire community, and *he should never give up calling people to the religion and urging Muslims to fulfill [the obligation of] jihad.* Whenever the imam calls the people for jihad, they should never disobey by refusing to go out [for fighting]. *The imam should never let those who associate others with God without calling them to Islam, or collecting jizya (tribute) from them, if he is able to do that [. . .]* And if those said to Muslims: 'Let us make a *reconciliation together,* stipulating that we would not fight against you, and you would not fight against us', Muslims *should not agree* to do that, for God says: 'And be not faint of heart, and grieve not, for you are bound to rise high [. . .] ' (3:139); *unless those have an enormous power which Muslims cannot meet".*

Al-Sarakhsi, the commentator and elaborator on al-Shaybani's book, added:

76

"And every Muslim is a successor of the Prophet, and he was sent to call people to Islam, and was commanded to fight against those who rejected it haughtily [...] [As for reconciliation for a permanent unconditional peace, one has to keep in mind that] jihad is an obligation, and asking for such a reconciliation that stipulates the abandonment of an obligation cannot be accepted [...] [And if the '*kuffar*' enjoy considerable military superiority] a reconciliation can be accepted until Muslims' power would prevail, and then they openly declare war against them [...], for the reality of jihad is in keeping up Muslims' power first, then in subduing those who associate others with God. Thus, if Muslims are unable to do the latter, they have to keep up their own power until they can prevail and have the power to subdue them [...], the same as the debtor who is in a hardship is given a delay until a time of ease to pay back his debt". However, an attempt to ease the strictness of the obligation was made through stipulating the permission of the parents and giving priority to the payment of debt when jihad is not for self-defense [79].

The problem in the argument of Muhammad ibn al-Hasan and other jurists for the permanent collective obligation of jihad is mainly about the approach itself, for the wrong approach by definition leads to an erroneous reading and use of the supporting Quranic texts.

Keeping in mind the historical context when looking at any Quranic text, and the historical perspective in looking to the Quran in its entirety, is an approach that is different from a lifeless mechanical chronology. The Quran, as it has been repeatedly stressed, addressed both the needs of a particular people in a given time and place, and the universal needs of humanity in its entirety during all times and places. Sometimes, the particularity is obvious, such as in the verses about pre-Islamic Arabian beliefs and practices (6:136-140). At other times, one has to find out what might be interim or permanent through the Quranic structural context and the historical background.

The circumstances of the revelation of a verse and the relevant socio-cultural history of the Arabs before and at the time of the Prophet have to be thoroughly considered. This requires a comprehensive perspective of the Quran (and the message of Islam as indicated in all its sources including the traditions, *sunna*, and life, *sira*, of the Prophet) and of the socio-cultural environment of the message before and during the time of the Prophet.

- As Mottahedeh and al-Sayyid have sharply articulated and accurately stated:

"The transition to a *formal legal theory of war* changed jihad from a theory primarily based on *historical memory* of the battles fought in the time of the Prophet and early Islamic period to a more precisely defined and normative theory rooted *in very specific events in the life of the Prophet and very specific interpretation of Quranic verses*. In the theory based on Quranic verses, an attempt was made to *organize the relevant verses in chronological order,* so that the so-called *verse* (or verses, according to some) *of the sword*, which made war perpetual and a permanent obligation of the Islamic community, *came last and therefore abrogated* verses that could clearly have allowed a different development of the law."

Earlier, Hamilton A.R. Gibb precisely pointed out:

"The fully developed *political theory of the Sunni jurists* was thus [...] not speculatively derived from the sources

78

of Revelation, but rather *based upon an interpretation of these sources in the light of later political developments,* and reinforced by the dogma of the divine guidance of the community and infallibility of its *ijma':* 'My community will never agree [altogether] upon an error'. Almost every succeeding generation left its mark upon political doctrine, as *fresh precedents were created and the theory was accommodated to them* [...] Sunni political theory was in fact only the *rationalization of the history of the community.* Without precedents, no theory; and all the imposing fabric of interpretation of the sources is merely the *post evnetum justification of the precedents* which have been ratified by ijma' [...] he [al-Mawardi] *often omits all but a brief reference to the disputes out of which the actual decisions arose,* and thus gives to his statements [in spite of their framework of scholastic discussion] a somewhat final and assertive air, as if they merely recapitulated what always was, is now, and ever should be." [80]

Gibb's observation is very accurate with regard to the juristic presentation – whether that of al-Mawardi (d. 450 AH/ 1058 CE) or of other jurists – of the position of "imamate or caliphate," its function, and its religious and worldly importance and role. This is especially significant at a time when factual power throughout the Muslim lands was seized by several independent rulers, some of whom expressed a nominal acknowledgement of the Abbasid caliphate, and some of whom did not. Similarly, qualifying jihad as a collective obligation for the Muslim umma to subdue all those who might stubbornly reject Islam throughout the world after being called to it and also refuse to pay jizya, at a time when Muslims were politically and militarily in general forceless, is highly unrealistic. Such a fact was subsequently proven through the end of Muslim rule in Southern Spain (Andalusia) in 898 AH/ 1492 CE, the invasion of the Muslim lands by the Crusaders starting from 491 AH/ 1097 CE, and the complete and terminal fall of the caliphate under the sweeping Mongol attacks in 656 AH/ 1258 CE.

- It is well known that the revelation of the Quranic verses was distributed over 23 lunar years. Relating the verses to their time of revelation, and structuring the verses related to a certain topic in a comprehensible topical integration would be necessary and very useful in order to put each verse in its structural and historical context. But taking them as split fragments and organizing them without decisive or sufficient evidence into a chronological order, merely to establish a concept of *"abrogation"* that is not explicit and is based on a mere assumed sequence of time within each topical group is an approach that is devoid of any conclusive historical, logical, or linguistic evidence. Yet such an approach was what was applied to the verses on jihad and followed by Muhammad ibn al-Hasan al-Shaybani and most jurists. It was this approach that led to seeing the so-called "verse – or verses – of the sword" as a final and permanent obligation of war for the entire Muslim community.

Yet, there is no consensus among scholars of the Quran, jurists and other authorities, past and present, on one chronological order for a certain topical group of Quranic verses, on the acceptance of such a concept of abrogation in the Quran, or on the application of this concept to the so-called *"verse or verses of the sword."* Abu Muslim Muhammad ibn Bahr al-Asfahani (d. 322 AH/ 934 CE), was of the opinion that no abrogation had ever occurred within the Quran, even though the Quran as a whole abrogated the laws included in previous divine messages [81]. Shaykh Mahmud Shaltut the former Shaykh of al-Azhar (d. 1963), quoted and apparently supported Abu Muslim's view [82]. In his commentary on the verse 2:106, Muhammad Asad wrote: "Any message

80

which We annul or consign to oblivion, We replace with a better or similar one" is related to the Quran's supercession of previous messages. He continued,

"The word 'ayah' (message) occurring in this context is also used to denote 'a verse' of the Quran (because every one of those verses contains a message). Taking this restricted meaning of the term 'ayah', some scholars conclude from the above passage that certain verses of the Quran have been *'abrogated'* by God's command before the revelation of the Quran was completed [...], *there does not exist a single reliable tradition* to the effect that the Prophet ever declared a verse of the Quran to have been 'abrogated'. At the root of the so-called *'doctrine of abrogation,'* may lie the inability of some of the early commentators to reconcile one Quranic passage with another, a difficulty which was overcome by declaring that one of the verses in question had been 'abrogated'. The arbitrary procedure explains also why there is *no unanimity* whatsoever among the upholders of the 'doctrine of abrogation' as to which, and how many, Quranic verses have been affected by it; and furthermore, as to whether this alleged abrogation implies a *total elimination of the verse in question from the context of the Quran, or only a cancellation of the specific ordinance or statement* contained in it. In short, the 'doctrine of abrogation' has no basis whatsoever in historical fact, and must be rejected. On the other hand, the apparent difficulty in interpreting the above Quranic passage (2:106) disappears immediately if the term 'ayah' is understood correctly as 'message', and if we read this verse in conjunction with the preceding one which states that [the People of the Book] refuse to accept any revelation [which might supersede that of the Bible], for if read in this way, the abrogation relates to earlier divine messages and not to any part of the Quran itself" [83].

The prominent scholar of Quranic sciences, al-Suyuti (d. 911 AH/ 1505 CE), was among the supporters of the "abrogation" view, but he brought down the cases of the assumed abrogation only to *twenty,* while other authors have argued that the number is as high as 290 [84]. Al-Suyuti did not agree about applying 'abrogation' to the so- called 'verse of the sword' (9:5). The word *"nunsiha / consign it to oblivion"* is read *"nansa'uha/ delay"* in the recitation of Abu 'Amr and ibn Kathir, following the Companions Umar ibn al-Khattab, 'Abd Allah ibn 'Abbas and 'Ubayy ibn Ka'b, and the Successors Mujahid (d. 104 AH/ 722 CE), 'Ata' (d. 114 AH/ 732 CE) and others. For al-Suyuti, a command has to be obeyed *for a certain reason* (*'illa*)*,* but if the reason ceases to exist, *another later command is applied* according to the people's need. The former command still exists to be applied whenever its reason materializes. This is *distinct from abrogation,* which stops the former command from being applied in any case and terminates its effect. Thus, *the commands of patience and forgiveness have their permanent effect whenever their reasons exist,* and the command of fighting has also its effect side by side with the commands of patience and forgiveness, and it has to be followed when its reasons exist [85]. Mustafa Zayd, who supports the view of abrogation, devotes a complete chapter to arguing against the claimed abrogation of the verses related to patience and forgiveness by the so-called "verse of the sword" [86].

• Furthermore, there were moral and psychological matters in addition to the historical, textual, and methodological considerations that led to the prevalence of the view about the permanent obligation of the Muslim community as a whole in carrying out "jihad" all over the world, whenever they are able to do so. In this way, the message of Islam would be spread, and any power that may bar the people from hearing it should be fought against. Thus, the goal appointed by God can be reached "to make it [the message of Islam] *prevail over all religion,* however hateful this may be to those who associate others with God" (61:9). Although prevalence of a faith is not necessarily determined by the number of its followers, and the Quran's principle strictly states: "No coercion should ever be in matters of faith" (2:256), advocates of the view have their argument and justification. They simply think that *Islam is the mere and plain truth,* and so it would be convincing to any normal and sensible person, and any refusal of this truth would be due to egotism, arrogance, stubbornness, and viciousness, as it means rejection of justice and common welfare. Therefore, as proponents of universal justice and welfare, Muslims should have the right and the responsibility to use force to spread their message for the benefit of the masses against the limited unfair obstructers of universal righteousness. However, a recognition and acceptance of the Muslim political authority by paying the jizya was deemed sufficient, and embracing Islam was not stipulated as the only condition for peace. Instead, it was argued that such an acceptance of the Muslim political authority would allow the people in the long term to know Islam more in its sources and through the behavior of Muslims, leading them to accept it sooner or later.

Such an oversimplification of the matters of belief and faith has made such a concept of jihad as an Islamic permanent obligation for the entire umma very reasonable and fair for the majority of Muslim jurists throughout the generations. They have believed that imposing a humiliating *jizya* on others is nothing in comparison to the great benefits that the people will gain, and then no material coercion will practically occur in matters of faith. Apparently, paying a tribute or *jizya'* to any conqueror was a model that was used throughout history, and not many people considered it as serious suppression. Leaving an inherited faith and accepting a new one has not been viewed historically as a difficult thing, especially when it is stressed that the sensible human being ought to use his mind in judging the inherited faith and the offered one. Common sense, as Muslims think, would naturally lead a person to accept Islam.

In the fervor of faith and wishful thinking, Muslim jurists through their milieu of conquests and successive wars, including the battles fought by rulers to seize power, could not properly appreciate the complexity of the human psychology and sociology in matters of faith, and could not grasp the profound message of the Quranic verse: "And do not revile those that they invoke instead of God, lest they revile God out of spite and in ignorance, *for goodly indeed have We made their own doings appear to every community;* and in time [however] unto their Lord they must return, and then He will make them [truly] understand all that they were doing" (6:108). Muslims are taught to be objective, fair, and well-mannered, whatever their faith about the truth may be, in their conversation with others, *"call to your Lord's path with wisdom and goodly exhortation, and argue with them in the most kindly manner"* [16:125]. A significant model of dialogue with "others" is given by the Quran: *"and, behold, either we [who believe in God], or you [who associate others with Him] are on the right path or have clearly gone astray. Say: 'Neither shall you be called to account for whatever we may have become guilty of, nor shall we be called to account for whatever you are doing'"* (34:24-25). Thus, numerous verses in the Quran remind Muslims that *the final and just judgment of any human being is only with God*, who is fully aware of a person's intention, knowledge, ability, and all his/her circumstances.

84

In addition, Muslims, after the unanticipated collapse of the Sassanian Persian Empire, believed that the Byzantine Empire and the entire world would follow, if only they fulfilled their obligation and did their best to make God's guidance and the religion of truth "prevail over all religion, however, hateful this may be to those who associate others with God" (61:8). In a climate of victorious conquests, zeal led them to see Islam as encompassing the entire world for the benefit of all humanity. When this ceased to occur, and on the contrary successive attacks against the Muslim lands were undertaken by the Crusaders, the Mongols, and then the European colonists, Muslims looked for a consolation in past glories, and believed that it was their guilt and deviation from the right path that brought upon them such adversity. It did not enter their minds that they have to change their understanding of the Quran, and review their political and military history as well as their intellectual and juristic heritage, in order to respond to their time and build up their present and future. They have thought that if they merely promoted their morality and religiosity, then all the glories of the past would be automatically regained.

☐ *Domination of the Permanent Aggressive View of War throughout the Centuries*

The view of the permanent obligation of *jihad* on the entire Muslim community/ *umma*, in order to confront by force the ruling authorities that use their power to obstruct the spread of Islam and block its peaceful propagation and dissemination, has continued to dominate the Islamic works through the successive centuries until today. This approach embodies the understanding of "the verse or verses of the sword" (9:5, 36 and sometimes others) as the final phase in defining relations of the Muslim umma with the non-Muslim world. Later Muslim generations became mere followers and imitators of what had been written before, and their weakness in facing the successive attacks of the Crusaders, the Mongols, and the European colonists has made them liable to ideas that nurture in them, in whatever way, self-assertion, responsibility, struggle and hope.

The prominent commentator on the Quran, Muhammad ibn Ahmad al-Qurtubi (d. 761 AH/ 1359 CE), stated in his comment on the verse 9:5 that its command is *"general, related to any place."* He quoted a view related to al-Husayn ibn al-Fadl ibn 'Umayr al-Baji (d. 282 AH/ 895 CE, a commentator on the Quran originally from Kufa who lived in Nisapur) that the verse "abrogated every verse in the Quran that mentions ignoring the enemies' offences and meeting them with patience." Al-Qurtubi mentioned that according to the Maliki jurists to whom he belonged, the payment of *jizya* "was required as a *substitute for killing because of kufr* (denial of the truth)" [(87)].

However, the prominent scholar Ahmad ibn Hajar al-'Asqalani (d. 852 AH/ 1448 CE) in his commentary on al-Bukhari's collection of traditions (*Sahih al-Bukhari*), broadened the definition of *al-jihad*. Under this definition, the term referred to *firstly: jihad against one's own self* by learning the teachings of the religion, practicing them and teaching them, *secondly: jihad against the devil's insinuations, thirdly: jihad against the dissolute (al-fussaq), and last: jihad as making the utmost effort in fighting against the kuffar*. Ibn Hajar followed the dominant view that jihad in the last case after the Prophet's death is a *collective duty* of the entire umma, unless Muslims are attacked then jihad becomes *an obligation for every Muslim individual* on the attacked land. The collective duty is required to be fulfilled *at least once a year* according to the majority of jurists [88].

The prominent Shafi'i jurist al-Mawardi (d. 450 AH/ 1058 CE) stated among the responsibilities of the head of the Muslim state (*al-imam*): "carrying out *jihad against whomever is called to Islam then stubbornly resists it, until he becomes a Muslim or enters in Muslims' protection (dhimma),* in order to fulfill what God requires of *making Islam prevail over all religion*." As for a region that is on the borders of an enemy, its governor has the responsibility of carrying out jihad against the bordering enemy [89]. Ahmad ibn Muhammad ibn Ahmad ibn Rushd (d.595 AH/ 1198 CE) stated that *jihad* is a collective duty for the entire umma (*fard kifaya*), indicating that *those who are to be fought against* are all polytheists (*al-mushrikin*) drawing on the verse: "And fight against them until there is no more oppression and all matters of faith would be straight with God alone [...]" (2:'193, also 8:39).

Ibn Jama'a, Muhammad ibn Ibrahim ibn Sa'd Allah (d. 733 AH/ 1332 CE) indicated that *"jihad"* is one of the main responsibilities of the head of the Muslim state *'the sultan,'* to be fulfilled *at least once a year*. It is a collective duty, *fard kifaya* if the *kuffar* stay in their lands and do not come to Muslim lands or interfere with them. In such a case, one who wants to go for jihad *has to get the permission of his parents*, and if he is *in debt* he has to get *the permission of his creditor* [90]. Ibn Taymiyya (d. 728 AH/ 1327 CE) simply stated that whoever was informed by God's message that had been conveyed by Prophet Muhammad, had to be fought against "until there is no more oppression and all matters of faith would be straight with God alone" (2:193), but he restricted those who should be fought against *to those who are able to fight*. Therefore, he excluded from those who should be fought against the elderly, the disabled, children, women, and monks [91].

In Focus

The late outstanding contemporary jurist and professor of Shari'a at the Law School in Cairo University, Shaykh Abd al-Wahhab Khallaf (d. 1956), concisely and sharply presented the view and argument of permanent aggressive war as the principle of universal relations between Muslims and the non-Muslim world, as well as the opposite view and argument of permanent peace and confinement of war to self-defense in Muslim relations with the non-Muslim world. Both views represent a *human effort, ijtihad*, in understanding and interpreting the various verses in the Quran and the oral and practical traditions of the Prophet, for there is no simple explicit divine rule in the matter.

View I: *War is the Principle in Muslims' Relations with the Non-Muslim World*

The supporters of *the permanent state of war* between the Muslims and the non-Muslim world have built their view on the fact that Islam commands the believers to call others to its message. This call has *two forms*: a call with *the tongue* and another with *the sword*. According to this view, *Muslims have to use force against* those who are called to Islam *by the tongue*, thereby receiving the proper information about Islam that reveals its truth, but still do not accept its message. If they are *Arab polytheists,* they have to be fought against until they accept Islam, but if they are Arabs who believe in the earlier divine messages as (*"People of the Book"*) or non-Arab polytheists, they have to be fought against until they accept Islam or pay the *jizya* tax and submit to the Muslim political authority. Until one of these goals is reached, *no peace is*

89

allowed by Islam for these people, except *temporarily* when a failure in reaching either goal is due to some sort of forcing pressures, and then this failure should not exceed the limits of necessity.

The supporters of this view have argued for it on the grounds of *these verses*: "And fight against those who associate others with God all together just as they fight against you [O believers] all together" (9:36), "Fight against those from among the receivers of the Book who do not [truly] believe either in God or the Last Day, and do not consider forbidden that which God and the Conveyor of His Message have forbidden and do not follow the religion of truth, till they [agree to] pay the exemption tax (*jizya*) with a willing hand, after having been humbled [in war]" (9:29). They also quote the Prophet's tradition, "I have been commanded to fight against people until they say: 'there is no god but the One God', and when they say it their blood and property become secure except for a right established by law, and their judgment belongs to God" [reported by al-Bukhari and Muslim]. Thus, those who hold this view believe that people who are properly called to Islam have no excuse in continuing to be followers of another faith. Therefore, there is no way to push them to their own good and benefit other than the use of force, and those who persist in their resistance should be killed, in order to remove their evil.

Thus, the rules of the international policy of the Muslim state according to this view are:

1) *Jihad is an obligation* that cannot be neglected through a guarantee of peace (*aman*) or a non-aggression agreement, unless such an agreement may buy the Muslims time to reach military readiness for war, especially when facing a stronger enemy.

90

However, if *war is initiated against Muslims, jihad is an obligation for every individual Muslim able to carry it out.* If war is not initially waged against the Muslims, jihad is a *collective obligation for the entire Muslim community/ umma.* If part of the umma fulfills the jihad, then the whole would be cleared of the obligation, but if none fulfills it, the entire umma is guilty.

2) *The basis in Muslims' relations with the non-Muslim world is war, unless there is a reason that necessitates peace,* such as faith, [i.e. Islam or being among the People of the Book] or a *guarantee of peace* that is either *temporary or permanent. The temporary peace may be general* for the entire people of a land, and has to be granted by the head of the Muslim state *(al-imam)* or one who stands for him, as was the case in the agreement of Hudaybiya made by the Prophet in the year 6 AH/ 627 CE. As for the special guarantee of peace, it is granted to certain persons for carrying out a certain work such as trade. A *temporary* guarantee of peace in all its kinds is allowed when it is beneficial for the Muslims. If the imam finds the temporary agreement no longer beneficial to the Muslims, he is authorized to cancel it, but he has to declare such a cancellation openly, avoiding any treachery or surprise attack.

The *permanent* guarantee of peace is granted only in the case when the *imam* or one who stands for him gives the *pledge of protection* (*'ahd al-dhimma*) to the People of the Book in general, Arabs or non-Arabs, or to non-Arab polytheists. Such a guarantee of peace should be permanent, and it is ever binding for Muslims. It may be revoked by the *dhimmis* through conversion to Islam, defection to the land of war, or rebellion against Muslims and their acquisition of dominance over a certain area. The agreement of the *dhimma* cannot be broken by refraining from paying *jizya*, or committing any individual crime. In principle, any transgression by a *dhimmi* that can be explained by any reason other than breaking the agreement of *dhimma*, should be accepted as such.

3) According to this view, the world is divided into "the abode of Islam" (*dar al-Islam*), where the laws of Islam are executed, and the Muslims' guarantee of peace for Muslims or *dhimmis* is enforceable, and "the abode of war" (*dar al-harb*) where no laws of Islam are implemented, and no Muslim guarantee of peace is enforceable.

View II: _Peace is the Principle in Muslims' Relations with the Non-Muslim World_

Other jurists have stated that _Islam inclines to peace, not to war, does not allow that a human being to be killed merely because he is not a Muslim._ According to these jurists, Islam does not allow Muslims to fight against others just because they have a different faith. Islam _stipulates aggression only in the case of a deliberate obstruction of a propagation of the message of Islam._

This view has been supported by these arguments:

1) The Quranic verses about fighting indicate _the reasons_ for it, which are _removing injustice, stopping oppression, or defending the right of propagating the faith:_ "And fight in God's cause _against those who have initially fought against you, but do not commit aggression,_ for verily God does not love aggressors. And kill them [the initiators of war] wherever you may come upon them, _and drive them away from wherever they drove you away, for oppression is even worse than killing._ And fight not against them near the Inviolable House of Worship (_al-Masjid al-Haram_), unless they first fight against you there, _but if they fight against you, kill them [...] But if they desist, behold, God is much-forgiving, mercy giving._ Hence, fight against them _until there is no more oppression,_ and all matters of faith would be straight with God alone [and free from any person's pressure], but if they desist, then all hostility shall cease, save against those who [willfully] commit injustice [...] Thus, if anyone commits aggression against you, _just attack_

93

him as he has attacked you, but remain conscious of God and know that God is with those who are conscious of Him" (2:190-194), "And how could you refuse to fight in the cause of God and of *the utterly helpless oppressed men and women and children* who are crying, 'O our Lord! Lead us forth out of this land whose people are oppressors' [...]" (4:75), "*Permission [to fight] is given to those against whom war has initially been wrongfully waged* [...] those who have been *driven out of their homes* against all right, for no other reason than their saying, 'Our Lord is God' [...]" (22:39-40).

2) It is forbidden to kill women, children, monks, the elderly, the blind, the disabled, or whoever may be in a similar situation, because all those are not combatants. If fighting was to force people to embrace Islam, the exception of those individuals would be unreasonable, especially with regard to the monks.

3) The Quran sharply states: "*No coercion should ever be in matters of faith*" (2:256), "*do you think that you could compel people to believe?*" (10:99).

The rules of the international policy of the Muslim state accordingly would be:

1) *Calling peacefully the non-Muslim to Islam is a collective duty (fard kifaya) for the umma as a whole.*

2) The basis for the Muslims' relations with others *is peace, unless a legitimate reason for war emerges,* such as *an attack waged against Muslims, or an obstruction of their message* by the state authorities.

3) The "abode of Islam" (*dar al-Islam*) is as defined before by the supporters of permanent war, but the difference exists with regard to the "abode of war" (*dar al-harb*). For this second group, *dar al-harb* is the land that had previously enjoyed peaceful relations with the Muslims but changed its situation because of its attack on Muslims, Muslim lands, or Muslims' right of propagating their message. No fighting is allowed against any people who can not be accused of such wrongdoing, and peaceful relations with them cannot be severed. The Muslim guarantee of peace to such a people is well-established not on the basis of a grant or a contract, but on the basis of the fact that the original principle in Muslims' relations with the non-Muslim world is peace, and nothing has happened to contradict it.

The Pointed Difference

After crystallizing each of the two views, Shaykh Khallaf underlined the pointed difference between them as follows:

1) According to the *first* view, *jihad is an obligation in dealing with those who did not positively respond to the message after it was delivered to them properly* and completely. So the *non-Muslims have to embrace Islam voluntarily or involuntarily.*

   The *second* view considers *jihad as only legitimate for self-defense when Muslims are attacked or when their spreading of the message of Islam is obstructed.*

2) According to the *first* view, *no guarantee of peace can be offered by Muslims to non-Muslims except temporarily or when a pledge of protection/ dhimma to non-Muslims is held by the Muslims* and this pledge is permanent by its nature.

   The *second* view *conceives of peace as the original general permanent state of relations between Muslims and non-Muslims throughout the world.* The state of war is only incidental when certain justifying reasons occur for defending Muslim land or people against an attack, or defending the right of spreading the message of Islam.

3) According to the *first* view, *the difference in the abode or territory (al-dar) between Muslims and non-Muslims is based on the difference of religion,* while the *second* view considers that *the abode of war (dar al-harb) is only that whose people have*

96

committed aggression against Muslims. Thus the basis of qualifying a land as such is merely its place as a source of security or threat for Muslims, not just the difference of religion of its population.

Preponderance of the View of Permanent Peace in World Relations

In conclusion, Shaykh Khallaf gives preponderance to the view that considers peace the permanent state in world relations between Muslims and non-Muslims, and argues that war is only legitimate against those who initiate hostility and commit aggression against Muslims. He gives his reasons as follows:

1) The Quran justifies reasons for the general normal state of peace and the occasional war in the verses: "It may well be that God will bring about [mutual] affection between you [O believers] and those from among them [the unbelievers] whom you [now] face as enemies, and God is all-powerful and God is much forgiving, mercy-giving. *As for such [of the unbelievers] as do not fight against you on account of [your] faith, and neither drive you forth from your homelands, God does not forbid you to be kind to them and to behave towards them with equity,* for verily God loves those who act equitably. *God only forbids you to turn in full alliance towards such as fight against you because of [your] faith, and drive you forth from your homes, or aid [others] in driving you forth [. . .] "* (60:7-9). It may be necessary to add that according to al-Zamakhshari (d. 538 AH/ 1143 CE) in *al-Kashshaf,* the expression "God does not forbid you" in the above verse (60:8) indicates in this context a *positive exhortation.* Moreover, the Quran states: *"Thus, if they let you be, and do not make war on you, God does not give you any way [for use of force] against them"* (4:90), *"And if they incline to peace, incline you to it as well, and place your trust*

in God [...]. And should they seek but to deceive you, behold, [reliance on] God will be enough for you" (8:61-2).

2)   *Verses that talk about fighting in a generalized way cannot be taken as supporting war as a rule, but they have to be conceived inseparably from and in connection with the other specifying verses* that restrict war and indicate reasons and conditions for it. There is *no way for a claimed abrogation*, since the verses that restrict war to be against aggression are consensually qualified as permanently operative and binding. A claim of abrogation here cannot stand, and abrogation in the Quran is not unanimously accepted in principle, nor are the assumed abrogations agreed upon by the upholders of the principle. Some commentators raised the number of verses abrogated by the so-called "verse or verses of the sword" to exceed a hundred verses, including all verses that command patience and forgiveness or forbid coercion in matters of faith.

3)   As for the Prophet's tradition "I am commanded to *fight against people until they say, 'There is no god but the One God'* [...] ", it is <u>consensually</u> agreed by Muslims that it was related to the <u>Arab polytheists</u> in particular. The People of the Book among the Arabs and the non-Arab polytheists are dealt with differently.

4)   The prohibition against the Muslims' *taking the unbelievers or certain People of the Book as close allies* is related to close alliance and support, not mere peaceful relations, good behavior, and contacts for mutual benefit. The prominent classical commentator

on the Quran al-Fakhr al-Razi (d. 604 AH/ 1207 CE) mentioned that harmonious co-relations in this life are not forbidden. In his commentary on the verse "No coercion should ever be in matters of faith" (2:256), he stated that imposing faith by force on a person who chooses to be an unbeliever after being told the evidence would mean an abolition of *testing human beings in this life* based on their freedom of choice [92].

Modern Jurists and Thinkers Advocate Peace in Muslims' Relations with Non-Muslims in the World

What Khallaf has preponderated of the two juristic views about Muslims' relations with non-Muslims in the world has become dominant in modern Islamic jurisprudence and thought. The so-called "verse(s) of the sword", has/ have been put in their Quranic and historical context. *Tafsir al-Manar* by Muhammad Abduh (d. 1905) and Muhammad Rashid Rida (d. 1935), refuted the claimed abrogation of the verses commanding peace and forgiveness by that – or those – verse(s). In the commentary on the verse 2:194: "Fight during the sacred months if you are attacked, for sanctity and its violation should be reciprocal. Thus, if anyone commits aggression against you, attack him just as he has attacked you, but remain conscious of God, and know that God is with those who are conscious of Him" (2:194), the commentary indicates:

"Some commentators claimed that this verse was abrogated by the verse of Sura al-Tawba that they called 'the verse of the sword' (9:5). Imam Muhammad Abduh said that the outcome of the verse is giving Muslims permission to fight back while they are in the state of pilgrimage in the sacred city during the sacred month if the polytheists there initiated fighting against them [for they merely respond to the attack of those who have attacked], and its rule is constant and there is neither what abrogates nor what is abrogated [...]. In the battles of Badr and Uhud to which the verses in Sura Āl-'Imran (no. 3) and Sura al-'Anfal (no. 8) are related, the polytheists were the initial aggressors, and the verses of Sura al-Tawba (no. 9) are about polytheists who broke

101

their agreements and promises with Muslims, and the sura indicated that peace should be maintained with those who kept their promises [9:7]. The verse emphasized: 'Would you fail to fight against people who have broken their solemn pledge and have done all that they could to drive the Conveyor of God's message away, and have been first to attack you?' (9:13). The polytheists started their oppression and war against Muslims so as to turn them back from their faith [...] and the early wars of the Prophet's Companions were to defend the message and the believers against the unjust [oppressors] not to commit aggression [...] *Later conquests followed the nature of domination and did not always comply with the laws of religion"* [(93)].

Shaykh Mahmud Shaltut, the former Shaykh of al-Azhar (d. 1963), stressed that peace is the original general principle in human relations, and refused the argument that compulsion can be a way for spreading the message of God. Fighting back is only allowed for self-defense against aggression as an exception to the general principle of peace. Its aim in such a case is to stop the aggression, and it does not require that the aggressors accept Islam if they are defeated [(94)]. Dr. Muhammad Abd Allah Diraz, former dean of the Faculty of Usul al-Din at al-Azhar (d. 1958), advised the reader of the Quran not to be confined to and secluded within the verses revealed in Mecca about peacefulness, forgiveness, patience and non-confrontation in dealing with the polytheists who behaved offensively towards Islam and the Muslims, nor be confined to and secluded within the verses revealed in Medina about fighting back against those who initially committed oppression and aggression against Muslims. Looking to the *two divaricated lines* should not obscure *the joint angle or base* of both, since the Quran contains *comprehensive verses that sharply indicate that*

102

war is not the general rule but the exception, that the state of war is not created by Islam or Muslims but by their enemies, and that it is restricted to legitimate self-defense.

Diraz quoted the verses that have been repeatedly mentioned above, and a reference to their places throughout the Quran may be sufficient here (2:190-193, 4:90-91, 8:61-62, 60:8-9). On the other hand, Islam forbids war that is merely waged for *religious fanaticism*: "No coercion should ever be in matters of faith" (2:256, also 10:99). Self-conceit has to be always resisted by Muslims and never be given a chance to fuel a war: "And never let your hatred of people who once barred you from the Inviolable House of Worship lead you into aggression, but rather help one another in furthering the good and virtue and God-consciousness, and do not help one another in furthering evil and enmity" (5:2). Muslims should never fight to cause *destruction or gain expansion:* "As for that [happy eternal] life in the hereafter, We grant it [only] to those who do not seek to exalt themselves on earth, nor yet to spread damage, but the future belongs to the God-conscious" (28:83). Muslims should also never declare war to compete with others in showing power and reaching superiority, "And be not like one who breaks and completely untwists the yarn that she [herself] has spun and made strong, [be not like this by] using your oaths as a means of deceiving one another, simply because some of you may be more powerful than others" (16:92) [95].

On the Obstruction of the Propagation
of the Message as a Reason for War

Modern Muslim jurists and thinkers, then, emphasize that peace is the Islamic principle in world relations, and that the only legitimate war in Islam is that of self-defense, when Muslims and their land are attacked. They do not accept the claim that the verses of Sura al-Tawba have abrogated verses of peace, patience and forgiveness, since these verses obviously were addressing a particular historical situation in Arabia during the Prophet's time, where the Arab polytheists broke their promises and agreements with the Muslims and turned against them. As for those who observed their agreements, and kept their promises, Muslims were commanded to maintain peace with them (9:4, 7). In all this, Muslims are not different from the universal principles of justice and common sense. However, modern authors – starting with those of *Tafsir al-Manar* – add another justifying cause for a Muslim war, which is *obstructing the spreading of the message of Islam.*

The Universal Declaration of Human Rights issued by the General Assembly of the United Nations on December 2, 1948, secures in its 18th article *freedom of thinking, conscience and religion,* which comprises the freedom of expression through practice, *individual and collective performance of rituals, and education.* The freedom of changing the faith is considered a form of the freedom of thinking, conscience, and religion. In the next article, the Declaration secures the freedom of opinion and expression, which includes the freedom of adopting an opinion without interference and *receiving news and ideas and spreading them by any means without being restricted by geographic borders* (article 19).

Accordingly, a *peaceful propagation of the message of Islam* may be considered within the basic human rights. The Universal Declaration *secures the freedom of adopting, receiving, and spreading news and ideas.* However, would mere forbidding of a peaceful propagation of the message of Islam, within reasonable limits and without pursuing oppressive measures against the believers in or propagators of the message, justify a Muslim war in theory or in practice?

I think that such an obstruction of spreading the message of Islam, within the previously mentioned lines, can be struggled against peacefully through universal political, informational and juridical measures. The United Nations and its affiliated and related bodies have to be benefited from in their full potential to place the necessary political, legal, and economic pressures against any country that does not secure human rights in full for its people, individually and collectively. The mass media in our era of globalization can expose and condemn any violation of individual and collective human rights.

Furthermore, universal alliances of the advocates of comprehensive human rights, especially those securing freedom of opinion, faith, expression and association, ought to coordinate their efforts in defending and securing human rights in full all over the world. Initiating and strengthening a peaceful defense of human rights, within the United Nations and outside it, is timely and necessary, especially when technological development has made global information enormously fast and viable, and made war and its damage very costly and widely destructive for all parties involved in the war, as well as for the entire world.

Jihad as an Alleged Universal Collective Duty for Spreading the Message

Jihad as a collective duty for spreading the message of Islam is not supported by the Quran or the Sunna. Even the practice of the two early Caliphs Abu Bakr and Umar can be understood as aiming initially to secure the borders of Arabia with the Byzantine Empire and the Sassanian Persian Empire. Furthermore, it was accompanied with strict instructions forbidding penetration into the neighboring lands. Through battles that the Muslims could not anticipate and for which they were not prepared, the war on the Sassanian Persian front resulted in a complete collapse of the empire, and the war on the Byzantine front ended in annexing to the Muslim state Syria, Egypt, and later North Africa at the time of Caliph Uthman. However, those results stimulated the appetite of subsequent Muslim leaders, *especially the Umayyads,* for *mere conquests, and so war for the sake of expansion began to be considered a virtue* of the Muslim monarch or ruler (*ghazi*), and the spread of Islam was the legitimization given for such warfare. Aspiration towards the fall of the Byzantine Empire and its capital Constantinople into Muslim hands – in the style of the Sassanian Empire – became an obsession in the Muslim psyche and literature.

In such a climate of expansion, the scholars of Islam, inspired by the rulers, forged the connection between jihad and spreading Islam, which cannot be explicitly based on the Quran and Sunna, nor on clear-cut statements or policies of Caliphs Abu Bakr and Umar. As the Quran states that God sent Prophet Muhammad with the guidance and message of the truth "to the end that *He makes it prevail over all religion*" (48:28, 61:9), an obligation for Muslims to achieve such an end has been assumed from the verses. The Quranic verse

"O you who have attained to faith! Fight against the deniers of the truth" (9:123), may be used as a general command to all Muslims in all times and places, taken out of context of the sura that addressed the particular case of the Arabs who initiated aggression and frequently acted offensively against Muslims. Similarly, the so-called "verse of the sword" was taken out of context and claimed to have abrogated all verses related to peace and peacefulness.

From that point on, a Muslim permanent world war was declared whenever and wherever Muslims believed that it was legitimate and felt that they were ready for it. As this is a long-term goal for which successive generations have to work, then the obligation was qualified as "*collective*" for the entire Muslim umma throughout all times and places. At the same time, it was conceived to be *within the ability and the available means* (*fard kifaya*), as long as there was no urgent danger faced by the Muslims. In the case of attack, self-defense becomes an individual obligation for every Muslim who is able for fighting back (*fard 'ayn*).

Using force to spread Islam in the world is against the essential principle of the Quran, "No coercion should ever be in matters of faith" (2:256). Making this a *collective* duty for the entire umma according to its existing *ability* at a certain time and in a particular place would not remove that contradiction. Arguing that such a war would only be waged against the state authorities who forbid the peaceful propagation of Islam cannot be convincing, for it may be responded to with the argument that the people themselves do not wish such a spread of the message, and that the state authorities are simply representing and fulfilling their will. Fighting for expansion in the name of Islam might have taken place in the past when the expansion of the powerful was a world tradition, but it cannot be accepted in the law of Islamic justice nor in the contemporary world. Muslims reject translating "jihad" as "holy war," but how then may a collective jihad for spreading Islam be described? And what would be the response to an allegation that Islam legitimizes its spread by force?

Such a juristic formulation presumes that Islam by its merits is acceptable to every human being who has common sense, and that any objection indicates personal bias, unfairness, self-interest or malignancy. We know that human psychology, sociology, and accordingly human thinking are not simple, and various correlated factors interact for an individual or group to reach a decision, especially with regard to embracing a religious faith. The Quran repeatedly emphasizes that God only is the One who can judge comprehensively and justly the human deed of any individual, since He is the only One whose knowledge encompasses the internal (e.g. intentions, knowledge, and intellect) and the external (e.g. social environment, information, education, and state pressures) circumstances of every individual in all their various dimensions and angles. The appreciation of the truth, the deliberate denial of the truth, and the unambiguous belligerent action against it are serious conclusions that cannot be claimed at random, and peace and war cannot be decided by assumptions and presumptions.

Some may argue: if Islam does not allow by any means coercion in matters of faith, and any spreading of the faith by force, and secures the freedom of opinion, faith, and expression, then why does it forbid and punish an abandonment of Islam, calling it *apostasy*?

In my understanding, *apostasy historically was not a result of individual free thinking, but was a tribal rebellion against the unifying central authority of the Islamic state,* whose leadership in its early stage was represented in the Prophet and Caliphs, seen as relatives of the Meccan tribe of Quraysh. That rebellion against the dominance of that tribe saw in the Prophet's death an opportunity for wide-range action. A rejection of the Islamic state authority and its leadership was merely a tribal rebellion that saw Islam as a domination of a certain tribe or clan within the tribe, and saw the social welfare dues, *zakat*, as a tribute and sign of submission to that tribe or clan. Those who claimed prophethood, such as Musaylima in Bani Hanifa, Sajah in Bani Tamim, Tulayha ibn Khuwaylid in Bani Asad, Tayyi' and Ghatafan, and al-Aswad al-'Ansi in Yemen, had no constructive reform, be it intellectual or behavioral, individual or social, but merely represented tribal and regional challenges against Quraysh, Bani Hashim or Mecca in general.

Consequently, rejection of the authority of the Islamic state spread throughout Arabia. Among the rejectionists were those who did not claim prophethood, such as the people of al-Bahrayn, Bani Sulaym, and Kinda. In Ta'if and Mecca itself some signs of rejection emerged, but did not continue [96]. The Arab tribes were not used to being part of a unified entity with a central authority that secured law and order in the entire peninsula. Instead, they could easily see Muhammad as an incidentally winning chieftain, whose domination was irrelevant once he became old or died.

The Shafi'i jurist al-Mawardi considered such a *rebellious collective movement* and its confrontation by the Muslim authorities as a *"group war*," a categorization obviously different in its nature and practice from an individual change of faith. Abu Hanifa believed that a woman would not be punished if she rejected Islam since she cannot physically fight against it and its forces. Thus, the military dimension of the incriminated act of apostasy (*ridda*) was thoroughly recognized by some jurists (97). The Prophet's tradition: "One who changes his faith is to be killed" [reported by al-Bukhari, Ibn Hanbal, Abu Dawud, al-Nisa'i, al-Tirmidhi and Ibn Majah] cannot be taken out of its historical context: it referred to a collective rebellion against the state, not to a mere individual change of faith. If the text were taken literally, it could apply to any conversion from one religion to another, even between religions rather than Islam, and this logically cannot be what was meant. Thus, the text has to be understood within its well-known particular historical circumstances, and it cannot be extrapolated to refer to an individual change of faith punished by death. As jurists such as the prominent al-Qarafi pointed out, the Prophet's tradition and action in this matter were within his authority as a leader of the community (*imam*) and were limited to the given circumstances, as opposed to a part of his permanent message and binding teachings as a Prophet (98).

The Hypothetical Division of the World

A theoretical division of the world into an *"abode of Islam"* and another *"abode of war"* or *of denial of the truth, kufr*, was not widely used in the past by serious authors, apart from the jurists, and cannot be acceptable in our era of globalization and mass communications. Such terms were not used by businessmen, travelers, geographers, many historians, or other serious authors. Even if they were used in the past in common talk about the area of Muslim-Byzantine frontiers where constant warfare was taking place, it could not be broadened to encompass all non-Muslim lands. Most Muslim travelers, geographers, and historians dealt with cities, countries, states, their peoples and their inter-relations with Muslims, without mentioning such division. The geographer al-Maqdisi (d. 380 AH/ 990 CE) limited his work *Ahsan al-Taqasim* to Muslim countries, but other geographers and historians dealt with countries around the world without mentioning that bi-division. Even the juristic use of the bi-division "appears by its nature to be more an expression of something that jurists had to deal with after it had occurred, and not as an expression of what they thought should happen" [99]. Al-Mawardi added to the bi-division the third area that he called the land of treaty or convention, *"dar al-'ahd,"* the area with which Islamic authorities have a relationship but that does not constitute part of the land of Islam, and whose people are not considered subjects to the Muslim state.

□ Muslims' Alliance with Non-Muslims

Related to the claimed division of the world into permanent war between Muslims and the non-Muslim world, is the view that *bars Muslims from any alliance with non-Muslims*. The Quran teaches: "O you who have attained to faith! Do not take the Jews and Christians as your *patrons and upholders*, they but defend one another, and *whoever of you becomes unyieldingly bound to them becomes, verily, one of them*" (5:51), "O you have attained to faith! Do not take for your *patrons and upholders such as mock at your faith and make a jest of it* – be they from among those who have been given the Book before your time, or [from among] those who stubbornly deny the truth [of the belief in God altogether] [...] *And when you call to prayer, they mock at it and make a jest of it* [...]" (5:57-58), "Announce you to the hypocrites that grievous suffering awaits them; those who take the stubborn deniers of the truth <u>as patrons and upholders in preference to believers</u>; do they hope to gain honor in their patronage? Behold, it is to God [alone] that all veneration belongs" (4:138-139).

These verses are taken out of their historical and structural context:
– *First,* they address the situation in Arabia at the time of the Prophet, rather than determining Muslims' relations with non-Muslims at all times all over the world. The historical significance is obvious in indicating that those whom the Muslims should not take as patrons and upholders "*mock at your faith and make a jest of it,*" which can not be a universal situation. If this is a general law that forbids all close relations with Jews and Christians, how then can be a marriage of a Jewish or Christian woman be allowed to the Muslim man according to the Quran (5:5)?

– *Second,* the Arabic word *awliya',* sing. *waliyy,* has many meanings. In some English translations of the Quran the word is translated as "friends," which is not correct in this context.

– *Third,* the Quran states that the *"People of the Book" "are not all alike; among the People of the Book there are upright people, who recite God's message throughout the night and prostrate themselves [before Him]. They believe in God and the Last Day, and enjoin the doing of what is right and forbid the doing of what is wrong, and vie with one another in doing good works, and these are among the righteous. And whatever good they do, they shall never be denied the reward thereof, and God has full knowledge of those who are conscious of Him"* (3:113-115). What would be wrong, then, in taking such people as supporters or friends?

– *Fourth,* the Quran stresses *fairness of judgment and avoidance of unfair and erroneous generalization, oversimplification, and stereotyping.* Thus, any Quranic description of a certain group under given circumstances, should not be taken out of its structural and historical context: *"And among the People of the Book there is many a one who, if you entrust him [/her] with a treasure, will [faithfully] restore it to you; and there is among them many a one who, if you entrust him [/her] with a coin of no big value will not restore it to you unless you keep standing over him [/her]"* (3:75). Even with regard to the Bedouins, whose behavior in general might psychologically and sociologically have its negatives as a result of their life environment and upbringing, *"more tenacious in [their] refusal to acknowledge the truth and in [their] hypocrisy and more liable to ignore the ordinances which God has brought down to the Conveyor of His message"* (5:97), the Quran teaches fairness and accuracy in setting the particular side by side with the general: *"However, among the bedouins there are [also] such as believe in God and the Last Day and spend [in God's cause] [...]"* (5:99).

113

‒ *Fifth,* the Quran *urges Muslims to interact with universal human diversity,* and know well its various components and what may characterize each of them. Only thus is humanity enriched with such diversity through universal knowledge and cooperation: *"O People! Behold, We have created you all out of a male and a female, and have made you into nations and tribes, so that you might come to <u>know one another</u> [and recognize the merits of each component in your diversity and the value of cooperation]. Verily, the noblest of you in the sight of God is the one who is most deeply conscious of Him"* (49:13). How can such a universal call be consistent with a division of the world into Muslim and non-Muslim blocks and a forbiddance of interaction between the two?

‒ *Sixth,* Muslims are taught by the Quran *"to invite unto all that is good and enjoin the doing of what is right and forbid the doing of what is wrong"* (3:104), and to cooperate *"in furthering virtue and God-consciousness,"* not *"in furthering evil and enmity"* (5:2). How can this moral responsibility be fulfilled through dividing the world and its human population, and through isolation from others or considering them permanent enemies?

Last but not least, it is understandable and desirable that Muslims should not be totally dependent on others and should rely on their own selves, and that they should not always wait for others to defend or uphold them, or look to others as patrons and to themselves as tributaries. That is the essence of what is taught by the Quran in the above mentioned verses whatever the historical particularities might be, rather than an erroneous generalized prohibition of merely taking others as friends or allies. Close relations and cooperation between equals and for a legitimate and righteous goal is a positive and constructive attitude for the Muslims, as well as for the entire world. Muslims are taught to develop pleasant relations based on fairness, care, and kindness with good people, whatever their beliefs may be (60:8): "It may well be that God will bring about [mutual] affection between you [O believers] and those from among them [the unbelievers] whom you [now] face as enemies" (60:7).

Muhammad Rashid Rida, in his monthly *Al-Manar*, correctly disagreed with the legal opinion (*fatwa*) given by the Ottoman mufti to the Muslim Bosnians in the year 1909, when their region came under the rule of Austria-Hungary. The Ottoman mufti had stated that the Muslim Bosnians should migrate to a land ruled by Muslim authorities, otherwise their marriages under the non-Muslim authorities would be void, as they must be held under the Shari'a of a Muslim authority. The "*fatwa*" reflected the bi-division of the world into "*dar-Islam*" and the other.

However, during the life of the Prophet, there were Muslims in Arabia who did not live under the authority of the Muslim state in Medina, yet naturally their marriages and other necessary dealings were valid without their having to migrate in order to live under Islamic law and its authorities in Medina. The only matter to which the Quran pointed with regard to those Muslims who did not migrate to Medina was that the Muslim authorities in Medina would not be responsible for taking care of them or protecting them: "*And as for those who have attained to faith and have not migrated [to the land which is under your power], you are not in charge of them [or responsible for securing their protection and needs (walaya)] until they migrate [to your land]. Yet, if they ask you for support against oppression that occurs due to their faith, it is your duty to give [them] the support except against a people with whom you have a covenant*" (8:72).

Forbidding the early Muslims from taking those who did not migrate as associates and allies "*awliya*" (4:89), was a warning against the hypocrites outside Medina, especially among bedouins, "*who would like to be safe from you as well as from their own [polytheist] folk, who wherever they are faced anew with temptation to evil, plunge into it headlong*" (4:91). However, those people were not necessarily required to migrate, as long as they were not claiming that they were the associates and allies of Muslims (*awliya'*); it was sufficient for them to let the Muslims be and offer them peace (4:91). Historically, Muslim minorities have lived all over the world under non-Muslim authorities, and their successive generations carried out their marriages, divorces and other dealings without any doubt that any of these acts were at any point null or void.

□ *Division of Annexed Lands into those Annexed by Force, and those Annexed through Peaceful Agreement*

The juristic attitude of dividing and qualifying established a division within the lands that came to be under the sovereignty of the Muslim state. They mainly were divided into lands that had been *annexed by force* (*'anwa*), and lands that were *annexed through a peaceful agreement* (*sulh*), according to whether their people – through their authorities – gave up the ownership of the land to the Muslims or kept it for the native people. In all cases, a land-tax, *kharaj*, was decided by Caliph Umar. However, in lands annexed by force, the amount would be determined by the Muslim administration and subject to change, while in lands annexed through peaceful agreement, the amount of *kharaj* was fixed and could not be changed, regardless of economic and monetary fluctuations.

This division led to administrative difficulties and complications, especially when the status was arguable or became arguable as time passed. Besides, when an owner of *sulh* land became a Muslim, or sold the land to a Muslim, would the *kharaj* stay unchangeable in time? This would lead to inequality in the payment of *kharaj* between Muslims who owned *'anwa* lands and Muslims who owned *sulh* lands, even if the value of both lands in certain cases might be the same. Even more significantly, would *the sulh lands qualify as "dar Islam"?* Abu Hanifa considered *sulh* lands as *dar Islam*. The Shafi'i jurist al-Mawardi, on the other hand, considered the *sulh* land kept by its people as *an abode of treaty or convention, dar 'ahd*, while people who gave up the ownership of their *sulh* lands were called

117

"people of treaty or convention" (*ahl 'ahd*) *but their lands became an endowment* (*waqf*) *for "dar al-Islam"* and could not be sold.

In such complex situations, any damage or loss in the financial records, as occurred under the Umayyad governor of Iraq al-Hajjaj ibn Yusuf (d.95 AH/ 714 CE), would have serious ramifications [100]. As conquests decreased during later Umayyad years, and setbacks were suffered under Hisham (105-125 AH/ 724-743 CE),

"Muslim jurists became more interested in fiscal problems – in particular the status of land – as determined by the earlier conquests. In this way the genres of 'land tax' and 'state finances' came into existence, and were more cultivated than was the literature on campaigns, which passed into biographies and histories, while the genre on 'the conduct of state' became a relatively (though not uniformly) static section of general law books [. . .] [The] relative stabilization of the frontier led to a truce and arrangements for furtherance of trade. By the time of al-Shafi'i a juridical theory of a third abode 'the realm of treaty relations' had emerged. These juridical developments had become necessary to deal with a new situation, and they seem to reflect rather than precede the appearance of this situation" [101].

The Spiritual, Moral, and Intellectual Jihad

At the start of the section on "Jihad" in his voluminous commentary on al-Bukhari's collection of authentic hadith, the prominent scholar Ahmad ibn Ali ibn Muhammad ibn Hajar al-'Asqalani (d. 852 AH/ 1449 CE) wrote that *determining the linguistic origin of "jihad" requires great effort.* It is used as an Islamic term to mean *striving hard against the evil desires and whims of one's own self,* against the *wrongdoers* and *against the devil,* and not only against the aggression of the deniers of the truth (*al-kuffar*). On the *first front,* jihad is carried out by learning the teachings of the religion, practicing them, and then teaching them. *With the wrongdoers* one may use the hand (if this does not worsen the situation), or the tongue, or merely the heart if neither is possible. Jihad *against the devil* would be in resisting the doubts that may arise in one's faith, or curbing the illegitimate desires in one's actions [102].

Such a spiritual, moral and intellectual jihad is basic in the accurate concept of the term, which cannot be restricted to merely physical fighting for which the Arabic word "*qital*" is used in the Quran and the Sunna. In the Quran, one reads: *"And strive hard in God's cause with all the striving that is due to Him"* (22:78), "And as for those who *strive hard in Our cause* – We shall most certainly guide them to paths that lead to Us, and behold, God is indeed with the doers of good" (29:69).

In his commentary on the Quran, Muhammad ibn Ahmad al-Qurtubi (d. 671 AH/ 1272 CE) indicated that the word "jihad" in the verses refers to obeying all what God commands and avoiding all what God forbids. Therefore, it *means striving hard against one's own self in the way of*

God's obedience, against the devil's rousing, against the unjust to stop their injustice, and against the aggression of the *kuffar* to repel it. Al-Qurtubi quoted Abu Sulayman al-Darani Abd al-Rahman ibn Ahmad ibn Atiyya (d. 215 AH/ 830 CE), a prominent ascetic and Sufi, who said that the "jihad" in the verse does not only mean fighting against the aggression of the *kuffar*, but also upholding the religion, responding to contenders, resisting despots, and – *the utmost jihad – enjoining the doing of what is good and right and forbidding the doing of what is evil and wrong.* Within jihad also is the moral striving for the obedience of God, which is the greatest jihad [103].

Another prominent commentator, al-Fakhr al-Razi Muhammad ibn Umar (d. 604 AH/ 1207 CE), quoted Abd Allah ibn al-Mubarak al-Mirwazi (d. 181 AH/ 797 CE) who stressed that striving hard against the evil desires and whims of one's own self is jihad. The commentator mentioned a Prophet's tradition following his return from the campaign to Tabuk: "*We come back from the minor jihad to the major jihad*" – referring to the spiritual, moral jihad. The commentator indicated that observance of doing all what God commands, and the avoidance of doing all what God forbids, is the real jihad [104].

In Sufi terminology, "*mujahada*" is a well-known term for spiritual and moral development. Abu Hamid Muhammad ibn Muhammad ibn Muhammad al-Ghazali (d. 505 AH/ 1111 CE), the outstanding Islamic theologian, jurist and sufi, used the word "*mujahada*" and the word "*riyada*" to discuss moral training for spiritual moral enhancement. He believed that there is no difference between worshiping an idol by someone and worshiping one's own ego, and suggested that one should firmly stand against his/ her capricious inclinations. He quoted the Quranic verse that

120

recounts what Prophet Joseph said, "*Verily, if one is conscious of Him [God] and firmly forbears and perseveres, behold, God does not fail to requite the doers of good*" (12:90) [105]. Ibn al-Mubarak also emphasized the spiritual discipline and merits of jihad, and in his book on asceticism, *Kitab al-Zuhd wa-al Raqa'iq*, he considered jihad an ascetic practice [106].

Jihad, which was originally meant military self-defense, evolved into an aggressive expansionist theory after a few early decades of Muslim history. It also continued to be probably "a sixth pillar" of Islam in the view of some such as Philip Hitti, who believed that it led Muslims "to an unparalleled expansion as a worldly power. It is one of the principal duties of the caliph to keep pushing back the [...] wall separating '*dar al-Islam*' from '*dar al-harb*'. The bipartite division of the world finds a parallel in the communistic theory" [107].

On the other hand, placing jihad into the depth of the human self and emphasizing its spiritual, moral, intellectual and social role always existed. Such an approach was sometimes broadened by Sufis, who deemed this to be the only permanent jihad. Modern Muslim thinkers and jurists have been sincerely and steadfastly developing the early concept of jihad as only self-defense in an era of universal human rights and peaceful constructive cooperation. They are gradually gaining the conviction of sensible people, Muslims and non-Muslims, while extremists are trying to benefit from the lifelong theory of permanent aggressive war, in order to reach their mistaken idea of making Islam "prevail over all religions."

The peaceful and whole-hearted striving or jihad for justice in its various dimensions, through spiritual-moral, intellectual-informative-educational,   social-economical-political, national and universal fields, would mean a genuine energetic non-violent struggle for the cause of God, the All-Peace and All-Just. It would require huge organized efforts and sacrifices, but would be constructive and rewarding for Muslims, and for the entire world. Meanwhile, such "*jihad without violence or bloodshed*" would save all humans the horrible losses and casualties on all sides, which technology now multiplies beyond imagination in any violent conflict, not only for the involved parties, but also for the peaceful civilians, including women, children, the disabled and the elderly, and for the entire world in an era of globalism.

In a remarkable precedent, Prophet Muhammad held a peaceful agreement with the hostile, oppressive and belligerent polytheist leaders of the Quraysh tribe at *al-Hudaybiya* in the year 6 AH/ 627 CE. It stated that a truce had to be observed by the two parties for 10 years, and that each party would *approach Arab tribes to persuade them to be on its side*. This significant peaceful treaty, which gave the chance for human reason and politically informative efforts, paved the way for the Prophet and the Muslims to mobilize a huge army to re-enter Mecca only 2 years later (in the year 8 AH/ 629 CE) with minimal losses, as a result of a violation of the truce terms by a tribe allied with Quraysh that attacked a tribe allied with the Prophet. Thus, the peaceful agreement was exactly as the Quran described it, "*a manifest victory (fath mubin)*" (48:1).

The late Muhammad Asad stressed *the moral victory* achieved by the truce of Hudaybiyah, which opened the door to the *subsequent triumph of Islam in Arabia*. He explains:

"The Truce was to prove of the greatest importance to the future of Islam. For the first time in six years *peaceful contacts were established* between Mecca and Medina, and thus the way was opened to the *penetration of Islamic ideas* into the citadel of Arabian paganism. The Meccans who had the occasion to visit the Muslim camp at Hudaybiya returned deeply impressed by the spirit and unity of Muhammad's followers, and many of them *began to waver in their hostility* towards the faith preached by him. As soon as the perennial warfare came to an end and people of both sides *could meet freely, new converts rallied* around the Prophet, first in tens, then in hundreds, then in thousands – so much that when pagan Quraysh broke the truce two years after its conclusion, the Prophet could [enter] Mecca almost without resistance" [(108)].

In this way God's promise to His Prophet was fulfilled, as the same sura states in verse 27: "*God has shown the truth in the vision of the Conveyor of His Message; <u>most certainly shall you enter the Inviolable House of Worship, if God so wills, in full security</u>...without any fear, for He has [always] known that which you yourselves could not know, and He has ordained [for you], besides this and before it, a victory soon to come*" (48:27).

Notes

All emphases in quotations are the author's.

(1)   Ibn Abd al-Salam, 'Izz al-Din 'Abd al-Aziz, ed. Taha Sa'd, *Qawa 'id al-Ahkam fi Masalih al-Anam*, Beirut: Dar al-Jil, 1980, vol. 2, pp. 189-190.

(2)   Ibn Qayyim al-Jawziyya, Muhammad ibn Abi-Bakr, *I'lam al-Muwaqqi'in*, Cairo: Dar al-Tiba'a al-Muniriyya, n.d. vol. 3, p.1.

(3)   Quoted by Shalabi, Muhammad Mustafa, *Ta'lil al-Akham*, Cairo: al-Azhar Press, 1947, pp. 37-8.

(4)   *Ibid.*, p. 71.

(5)   *Ibid.*, p. 214.

(6)   Ibn Abd al-Salam, *Qawa 'id al-Ahkam fi Masalih al-An'am*, vol. 2, p. 143.

(7)   *Ibid.*, pp. 305, 314.

(8)   Ibn Qayyim al-Jawziyya, Muhammad ibn Abi Bakr, *I'lam al-Muwaqqi'in*, Cairo: Maktaba al-Adab, n.d., p. 218.

(9)   See in general: al-Qarafi, Ahmad ibn Idris, *al-Ihkam fi 'Usul al-Ahkam wa Tasarrufat al-Qadi wa al-Imam*, ed. Abd al-Fattah Abu Ghudda, Maktab al-Matbu'at al-Islamiyya, 1967; esp. pp. 86-109; also: *al-Furuq*, Beirut: 'Alam al-Kutub, n.d. vol. 1, pp. 206-8.

(10)   Ibn Atiyya, Abd al-Haqq ibn Ghalib al-Andalusi, *al-Muharrar al-Wajiz fi Tafsir al-Kitab al-'Aziz,* ed. al-Majlis al-'Ilmi, Fez, Rabat: Ministry of Awqaf and Islamic Affairs, 1981, vol. 8, p. 133.

(11)   Quoted by Ibn Atiyya in *al-Muharrar al-Wajiz* (1975), vol. 2, p. 101. However, Ibn Atiyya himself is of the view that the verse is addressing the entire Muslim umma (pp. 100-101), in spite of its significant references such as: "*and drive them away from wherever they drove you away*", "*and fight not against them near the Inviolable House of Worship (al-Masjid al-Haram) unless they first fight against you*". Such references undoubtedly indicate the particular historical circumstances to which the verse is referring.

(12)   See for example: Amin, Ahmad, *Fajr al-Islam,* Beirut: Dar al-Kitab al-Arabi, 1969, p. 9.

(13)   See for the alliance between the Jews in Medina and the tribe of Ghatafan: Muhammad Ibn Sa'd, *al-Tabaqat al-Kubra*, Beirut: Dar Beirut, 1978, vol. 2, pp. 57-8, 91, 92.

(14)   Ibn Sa'd, *ibid.*, vol. 2, pp. 66, 69, 73.

(15)   *Ibid.*, vol. 2, pp. 149, 153-4.

(16)   *Ibid.*, vol. 2, pp. 34, 35, 123, 160.

(17)   Ibn Kathir, Isma'il ibn 'Umar, *al-Bidaya wa al-Nihaya*, Beirut: Dar al-Kutub al-'Ilmiyya, 1987, vol. 6, pp. 308-336.

(18)   See for example the Quranic verse 4:51 and the comments on it in the different commentaries.

(19)   See above note 13.

(20)   Ibn Kathir, *al-Bidaya wa al-Nihaya*, vol. 2 p. 190; Hasan, Hasan Ibrahim, *Tarikh al-Islam,* Cairo: Maktaba al-Nahda, 1964, vol. 1, pp. 19-21.

(21)   Ibn Sa'd, *al-Tabaqat,* vol. 2, pp. 128-130, 165-8.

(22)   al-Baladhuri, Ahmad ibn Yahya ibn Jabir, *Futuh al-Buldan,* ed. Radwan Muhammad Radwan, Cairo: al-Maktaba al-Tijariyya, 1959, pp. 71-2.

(23)   Ibn Kathir, *al-Bidaya wa al-Nihaya*, vol.6, pp. 331-3.

(24)   Watt, Montgomery, "Muhammad," in *The Cambridge History of Islam,* vol. 1, ed. P.M. Holt, Ann K. S. Lambton, & Bernard Lewis, London: Cambridge University Press, 1970, p. 53.

(25)   *Ibid.,* pp. 58-60.

(26)   al-Baladhuri, *Futuh al-Buldan*, p. 135.

(27)   Hitti, Philip K., *History of the Arabs,* London: McMillan, 1970, p. 80; Hasan, *Tarikh al-Islam,* vol. 1, p. 44.

(28)   Ibn Kathir, *al-Bidaya wa al-Nihaya,* vol. 7, pp. 2-4.

(29)   al-Baladhuri, *Futuh al-Buldan,* pp. 140-2.

(30)   Ibn Kathir, *al-Bidaya wa al-Nihaya*, vol. 6, pp. 347-8, vol. 7, pp 26-7; al-Baladhuri, *Futuh al-Buldan*, pp. 244-5.

(31)   al-Tabari, Muhammad ibn Jarir, *Tarikh al Umam wa-al-Muluk*, Cairo: al-Maktaba al-Husayniyya, n.d. vol. 3, p. 212, vol. 4, pp. 29, 61, 63, 195, 218.

(32)   Ibn Kathir, *al-Bidaya wa al-Nihaya,* vol. 7, pp. 31, 36, 48.

(33)   Butler, Alfred, *Fath al-Arab li-Misr*, Arabic translation of *The Arab Conquest of Egypt*, by Abu Hadid, Muhammad Farid, Cairo: Lajna al-Ta'lif wa al-Tarjama wa al-Nashr, pp. 112-4; Hasan, Hasan Ibrahim, *Tarikh al-Islam*, vol. 1, pp. 234-5.

(34)   Hasan, Hasan Ibrahim, *Tarikh al-Islam,* vol. 1, p. 219.

(35)   Hitti, *History of the Arabs,* pp. 136-9.

(36)   Hitti, *ibid.,* p. 158; Hasan, Hasan Ibrahim, *Tarikh al-Islam,* vol. 1, p. 221.

(37)   For some examples of governmental and ethical deficiencies in appointment, dismissal of top officials, and conducting of public affairs in general under the Umayyads see: *Ibn Kathir, al-Bidaya wa al-Nihaya,* vol. 8, p. 83 (regarding Sa'id ibn 'Uthman ibn 'Affan, the military leader of Khurasan), p. 84 (regarding the dismissal of Marwan ibn al-Hakam as governor of Medina), pp. 85-6 (regarding Ibn Umm al-Hakam the governor of Kufa), pp. 172-3, 188-190, 192 (regarding 'Ubayd Allah ibn Ziyad Shamar ibn dhi al-Jawshan,

and al-Husayn ibn Numayr's dealing with al-Husayn ibn Ali at the Battle of Karbala'); also: Majid, 'Abd al-Mun'im, *al-Tarikh al-Siyasi li al-Dawla al-Arabiyya*, Cairo: Maktaba al-Anglo al-Misriyya, 1971, vol. 2, p. 59 (regarding the harshness of 'Uqba ibn Nafi' in ruling al-Maghrib), p. 69 (regarding the harshness of Ziyad ibn Abi Sufyan in ruling al-Kufa), pp. 75-6 (regarding the cruelty of 'Ubayd Allah ibn Ziyad in Karbala'), pp. 86-8 (regarding Muslim ibn 'Uqba's cruelty in attacking Medina), pp. 92-100 (regarding the rotation of Marwan ibn al-Hakam and Sa'id ibn al-'As in governing Hijaz), pp. 239-40, 277 (regarding the dismissal of the leaders of the conquests due to personal grudges), pp. 101, 271-2, 317-323 (regarding the Umayyad exploitation of the contradictions between the two main Arab genealogical branches, the Yeminis and the Qaysis); also: pp. 121-2, 124 (regarding the cruelty of the two anti-Umayyad rebels al-Mukhtar ibn Ubayd al-Thaqafi and Mus'ab ibn al-Zubayr), pp. 132-149 (regarding the harshness of al-Hajjaj in Mecca and Iraq), pp. 259 (regarding cursing Ali ibn Abi Talib in mosques and poisoning his descendants), pp. 269, 273 (regarding the harshness of Yazid ibn al-Muhallab in governing the eastern lands), pp. 277-8 (regarding harshness in ruling the Maghrib and Transoxania *'ma wara'al-nahr*); al-Baladhuri, *Futuh al-Buldan*, p. 238 (regarding a strange agreement with Nubia to submit 300 slaves yearly and receive food in return).

(38)   Ibn Kathir, *al-Bidaya wa al-Nihaya,* vol. 7, p. 158.

(39)   Majid, *al-Tarikh al-Siyasi*, vol. 2, p. 207.

(40)   *Ibid.*, pp. 30-1.

(41)   al-Baladhuri, *Futuh al-Buldan,* pp. 200-205, 227-9, 238-9, 330; Hasan, Hasan Ibrahim, *Tarikh al-Islam,* vol. 1, pp. 258-262.

(42)   al-Khudari, Muhammad, *Muhadarat Tarikh al-Umam al-Islamiyya: al-Dawla al-Abbasiyya,* Cairo: Dar al-Fikr al-Arabi, n.d. pp. 136-7, Hasan, Hasan Ibrahim, *Tarikh al-Islam,* Cairo: Maktaba al-Nahda al-Misriyya, 1964, vol. 2, p. 61.

(43)   See for example: al-Baladhuri, *Futuh al-Buldan,* p. 115; for the spoils of war in the conquest of the Sassanian empire see Ibn Kathir, *al-Bidaya wa al-Nihaya,* vol. 7, pp. 68-9, 71-2; for the spoils of war in the conquests of North Africa, Andalus and Sind see Majid, *al-Tarikh al-Siyasi,* vol. 2, pp. 55, 207, 237.

(44)   Holt, P.M. & Lewis, Bernard (ed.), "Introduction," *The Cambridge History of Islam,* London: Cambridge University Press, 1970, vol. 1, p. xii.

(45)   Sourdel, D., "The Abbasid Caliphate," *The Cambridge History of Islam,* vol. 1, p. 139.

(46)   Spuler, B., "The Disintegration of the Caliphate in the East," *The Cambridge History of Islam,* vol. 1, p. 147.

(47)   Inalcik, Halil, "The Emergence of the Ottomans," "The Rise of the Ottoman Empire," *The Cambridge History of Islam,* vol. 1, pp. 263, 269-270, 283, 289.

(48)   See Majid, *al-Tarikh al-Siyasi,* vol. 2, pp. 138, 143, 176-183, 278-9, 287-8, 288-91, 292-3, 300-3, 321-3.

(49)   *Ibid.*, pp. 41-7, 170-6, 244-9.

(50)   See for the origin of the use of the word *"mawali"* at the time of Caliph Umar ibn al-Khattab, al-Baladhuri, *Futuh al-Buldan*, pp. 366-368.

(51)   See for example: Majid, *al-Tarikh al-Siyasi,* vol. 2, pp. 116-7, 161, 277, 288-292, 327; Hasan, Hasan Ibrahim, *Tarikh al-Islam*, vol. 2, pp. 14-15; see also Ibn al-Athir, Ali ibn Ahmad, *al-Kamil fi al-Tarikh*, Cairo: Matba'a Bulaq, 1306 AH, vol. 3, p. 45.

(52)   Majid, *al-Tarikh al-Siyasi*, vol. 2, pp. 327-330; Gibb, Hamilton A.R., *Studies on the Civilization of Islam,* ed. Stanford Shaw & William R. Polk, Boston: Beacon Press, 1968, pp. 12-13, 66-73.

(53)   See Majid, *al-Tarikh al-Siyasi*, vol. 2, pp. 30, 55, 201; cf. pp. 92-103, 105-7, 109-11, 154-160, 229-241, 272-9, 281, 285, 292-3, 308-323.

(54)   Majid, *al-Tarikh al Siyasi,* vol. 2, pp. 73-6, 86-9, 128-133; Hasan, Hasan Ibrahim, *Tarikh al-Islam,* vol. 2, pp. 286-7, 397-402, 411-3.

(55)   al-Baladhuri, *Futuh al-Buldan,* pp. 157-162, 200-213, 237-8; Majid, *al-Tarikh al-Siyasi*, vol. 2, pp. 30-49, 60, 170-6, 193-5, 244-8.

(56)   al-Baladhuri, *Futuh al-Buldan*, pp. 227-232; Majid, *al-Tarikh al-Siyasi,* vol. 2, pp. 49-60, 176-183, 195-207.

(57)   al-Baladhuri, *Futuh al-Buldan,* pp. 232-4; Majid, *al-Tarikh al-Siyasi,* vol. 2, pp. 202-7, 305-7.

(58)   al-Baladhuri, *Futuh al-Buldan,* pp. 317-326, 330-5, 385-433; Majid, *al-Tarikh al-Siyasi,* pp. 220-7, 233-8, 250-5, 299-306.

(59)   Majid, *al-Tarikh al-Siyasi,* vol. 2, pp. 259-267.

(60)   Abduh, Muhammad & Rida, Muhammad Rashid, *Tafsir al-Manar*, Cairo: Maktaba al-Qahira, n.d., vol. 2, comment on the verse 194, p. 215, also: Khallaf, Abd al-Wahhab, *al-Siyasa al-Shar'iyya*, Cairo: Dar al-Ansar, 1977, p. 84.

(61)   Hasan, Hasan Ibrahim, *Tarikh al-Islam,* vol. 2, p. 62, quoting Ahmad al-Qalqashandi *Subh al-A'sha.*

(62)   Lapidus, Ira M., *A History of Islamic Societies*, Cambridge & New York: Cambridge University Press, 1988, p. 349.

(63)   Mu'nis, Husayn, *Tarikh al-Maghrib wa Hadaratuh*, Beirut: Al-'Asr al-Hadith Publications, 1992, vol. 1, pp. 282-3.

(64)   See for the bedouin hostilities towards Muslims in Medina above notes 14-16, referring to Ibn Sa'd, *al-Tabaqat.*

(65)   See above note 9.

(66)   Ibn Atiyya, *al-Muharrar al-Wajiz*, vol. 8, p. 133; al-Suyuti, Abd al-Rahman ibn Abi Bakr, *al-Itqan*, Beirut: Dar al-Fikr, n.d., vol. 2, p. 24.

(67)   See above note 11.

(68) Amin, Ahmad, *Duha al-Islam*. Beirut: Dar al-Kitab al-'Arabi, 10ᵗʰ ed., n.d., vol. 2, pp. 319-338.

(69) al-Afghani, Abu al-Wafa, editor of: Abu Yusuf, *al-Radd 'ala Siyar al-Awza'i*, Beirut: Dar al-Kutub al-'Ilmiyya, 1357 AH (1938), Introduction, p. 2.

(70) al-Afghani, Abu al-Wafa, *ibid.*, pp. 2-4.

(71) al-Haydarabadi, Muhammad Hamid-Allah, "Muqadimma fi 'Ilm al-Siyar", in Ibn Qayyim al-Jawziyya, Muhammad ibn Abi Bakr, *'Ahkam 'Ahl al-Dhimma*, ed. Subhi al-Salih, Beirut: Dar al-'Ilm lil-Malayin, 1981, vol.1, pp. 74-84.

(72) al-Shaybani, Muhammad ibn al-Hasan, *al-Siyar al- Kabir*, dictated by al-Sarakhsi, Muhammad ibn Ahmad, ed. Salah-al Din al-Munajjid, Cairo: Ma'had al-Makhtutat at Jami'a al-Duwal al-Arabiyya, 1971, vol. 1, pp. 12-16.

(73) al-Hajawi al-Tha'alibi, *al-Fikr al-Sami fi Tarikh al-Fiqh al-Islami,* Tunis: Maktaba al-Nahda, n.d. vol. 2, pp. 146-7.

(74) al-Shaybani, dictated by al-Sarakhsi, *al-Siyar al-Kabir*, vol. 1, pp. 187.

(75) Ibn Atiyya, *Al Muharrar al-Wajiz*, vol. 8, p. 159.

(76) Ibn Rushd, Muhammad ibn Ahmad, *Bidaya al-Mujtahid*, Beirut: Dar al-Fikr, n.d. vol. 1, p. 278.

(77) al-Zirikli, Khayr al-Din, *al-A'lam*, Beirut: Dar al-'Ilm lil-Malayin, 1980, vol. 4, p. 78.

(78)   Mottahedeh, Roy Parviz & al-Sayyid, Ridwan, "The Ideas of the Jihad in Islam before the Crusades," Angleki E. Laiou & Roy Parviz Mottahedeh (eds), *The Crusades from the Perspective of Byzantium and the Muslim World,* Washington D.C.: Dumbarton Oaks Research Library and Collection, 2001, p. 258.

(79)   Al-Shaybani, dictated by al-Sarakhsi, *al-Siyar al-Kabir,* vol. 1, pp. 187-196, 182-3, vol. 4, ed. Abd al-Aziz Ahmad, pp. 1449, 1454. See below for more detail.

(80)   Gibb, Hamilton A.R., "Al-Mawardi's Theory of the Caliphate," *Studies on the Civilization of Islam*, (ed.), Boston: Beacon Press, 1968, pp. 154-5, 162.

(81)   See for Abu Muslim al-Asfahani and his views: Zayd, Mustafa, *al-Naskh fi al-Quran al-Karim,* al-Mansura, Egypt: Dar al-Wafa', 1987, pp. 236-241, 267-277. The author disagrees with Abu Muslim in this rejection of abrogation in the Quran.

(82)   Shaltut, Mahmud, *al-Islam 'Aqida wa Shari'a,* Beirut & Cairo: Dar al-Shuruq, 1983, p. 282.

(83)   Asad, Muhammad, *The Message of the Quran*, Gibraltar: Dar Al-Andalus, 1984, pp. 22-3, note 87.

(84)   al-Suyuti, Abd al-Rahman ibn Abi Bakr, *al-Itqan*, Beirut: Dar al-Fikr, n.d., vol. 2, pp. 22-3; Zayd, Mustafa, *al-Naskh Fi al-Quran al Karim,* vol. 1, pp 400-1.

(85)   al-Suyuti, *al-Itqan*, vol. 2, pp. 21-33; also Abduh &
         Rida, *Tafsir al-Manar*, vol. 10, comment on verse
         9:5 p. 199.

(86)   Zayd, Mustafa, *al-Naskh fi al-Quran al-Karim,* vol.
         2, pp. 503-583.

(87)   al-Qurtubi, Muhammad ibn Ahmad, *al-Jami' li-
         Ahkam al-Quran*, Cairo: Dar al-Kutub al-Misriyya,
         n.d., vol. 8, pp. 73, 113. For al-Husayn ibn al-Fadl
         see al-Zirikley, Khayr al-Din, *al-A'lam,* vol. 2, pp.
         251-2.

(88)   Ibn Hajar al 'Asqalani, Ahmad ibn Ali ibn
         Muhammad, *Fath al-Bari fi Sharh Sahih al-
         Bukhari*, ed. Taha Sa'd & Mustafa al-Hawwari,
         Cairo: Maktaba al-Kulliyat al-Azhariyya, 1978,
         vol.11, pp. 260, 301-3.

(89)   al-Mawardi, Abu al-Hasan Ali ibn Muhammad ibn
         Habib, *al-Ahkam al-Sultaniyya*, Cairo: Maktaba
         Mustafa al-Babi al-Halabi, 1973, pp. 16, 30.

(90)   Ibn Jama'a, Muhammad ibn Ibrahim ibn Sa'd-Allah,
         Tahrir al-Ahkam fi Tadbir Ahl al-Islam, ed. Fu'ad Abd
         al-Mun'im Ahmad, Doha, Qatar: Ri'asa al-Mahakim
         al-Shar'iyya, 1985, pp. 67, 154-8.

(91)   Ibn Taymiyya, Ahmad ibn Abd al-Halim, *al-Siyasa
         al-Shar'iyya,* Cairo: Dar al-Kitab al-Arabi, 1969,
         pp. 117-8, 123-4.

(92)   Khallaf, Abd al-Wahhab, *al-Siyasa al-Shar'iyya*, pp.
         64-80.

(93)   Abduh & Rida, *Tafsir al-Manar*, vol. 2, pp. 214-6, vol. 10, p. 199.

(94)   Shaltut, Mahmud, *al-Islam 'Aqida wa Shari'a*, pp.453-5.

(95)   Diraz, Muhammad Abd Allah, "Ra'y al-Islam fi al-Qital", *Al-Azhar Monthly*, Cairo: al-Azhar, issue 1, vol. 24: Muharram 1372 AH/September 1952; also: *Dirasat Islamiyya fi al-'Alaqat al-Ijtima'iyya wa al-Dawliyya*, Kuwait: Dar al-Qalam, 1973, pp. 142-8.

(96)   See for example: al-Baladhuri, *Futuh al-Buldan*, pp. 97-115; Hasan, Hasan Ibrahim, *Tarikh al-Islam*, vol. 1, pp. 346-352.

(97)   al-Mawardi, *al-Ahkam al-Sultaniyya*, p. 55.

(98)   See above note 9. For a discussion of the change of faith (*ridda*) and how Shari'a deals with it see: Osman, Fathi, *Huquq al-Insan Bayna al-Shari'a al-Islamiyya wa al-Fikr al-Qanuni al-Gharbi*, 2nd ed., Los Angeles: Omar Ibn al-Khattab Foundation, 1997, pp. 137-142.

(99)   Mottahedeh & al-Sayyid, "The Idea of Jihad in Islam before the Crusades," *The Crusades from the Perspective of Byzantium and the Muslim World*, ed. Laiou & Mottahedeh, p. 28.

(100) See al-Baladhuri, *Futuh al-Buldan*, pp. 265-6, 268, 271, 272, 433-4; al-Mawardi, *al-Ahkam al-Sultaniyya*, pp. 137-8, 147-8, 172; Ibn Sallam, Abu 'Ubayd al-Qasim, *al-Amwal*, ed. Muhammad Khalil Harras, Cairo: Dar al-Fikr, 1975, pp. 69-77, 86-98, 189, 189-191.

(101) Mottahedeh & al-Sayyid, "The Idea of Jihad in Islam before the Crusades," *The Crusades from the Perspective of Byzantium and the Muslim World*, ed. Laiou & Mottahedeh, p.28.

(102) Ibn Hajar al-'Asqalani, *Fath al-Bari*, vol. 11, p. 260; and for due caution in using the hand to stop wrongdoing see: Ibn Qayyim al-Jawaziyya, *I'lam al-Muwaqqi'in*, Cairo: Idara al-Tiba'a al-Muniriyya, n.d, vol. 3, pp. 2-3.

(103) al-Qurtubi, *al-Jami' li-'Ahkam al-Quran*, vol. 12, p. 99, comment on the verse 22:78

(104) Fakhr al-Din al-Razi, Muhammad ibn Umar, *Mafatih al-Ghayb* or *al-Tafsir al-Kabir*, Beirut: Dar al-Kutub al-'Ilmiyya, 1990, comments on the verse 22:78 vol. 23, pp. 63-4. Regarding the Prophet's tradition: "We come back from the minor jihad to the major jihad" al-Suyuti graded it as "weak" and indicated that it was reported by al-Khatib al-Baghdadi (d. 463 AH/ 1070 CE) on the authority of Jabir. Al-Hafiz al-'Iraqi, in tracing and grading the traditions of al-Ghazali's work *"'Ihya' 'Ulum al-din"* mentioned that the tradition was reported by al-Bayhaqi (d. 458 AH/ 1066 CE) and that there is weakness in its chain of narration. However, it is well known that the grade "weak" does not mean "false" or "rejected", but only lower in the

credibility grade than the "authentic" and the "good," and in some cases just second to the authentic for scholars who followed a twofold division rather than a threefold one. Besides, the meaning of the tradition is valid and can be supported in its general indication by texts from the Quran and the Sunna, such as the above mentioned verses 22:78 and 29:69, and other verses as: "But for one who observes in fear his (/her) stand before God and holds back his (/her) innate self from base desires, paradise will truly be the abode" (79:40-41).

(105) al-Ghazali, Abu Hamid Muhammad ibn Muhammad, *Ihya' 'Ulum al-Din*, introduced by Tabana, Badawi, Cairo: Dar Ihya' al-Kutub al-'Arabiyya, 1957, vol. 2, pp. 54-77.

(106) Mottahedeh & al-Sayyid, "The Idea of Jihad in Islam before the Crusades," *The Crusaders from the Perspective of Byzantium and the Muslim World*, ed. Laiou & Mottahedeh, p. 29.

(107) Hitti, Philip K., *History of the Arabs*, pp. 137-8.

(108) Asad, Muhammad, *The Message of the Quran*, Introduction to Sura 48 "al-Fat-h" and comment on verse 1, pp. 784-5.

II

Non Arabs

Not Second Class Citizens
in the Muslim State

Arabs in the Arabian Peninsula had been a tribal people before Islam. They continued to be so after Islam, and traces of the tribal structure can be found there now. The early Muslim armies were tribally organized: every tribe had its place and flag in the army, and proudly narrated the events of the battles in which its members participated. The tribal structure and spirit extended to the annexed lands and the established cities there after Islam, until gradually a sense of belonging to the city emerged [1].

Organized Attachment of the Peoples of the Annexed Lands to the Arab Tribes

It was narrated that some Persian military leaders were inclined to embrace Islam after the collapse of the Sassanian Empire. They took the initiative to express this wish to the Arab Muslim leadership in their lands, at the same time asking for assurance from the Muslim Arabs that they would never attack them. They would join Muslim Arabs in fighting against Persians, but not in any conflict between the Arabs themselves, and they would be equally paid as the Muslim Arabs. They would have the choice to stay wherever they wanted, and the agreement on these conditions would come to them from the highest Muslim Arab leader who sent the Muslim Arab army to their land.

The message was forwarded to Caliph Umar, who agreed to the terms of the request. Those Persian leaders joined the Muslims in Basra, and chose to connect with the closest tribe in kinship to the Prophet, Bani Tamim. Caliph Umar instructed the Muslim Arab leaders to attach the Persians who embraced Islam to the Arab tribes as adherents, *mawali*, and to make them equal to the members of those tribes in all rights and obligations. He also gave them the option to be a separate tribe with equal payment to Arab tribes if they so chose [2]. Muslim tribes acquired further adherents from former Persian cavalry units, as well as from peasants without land property, slave laborers and weavers. In spite of the Islamic principles of equality and Caliph Umar's sharp instructions, a conflict between the Muslim *mawali* and the Muslim Arabs emerged, developing and culminating under the Umayyads. Since the Arabic word *mawla* (sing.), *mawali (pl.)* may mean an adherent or supporter, and also may mean a slave, it was used to express inferiority. Even those who practiced skilled work in the army, administration, commerce, and medicine, or held religious positions, were looked down upon by Muslim Arabs [3].

Development of Hostilities against the Mawali on Tribal Grounds

The Umayyad dynasty exploited tribal discords such as the pre-Islamic one between the southern Yemenis and the northern Mudaris or Qaysis, shifting from supporting and favoring one tribal ancestry to the other according to the ruler's whim or benefit. The damaging consequences of such clannish favoritism were not limited to the state base in Syria, but spread all over the state lands from Andalusia to Khurasan. On the opposite front, within the Umayyads' enemies, the contradictions between the noble Shi'i Arabs in Kufa and the Shi'i *mawali* were appalling. Al-Mukhtar ibn Abi 'Ubayd al-Thaqafi was supported mainly by the *mawali* in his rebellion against the Umayyads. He was confronted by another rebel against the Umayyads, Mus'ab ibn al-Zubayr, who defeated and killed al-Mukhtar in 68 AH/ 687 CE, massacred thousands of his army, and called himself "the butcher." However, he was then defeated by the Umayyads and killed in 72 AH/ 691 CE [4].

The *mawali* began to feel justly treated when Umar ibn Abd al-Aziz became the head of the Umayyad state, but his rule was short (99-101 AH/ 717-720 CE). This just ruler treated compassionately those related to Ali ibn Abi Talib, against whom the founder of the Umayyad dynasty Mu'awiya had fought and upon whose murder he seized power. Furthermore, Umar ibn Abd al-Aziz arranged debates with the rebellious group *al-Khawarij* who had been constantly fighting against the Umayyads. As a result, his justice and care about the people persuaded many to embrace Islam in such annexed lands as North Africa, Egypt, Khurasan, Transoxiana, and Northern India. He used to listen to and look at any complaint sent to him about any injustice practiced against any person, Muslim or non-Muslim, Arab or non-Arab [5]. It was narrated that when some people in the area of Samarqand complained that the Muslim army under Qutayba ibn Muslim entered their city deceptively, he turned the complaint to a judge who enquired into it, ruled for the litigants, and ordered the army to evacuate and conduct the war honestly [6]. However, with the death of Umar ibn Abd al-Aziz, this short period of justice and care for the people came to an end, and injustice, clannishness, and ethnic haughtiness returned.

Under Hisham ibn Abd al-Malik (105-125 AH/ 724-743 CE), a delegation from Tunisia, called by Muslim Arabs of that time "Africa," consisting of 29 men led by Maysara al-Mataghri, came to complain to Hisham directly about the appalling practices of his top officials in their country. They were not allowed to see the caliph, so they told the court official whom they met to let *"Amir al-Mu'minin"* know that their governor in Africa involved them in fighting with his army, but whenever spoils of war were seized, he excluded them when distributing them among his army, saying that this would make their jihad more pure and sincere! In the battlefield the complainants and their people would be put in the front, while the governor's army would be put at the back, with the claim that this would increase the reward of these people with God! Furthermore, the governor's officials killed the people's sheep to use their white fur for the Caliph. They bore all this, until the officials began to take every beautiful girl among the people! The complainants, knowing that this was not justifiable in the Quran and Sunna, decided to find out if all these practices had been made according to Hisham's orders or not, for they believed that they should not rebel against a Muslim *imam* (head of state) for what his officials might do.

The delegation waited and waited for a meeting with Hisham or an answer from him, but neither was reached. When they spent all their money during their long wait, they left their names and went back to their country, where they started a rebellion against the Umayyad rule. For such accumulated injustice, North Africa harbored support and fought for the Khariji trend that stressed equality in what they propagated [7].

Political and Socio-Cultural Developments for the Benefit of the Mawali

In time, the cities became the nucleus of the population structure instead of the clan, thus helping to bridge the gap between the Arabs and the *mawali* through urban and professional, cultural developments. The *mawali* were socially strengthened through the urban and civilizational development, and became culturally closer to the Arabs. On the other hand, many Arabs—especially those at the top of society—were attracted to Persian civilized life. That development was accelerated by intermarriage between the two groups, and non-Arab maternal relationship became a coveted relationship alongside Arab patrilineality [8].

The Abbasid movement, with its Arab and *mawali* components, brought the two groups together even further. As Lapidus lucidly explains,

"Thus, within 50 years, the founding of new cities, transfer of economic opportunities and political power to new peoples and new places stimulated the interpenetration of Arab and non-Arab people. Non-Arabs permeated the Arab military caste as converts and associates; and Arabs became landowners, merchants, and settlers. Pressures, generated by sedentarization and urbanization, by the teachings of Islam and by contact with other Middle Eastern peoples, weakened old tribal society, fostered new group and communal structure, intensified stratification of the society, diversion of labor and led to formation of new mixed Arab and non-Arab communities. Social change also made possible the formation of new religious associations built around family chiefs, descendants from the Prophet, charismatic preachers, Quran readers, scholars, and mystics. The breakdown

146

of lineage structure made possible new forms of social organization. Social change took cultural expression through conversions to Islam and acceptance of Arabic or Persian as shared languages" [9].

In modern times, colonization, followed by a long struggle for independence and the achievement of independence, may have brought the Muslim Arabs and the Muslim non-Arabs closer, through their common suffering and struggle, and their subsequent social development.

Development of Ethnic Superiority among non-Arabs: Shu'ubiyya

In spite of the developing integration and equality between Muslim Arabs and Muslim non-Arabs, Persian opposition to the Arabs and sometimes to Islam was demonstrated through various movements. The harboring and supporting of dissenting sects such as Shi'is and Kharijis, the rise of rebellious movements with origins rooted in old Persian traditions such as Sinbad the Magian (d. 139 AH/ 756 CE), al-Muqanna' of Khurasan (d. 164 AH/ 780 CE) and Babak the Khurrami (d. 223 AH/ 838 CE), followed by the establishment of autonomous dynasties such as the Saffarids (254-291 AH/ 868-903 CE) in Sijistan and North and East Persia, and the Samanids (261-390 AH/ 874-999 CE) with their center of power in Khurasan, all represented the ongoing growth of non-Arab ethnic identity between the eighth and tenth centuries C.E.

These political events were accompanied by an intellectual development among non-Arab Muslims, especially Persians. This movement became known as *"al-shu'ubiyya"* in reference to *"shu'ub,"* or "nations" in the verse *"O people! We have created you all out of a male and a female, and have made you into nations and tribes, so that you might come to know [and recognize and thus complement] on another. Verily, the most honorable of you in the sight of God is the one who is most deeply conscious of Him"* (49:13). The verse emphasizes the equality of all individuals, tribes, and nations. Arab supremacy– particularly rampant under the Umayyads – was countered with pride in the splendor of the ancient Persian monarchies and their civilizations, which were compared with Arab bedouin life. As Gustave E. von Grunebaum noted, "On the whole, dispute was conducted in a manner not worthy of the excellence of scholarship of a goodly portion of the contestants" [10]. Furthermore, it seemed on the Arab side that the heated argument had escalated to something "not far from identification of the religious culture of Islam with the Arabic humanities. It is a strange phenomenon that while Islam began as a protest against Arab culture and tradition as a whole, by the end of this period, the literary history of ancient Arabia was indissolubly linked up with Islam" [11].

In modern times, nationalism took hold in most Muslim countries through their struggles for independence, and in their post-independence era. However, it was accommodated within the Islamic identity, and so it avoided any attitude of ethnic supremacy or contradiction to Islam and its early Arab defenders. Muslim non-Arab nationalists have in general always maintained a favorable, or at least non-aggressive, attitude towards the Arabs, even in contexts where Arab versus non-Arab sensitivities exist, such as between the Berbers and Arabs in North Africa, the Kurds and Arabs in Iraq, or the Iranians and the Arabs in general. The close historical and cultural relations between the Arabs and Islam have restricted the sensitivities from transgressing the limits of time or reason. As for Arab nationalism, even its secular and non-Muslim advocates have compounded the Muslim history with Arab glories.

Implications in Jurisprudence

- ***Qurashi Descent as a Requirement for the Position of a Caliph or Imam***

Among the requirements that must be fulfilled for the position of a caliph or imam, al-Mawardi argued, is descent from the tribe of Quraysh. He based this view on the Prophet's Traditions (Sunna) and on consensus [13]. This was one of the Arab arguments against the Ottoman Empire whose sultans claimed the title of "caliph." In the Arab nationalist separatist movement against the Ottoman Empire, for example, aspirations for an Arab caliphate were expressed by Syrian writer Abd al-Rahman al-Kawakibi (d. 1902) [12].

Ibn Khaldun (d. 808 AH/ 1405 CE) discussed at length this requirement of descent from Quraysh, arguing against its being permanently binding on the grounds of its reason and purpose (*'illa, maqsid*). Although he believed in its support by the Sunna and the consensus of the Prophet's Companions, he also held that the rules of Shari'a in worldly practices (*mu'amalat*, vis-à-vis acts of worship, *'ibadat*) should have their reasons and purposes. As the reason and purpose here have not been explicitly mentioned in the Sunna, Ibn Khaldun concluded that descent from Quraysh was historically required because of the social structural power (*'asabiyya*) of Quraysh. Due to Quraysh's number, solidarity and veneration among all who were related to the main Arab block of Mudar, and consequently among the entire people of Arabia in that time, the stipulation that the caliph come from that tribe was essential under those given circumstances in order to secure submission to the Muslim political leader, and avoid any conflict or disunity.

However, after the decline of the caliphate and of Arab power in the structure of the Muslim society – as Shari'a laws are for every time and place – the requirement of descent from Quraysh has to be turned into a general condition that the one who is trusted with authority by Muslims ought to enjoy social power, so that others would follow and obey him. Ibn Khaldun was of the view that such social power on the part of the state leader, caliph or monarch, is fundamental in seizing and securing authority. In his renowned sociopolitical system, Ibn Khadun argued that the close and fundamental supporters of a dynasty that had been connected to it from its beginning – whether as free supporters or freed slaves – would become a part of it and its structural power ('asabiyya), even if they did not share the same descent. As examples he mentioned Bani Barmak and Bani Sahl in relation to the early Abbasid period, and the Turks in later times [14].

A few traditions related to the Prophet stated that the "imam" and "amir," or the head of the Muslim state in general, had to be related to Quraysh [15]. However, it is noticeable that when Abu Bakr argued with the Medinese "al-Ansar/ the Supporters" that the caliph after the death of the Prophet should be from Quraysh, he did not mention any tradition related to the Prophet. He simply said in his own words that "the Arabs only know this matter [of leadership] in this group of Quraysh; they stand at the center of the Arabs in their lineage and homes" [16]. However, as Ibn Khaldun rightfully indicated, in Shari'a we have to figure out the reason "'illa" and the purpose "maqsad" behind rules related to worldly practices "mu'amalat," as opposed to acts of worship, "'ibadat," which have to be followed as long as they are commanded in an authentic text that indicates a definite meaning. Moreover, we have to analyze whether a tradition of the Prophet came from him as a Conveyor of

God's message and so is binding for the believer of any time or place, as a leader who might use his discretion according to the given circumstances, or as a wise and experienced human being dispensing advice.

A logical analysis of the very few texts requiring the imam's descent from Quraysh would result in what Ibn Khaldun concluded: Quraysh at that time had distinction among other tribes in the Arab social structure because of its role in taking care of the *Ka'ba* and the pilgrimage, and in the Arabian commerce system with neighboring countries. An Arab leader needed such significant and distinctive lineage in order to be supported and obeyed by the people of Arabia when he practiced his authority. As the binding effect of the legal rule follows the existence of its reason and the fulfillment of its purpose, the rule does not have to be binding when its reason and purpose are missing. Political and social powers have different factors and criteria according to changing circumstances [17].

• Compatibility in Marriage Based on Ethnic Origin and Descent

Different views about compatibility in marriage between two suggested spouses and their families were raised in the juristic heritage. Alongside religiosity, healthiness, financial ability, and freedom, ethnic origin and descent were also discussed. The Maliki school approved of the marriage between Arabs and *mawali* in general based on their equality as Muslims, while the view of Sufyan al-Thawri and Ahmad ibn-Hanbal was that an Arab female should not marry a man from the *mawali*. The view of Abu Hanifa and his companions was that a female from Quraysh should only marry a Qurayshi man, and an Arab female should only marry an Arab man [18]. However, many jurists consider compatibility only relevant in the realm of religious and moral behavior, regardless of descent, work, or wealth. Attributed traditions to the Prophet that considered ethnicity, descent, work, or wealth were scrutinized and disregarded. Ali ibn Abi Talib was reported to state that "All human beings are equal to one another and compatible in marriage, Arabs, non-Arabs, Qurayshis and Hashimis [are all equal] if they become Muslims and believers" [19].

Outstanding Achievements of the Mawali *in Islamic Knowledge*

In spite of the injustice and ill-treatment that the non-Arab Muslims suffered from the Arab Muslims under the Umayyads, many of them were sincerely and deeply attracted to Islam and its learning. Al-Mubarrad (d. 385 AH/ 995 CE), the distinguished scholar, reported in his eminent work *al-Kamil*, that the people of Medina had not liked to have children with non-Arab women, until they saw rising among them Ali Zayn al-'Abidin ibn al-Husayn (ibn Ali ibn Abi Talib, d. 92 AH/ 710 CE), al-Qasim ibn Muhammad (ibn Abi Bakr al-Siddiq) (d. 106 AH/ 724 CE) and Salim Ibn 'Abd 'Allah (ibn Umar ibn al-Khattab, d. 106 AH/ 725 CE), all excelling in Islamic knowledge and religiosity. From subsequent generations of *mawali* came serious learners of Islamic knowledge, and distinctive scholars in various fields, such as Quran, Sunna, theology, jurisprudence, and even Arabic linguistics and grammar. In Medina, Islamic scholars included *mawali* such as Sulayman ibn Yasar (d. 100 AH/ 718 CE), Nafi' the *mawla* of 'Abd Allah ibn 'Umar (d. 120 AH/ 737 CE) and Rabi'a (d. 136 AH/ 753 CE) who taught Malik (d. 173 AH/ 789 CE). In Mecca, there were *mawali* scholars such as Mujahid ibn Jabr and 'Ikrima who reported most of the knowledge of Abd Allah ibn Abbas (d. 68 AH/ 687 CE). Distinctive scholars from among the *mawali* included Sa'id ibn Jubayr (d. 95 AH/ 713 CE) in Kufa, al-Hasan ibn Yasar al-Basri (d. 110 AH/ 728 CE) and Muhammad ibn Sirin (d. 110 AH/ 728 CE) in Basra, Makhul ibn Abd Allah (d. 113 AH/ 731 CE) in Syria, and Yazid ibn Abi Habib (d. 128 AH/ 745 CE) in Egypt [20].

Feelings of Belonging to a Certain Land or People Are Natural and Legitimate

Feelings of belonging to a certain land or people are natural and legitimate, as long as they do not lead to chauvinism or supremacy of any sort. Such feelings should not contradict the essential Islamic principle of human equality, whether behaviorally or legally in individual or group relations. Human diversity is a natural law that cannot be denied. According to the Quran, it is among the wonders of the Creator in creating the human species: "*And among His wonders is the creation of the heavens and the earth, and the diversity of your tongues and colors; and in this, behold, there are signs and messages for all who have knowledge*" (30:22). God's wonder enriched humankind through complementarity of the diverse merits and cooperation of the various human groups: "*and We have made you into nations and tribes so that you might come to know [and recognize] one another*" (49:13).

The Quran states the legitimacy of feelings towards belonging to a certain people to which "*your fathers, and children, and brothers, and spouses, and clan*" are related, or towards the land "*in which you have a pleasant residence,*" or towards "*the worldly goods you have acquired and the commerce whereof you fear a decline,*" as long as these natural feelings do not surpass "*the faith in and the love of God and the Conveyor of His message and the struggle of His cause*" (9:24). True Islam is "*in accordance with the natural disposition which God has instilled into human beings*" (30:30), and the believer has only to set the natural human feelings in their proper order and balance, and not to let any of them be suppressed. The country of origin merely represents an extended neighborhood and partnership, and the

155

nation to which one is related merely represents an extended family. Healthy feelings of patriotism and nationalism, and strong regional and geographical relations are all natural and legitimate from the Islamic point of view, as long as they do not exclude others, and do not supersede the faith.

The historical and cultural relations between Islam and the Arabs, and between Islam and the Arabic language and culture, are naturally and historically firm and continuous. Considering Arab nationalism or any nationalism in essence and in principle as opposing to Islam is neither sound nor realistic. As for the secularism with which nationalism may be connected, a discussion of it will ensue.

Notes

(1)   Amin, Ahmad, *Duha al-Islam*, vol. 2, pp. 340-1.

(2)   al-Baladhuri, *Futuh al-Buldan*, pp. 366, 368, 444;
        Abu Ubayd al-Qasim ibn Sallam, *al-Amwal*, p. 300.

(3)   Lapidus, *A History of Islamic Societies*, p. 50.

(4)   See for example Majid, *al-Tarikh al-Siyasi*, vol. 2,
        pp. 101, 123-7, 316-323.

(5)   *Ibid*, vol. 2, pp. 259-261; al-Baladhuri, *Futuh al-
        Buldan*, p. 415.

(6)   al-Baladhuri, *Futuh al-Buldan*, p. 411.

(7)   Bajeya, Salih, *al-Ibadiyya fi al-Jarid fi al-'Usur al-
        Islamiyya al-'Ula*, Tunis: Dar Bu-Salama, 1976, pp.
        25, 28-31, 35-6.

(8)   Farrukh, Umar, *Tarikh al-Fikr al-Arabi*, Beirut: Dar
        al-'Ilm lil-Malayin, 1981, pp. 241-3.

(9)   Lapidus, *A History of Islamic Societies*, pp. 50-1.

(10)   von Grunebaum, Gustave, *Medieval Islam*, Chicago:
        University of Chicago Press, 1946, pp. 204-5.

(11)   Gibb, *Studies on the Civilization of Islam*, p. 13.

(12)   Amin, Tahir, "Abd al-Rahman al-Kawakibi," *The
        Oxford Encyclopedia of the Modern Islamic World*,
        ed. John Esposito, New York: Oxford University
        Press, 1995, vol. 2, pp. 405-6.

(13)   al-Mawardi, *al-Ahkam al-Sultaniyya*, p. 6.

(14)   Ibn Khaldun, Abd al-Rahman ibn Muhammad, *Muqaddima Ibn Khaldum*, Beirut: Dar al-Qalam, 1978, pp. 194-6; and see for Ibn Khaldun's general theory of "*'asabiyya*" pp. 128-9, 131-6, 139-140.

(15)   The well-known tradition of the Prophet "*al-'A'imma min Quraysh*" (the imams or heads of the Muslim states are from Quraysh) was reported by al-Hakim in *al-Mustadrak* and al-Bayhaqi in *al-Sunan* on the authority of Ali ibn Ali Talib, and was given the grade of "good" – one below the top rank of "authentic" – by al-Suyuti, Abd al-Rahman ibn Abi Bakr, *al-Jami' al-Saghir*, Beirut: Dar al-Kutub al-'Ilmiyya, n.d. vol. 1, p 124. Another tradition requires descent from Quraysh for "*al-'umara*'" (the leaders) but stipulates for their leadership that they should be merciful and fair in distributing what is due to the people and just in delivering rulings. This was reported by al-Hakim in *al-Mustadrak* on the authority of Anas ibn Malik and was given the grade of "good" by al-Suyuti, *ibid.*, vol. 1, p. 123.

(16)   Ibn Kathir, *al-Bidaya wa al-Nihaya*, vol. 5, p. 216.

(17)   See note 118 above.

(18)   Ibn Rushd, Ahmad ibn Muhammad ibn Ahmad, *Bidaya al-Mujtahid*, Beirut: Dar al-Fikr, n.d. vol. 2, pp. 12-13.

(19)   Sabiq, Sayyid, *Fiqh al-Sunna*, Beirut: Dar al Kitab al-Arabi, 1977, vol. 2, pp. 143-151.

(20)   Amin, Ahmad, *Fajr al-Islam*, pp. 91, 153-5.

III

*Non-Muslims
in a Muslim Country:
Equal Citizens*

The status of non-Muslims who live in a country populated by a Muslim majority should be equal citizenship with full rights and responsibilities, and without any reservation in this respect. This issue has been obscured by various conceptual, theological, historical, and consequently juristic confusions.

The *"other,"* whoever and wherever he/she may be, is an equal human being, created in the same way as the Muslim by the Lord Creator, and he/she is under the power and care and grace of the Lord of all beings, the All-Merciful and Mercy-giving. All human beings, with their diverse races, colors, tongues, ethnicities, genders, faiths and opinions are equal in their origin and their human dignity, and thus equal in their rights and responsibilities without any discrimination: *"O human beings! Be conscious of your Lord, Who has created you out of one living entity and out of it has created its mate, and out of the two has spread all over a multitude of men and women"* (4:1), *"And thus does their Lord answer their prayer: 'I shall not lose sight of whatever any of you may do, man or woman, both related to one another"* (3:195), *"And among His wonders is that He has created for you mates from among your own selves, so that you might find peacefulness and tranquility with one another, and He has engendered affection and tenderness between you [...] And among His wonders is the creation of the heavens and the earth, and the diversity of your tongues and colors [...]"* (30:21, 22), *"O human beings! We have created you all out of a male and a female, and have made you into nations and tribes, so that you might come to know [and recognize and complement] one another"* (49:13).

God has conferred dignity on all the children of Adam and his mate, whatever their inborn or acquired differences may be, with all the material and moral constituents and dimensions of dignity that have to be secured by the individual's genuine endeavor and the social and global cooperation and support: *"And We have conferred <u>dignity on all the children of Adam, and have borne them over land and sea,</u> and have provided for them sustenance out of the good things of life"* (17:70).

Furthermore, the entire human species has since its origin *a divine spiritual component* that works through and interacts with the human physical and psychological structure (15:29, 38:72). This divine spiritual element exists in every human being, whatever his/her faith may be: "And when your Lord brings forth from the loins of the children of Adam their offspring, *He calls upon them to bear witness about themselves, 'Am I not your Lord?', to which they answer 'Yes, we do bear witness thereto'* [...]" (7:172). Every human being is fully free in dealing with his/ her spiritual characteristic, for *"<u>No coercion should ever be in matters of faith</u>"* (2:256). In the end, diversity is the natural law for humankind, since the human being is endowed with the intellect and free will, and no conformity could be expected nor imposed: "And had your Lord so willed, *<u>He could surely have made all humankind one single community, but [He willed it otherwise, and so] they continue to hold divergent views; [all of them,]</u> except these upon whom your Lord has bestowed His grace [by following His guidance in dealing with one another through their diversity]*" (11:118-9).

The People of the Book

The Quran coined the term of "*the People of the Book*" for the believers in the earlier revelations of God's messages, especially the Jews and the Christians. It emphasizes the belief in all earlier messages of God and His books as part of Islamic belief (e.g. 2:285, 5:44-46, 42:13). The Quran stresses that the Jews and Christians should observe the guidance of God indicated in their books: "*And how they ask you for judgment, while they have the Torah containing God's injunctions, and thereafter turn away*" (5:43); "*And let the followers of the Gospel judge in accordance with what God has brought down in it*" (5:47); "*And if the people of the Book would but attain to faith and God-consciousness, We should indeed efface their bad deeds and bring them into gardens of bliss; and if they would but truly observe the Torah and the Gospel and all that has been brought down to them by their Lord, they would partake of all the blessings of heaven and earth*" (5:65-66).

In dealing with the People of the Book, the Quran addresses Prophet Muhammad: "*and say: 'I believe in whatever revelation God has brought down, and I am bidden to bring about equity with you. God is our Lord as well as your Lord. To us shall be accounted our deeds, and to you your deeds. Let there be no dispute between us and you; God will bring us together, and with Him is all journeys' end*" (42:15); "*And do not argue with the People of the Book otherwise than in a most decent manner, unless it be such of them as are bent on wrongdoing [and thus all argument should be avoided], and say, 'We believe in that which has been brought down to us, as well as that which has been brought down to you; our God and your God is one and the same, and it is unto Him that we [all] submit ourselves'*"

(29:46). The food of the People of the Book is lawful for a Muslim, and the marriage of a Muslim woman or a woman from the People of the Book is lawful for a Muslim man (5:5).

Kindliness and Justice in Dealing with Others

The Quran teaches Muslims that their initial and natural relations with all other human beings who do not share with them the faith should be based on kindness and justice: *"As for such [of the unbelievers] as do not fight against you on account of [your] faith, and neither drive you forth from your homes, God does not forbid you to deal with them kindly and to behave towards them with full equity"* (*60:8*). However, as for those who *"have fought against you because of [your] faith and have driven you forth from your homes, and those who have supported [others] in driving you out, they should not be taken as patrons or supporters"* (*60:9*). Justice has to be secured in dealing with the enemy as well as with the friend: *"and never let hatred of anyone lead you into deviating from justice. Be just: this is the closest to being God-conscious"* (5:8); *"do not, then, follow your own inclinations swerving from justice"* (4:135). Kindness to the enemy may urge him to re-think seriously about and possibly reconsider the existing hostility, and so *"It may well be that God will bring about [mutual] affection between you [O believers] and those from among you whom you [now] face as enemies, for God is All-Powerful and God is Much-Forgiving, Mercy-Giving"* (60:7). What is forbidden is to be the allies and upholders of those who initiated and persisted in their aggression against you, for those 'are the wrongdoers' (60:9).

The Quran indicates in detail that differences may exist between the teachings of the various messages of God, according to the divergent circumstances of the communities that receive the message. However, the basic faith in the One God and the accountability of the human being in the eternal life to come is one and the same in all God's messages. This is the purpose and the cornerstone of all these messages: "*Unto each [community] We appointed a law and a way of behavior; and if God had so willed He could surely have made you all one single community, but [He willed it otherwise] in order to test you through what He has given you; vie then, with one another in doing good deeds;* unto God you all must return, and then He will make you truly know all that on which you were used to differ*" (5:48).

If the behavior of some "People of the Book" in the Prophet's environment in Arabia was criticized by the Quran, any generalization is not true and should be avoided according to God's guidance: "*They [the People of the Book] are not all alike; among the People of the Book are upright people, who recite God's message throughout the night and prostrate themselves [before Him]. They believe in God and the Last Day, and enjoin the doing of what is right and good and forbid the doing of what is wrong and evil, and vie with one another in doing good deeds, and these are the righteous. And whatever good they do, they shall never be denied the reward thereof, and God has full knowledge of those who are conscious of Him*" (3:113-115).

Yet, the Quran teaches: "*O you who have attained to faith! Do not take the Jews and the Christians as your allies [upholders or even patrons]; they are but allies of one another; and whoever of you takes them as allies [upholders or even patrons] becomes verily one of them; God does not guide such evildoers*" (5:51),"*O you who have attained to faith! Do not take as allies [or patrons] those who mock at your faith and make a jest of it from among those who have been given the Book before your time, or from among those who stubbornly deny the truth (al-kuffar); and remain conscious of God, if you are [truly] believers. And when you call to prayer, they mock at it and make jest of it [...]"* (5:57-58).

It is obvious that these verses deal with taking <u>those hostile People of the Book in Arabia at the time of</u> <u>the Prophet as "allies" or "patrons"</u>, as the Arabic word *"awliya'"* indicates in this context, and not merely friends, for fairness and kindness may turn the present enemy into a future friend.

Naturally, the verses have to be understood within the historical context, as the Jews in Medina stood persistently against Islam and Muslims, and *"mocked at Islam and made a jest of it"*, – *"and when Muslims called to prayer they mock at it."* Such a description specified certain historical circumstances, and cannot be taken as a general rule.

However, a different tone exists in the subsequent juristic heritage and at times in the Muslim practice regarding dealings with non-Muslims. This is especially in later times, on which we will now shed some light.

Can the Christians be Considered "kuffar" (disbelievers, infidels), or "mushrikin" (polytheists)?

The Christians do not believe in the prophethood of Muhammad, but they believe in God, the accountability of the human being, and the eternal life to come. However sharply the Christian theological details differ from the oneness of God in the Islamic faith, and despite the fact that Christians believe in the "Trinity," they conclude that God is One. The Quran does not include the *"People of the Book"* with the "polytheists" (*al-mushrikin*), or the stubborn deniers of God (*al-kuffar*) but mentions each group separately even when they share a certain behavior (e.g. 2:105; 5:57; 98:1, 6).

When *some of the* People of the Book were described in a very few verses as *"alladhin kafaru"* or "those who denied," this is not meant to equate them with the *"kuffar"* who deny the existence of God and the eternal life to come. Linguistically speaking, the Arabic verb *"kafara,"* which means "to cover," may be used in general in the Quran for the denial of gratitude for God's blessings and favors, as well as in particular for the absolute denial of the existence of God and the eternal life to come (see in any Arabic linguistic dictionary the verb 'kafara', e.g. Mustafa Ibrahim et al, *al-Mu'jam al-Wasit*, Majma' al-Lugha al-Arabiyya; Cairo: Dar al-Ma'arif, 1972). As examples, the Quran says: *"and should you try to count God's blessings, you could never compute them. [And yet] behold, the human being is indeed most persistent in wrong doing, stubbornly <u>ungrateful (kuffar)</u>"* (14:34); *"They are fully aware of God's blessings but nonetheless they refuse to acknowledge them, and most of them are given to denying the truth (al-kafirun).*

168

Will they, then, God's blessings [thus] deny" (16:71); *"and God's blessings they deny"* (29:67); *"and be grateful to Me and deny Me not"* (2:152).

Therefore, when the Quran describes *some* of the People of the Book in a few verses as denying the truth *"al-ladhin kafaru"* (2:105; 59:2, 11; 98:1, 6; see also 2:98-9), it refers to certain historical actions of a certain number of the People of the Book, the Jews of Medina in particular, which the Quran considers to have contradicted the due gratitude towards God's blessings from those who believe in Him. The Quran also states that *"Those of the children of Israel who denied the truth (al-ladhin kaffaru) had been condemned by David and Jesus"* not because of denying the One God or the eternal life to come, but merely because *"They would not prevent one another from doing whatever hateful things they did [...] And you can see many of them allying themselves with those who are stubbornly denying the truth ['alladhin kafaru]"* (5:78-80).

It is obvious, then, that the very few verses in which *some* of the People of the Book were described as denying the truth *"alladhin kafaru,"* do not refer to a denial of the fundamental belief in the One God and the eternal life to come, but to particular actions of *some* of them in given historical circumstances of time and place. It is crucial that we heed the dominant use of the "People of the Book" in the Quran, distinctively from the stubborn deniers of the truth (*al-kuffar*) and the polytheists (*al-mushrikin*). The Quran sharply states what has been quoted before: *"They are not alike;* <u>*among the People of the Book there are upright people,*</u> *who recite God's message throughout the night and prostrate themselves [before Him].* <u>*They believe in God and the Last Day,*</u> *and enjoin the doing of what is right and good and forbid the doing of what is wrong and evil, and vie with* one another in doing good works; and those are among the righteous. And whatever good they do, they shall never be denied the reward thereof" (3:43-5). Such a divine teaching of fairness and accuracy has to be learned and observed by all the believers in the Quran.

However, the Quran states: "The truth [and God's blessings] deny they who say: 'God is the Christ son of Mary' [. . .]" "*The truth [and God's blessings] deny they who say: 'God is the third of a trinity'*" (5:72-73). As was indicated previously, the Arabic verb "*kafara*" literally means "to cover." It is used frequently in the Quran to denote ingratitude towards God's favors, as well as the denial of God's existence, which represents extreme ingratitude towards God's favors and a denial of His blessings. This last type of "*kufr*" is called by some commentators and theologians "the greatest denial/ *al-kufr al-akbar*." Such a manifest denial of God – despite being convinced by it for material or socio-psychological considerations – is connected with a deliberate covering and stubborn rejection of the truth: "*They verily do not consider you a liar, they stubbornly reject God's messages*" (6:33); "*And they knowingly and stubbornly rejected them [God's messages] because of their unrighteousness and self-exaltation, although within themselves they were convinced of their truth*" (27:14); "*Yet, none could knowingly and stubbornly reject our messages unless he [/she] be utterly perfidious and stubborn rejector*" (31:32).

"*Kufr*" as denying the existence or the divine power of God should be explicitly expressed and thus judged. Similarly, "*shirk*" cannot be attributed to any who say that God is one but differs from the Muslim in the theological details. The Quran qualifies the Christian belief in Jesus as simply "overstepping" or "exceeding the bounds/ *ghuluww*:" "Say, '*O People of the Book! Do not overstep the bounds in*

170

your religious beliefs and do not follow the errant views of people [...]" (5:77). Such a particularized difference ought to be put in its correct perspective and clearly distinguished from the greatest denial of the truth, *al-kufr al-akbar*, which is the absolute denial of God. Nor should the Quran's specific description of certain People of the Book as deniers of God's favors (e.g. 2:105; 59:2; 98:1, 6) be extended or confused as equating this group with the deniers of God, "*al-kuffar*," or the polytheists, "*al-mushrikin*."

The Historical Status of the "dhimmi"

The Arabic word *"Dhimma"* as mentioned in the Prophet's traditions means promise, safeguard, and guarantee. Therefore, "the *dhimma* of Muslims," is the promise or guarantee given by the Muslims collectively to a non-Muslim individual or group. The "*dhimmi*s" were those non-Muslims who were given a promise or guarantee of security and protection by Muslims as a whole. For example, the Prophet offered Najran and its close neighboring areas his protection and promise (*jiwar* and *dhimma*) "for themselves, their possessions, their clan, and their faith and for their acts of worship and their houses of worship." One of the last teachings of the Prophet: "Honor me in observing what is due to those who have acquired my promise of [security and protection] '*dhimma*'" (transmitted by Nafi' from Abd-Allah ibn Umar). A tradition of the Prophet states: "I am a litigant against any who causes harm to any *dhimmi*, and whoever against whom I am a litigant, I shall prevail over him [/her] on the Day of Resurrection" (transmitted by al-Khatib al-Baghdadi in his work on 'History').

The "*dhimma*" was later qualified by the jurists as *a contract* between two parties: the Muslims represented by their head of state (*imam*) or whoever is delegated by him, and the non-Muslims in general. A request of *dhimma* status has to be accepted according to Hanafis, Hanbalis, and Zaydis. Shafi'is also were of this opinion, but excepted those who may cause Muslims harm, such as spies. A non-Muslim woman who is not a *dhimmi* can acquire *dhimmi* status through marrying a *dhimmi* man. Children born of *dhimmi* fathers or mothers acquire *dhimmi* status according to Hanafis, Malikis, Hanbalis, and some Shafi'is.

The contract of *dhimma* is permanent according to most jurists, and *dhimmi*s are considered among the people of the Muslim land. A statement related to Caliph Ali ibn Abi Talib and supported by many jurists indicated: "*Dhimmi*s have accepted the *dhimma* agreement with a view that their possessions and blood would be equal to our possessions and blood" [1]. The prominent jurist Abu Yusuf stated:

"The peaceful [agreement] was made between the Muslims and the *dhimmi*s that they pay *jizya*, and thus the cities were opened to the Muslims on condition that their houses of worship and churches within the cities and outside of them would be preserved, and their life would be secured, and they would be defended by Muslims in case of any attack against them. All Syria and most of Hira were opened to Muslims on such conditions. It was reported that Caliph Umar ibn al-Khattab said, 'I entrust the caliph who would succeed me with the responsibility towards those who are under the *dhimma* [promise] of the Prophet: fulfill what they are promised, defend them, and do not ask them of whatever is beyond their ability'" [2].

According to considerable juristic statements and historical practices, the general rule has been equality of the rights and responsibilities of Muslims and non-Muslims in Muslim lands. The exception to this equality are religious obligations such as the payment of *zakat* by Muslims or the payment of jizya by non-Muslims, the holding of certain positions that require religious qualifications such as judges, imams of mosques, and teachers of religion, and that therefore are assigned to Muslims only. The head of state (a caliph or an imam) and the military leader also have to be Muslims due to the requisite knowledge of Shari'a for the position [3]. Otherwise, al-Mawardi stated that a *dhimmi* can be an executive minister if he has the skills for the job, and is eligible for other military, administrative, and financial positions [4]. A *dhimmi* can also be a judge with jurisdiction over *dhimmi* cases, according to juristic views as well as historical practices.

The prominent Syrian jurist al-Awza'i (d. 157 AH/ 774 CE) strongly criticized the Abbasid governor of Syria, Salih ibn Ali ibn Abd Allah ibn Abbas, a close relative of the Abbasid Caliph, for forcing a collective transference of *dhimmi*s from Mount Lebanon on the grounds of suspicion of treason. Al-Awza'i highlighted that these people "*were not slaves, but free dhimmis*," stressed that legal responsibility, according to Shari'a, is individual, and emphasized that a criminal indictment cannot be indiscriminately made against an entire community. The Quran repeatedly indicates "and no bearer of burdens shall be made to bear another's burden" (6:164; also 17:15; 35:18; 39:7; 53:38) [5].

Jizya

The payment of *jizya* cannot be considered a penalty, for Islamic law does not punish any non-Muslim for his/ her faith: "*No coercion should ever be in matters of faith*" (2:256). The payment of jizya is in return for Muslim protection of *dhimmi*s and the exemption of non-Muslims from military service, according to the outweighing juristic view based on the early historical practices. Jizya was taken only from men who were fit for fighting; the elderly, children, women, priests, monks, and peaceful peasants were exempt from paying jizya. The Muslim military leader Suwayd ibn Muqrin wrote to the people of Dahistan and Jirjan, "You have the *dhimma*, and we are responsible for security and defense." Khalid ibn al-Walid wrote to Saluba ibn Nastuna and his people: "If we defend you we take the jizya; if not we will not take it". When Muslims became totally engaged in facing the huge Byzantine army in the battle of Yarmuk, they returned to the people of Hims the jizya they had collected and said to them "We have been distracted from defending you, and you have to take care of yourselves." Whenever non-Muslims had military responsibilities, they were exempt from the payment of jizya, as occurred in Palestine, Lebanon and other areas [6].

The Quranic verse about the payment of jizya has been discussed above in the examination of "jihad." The pertinent verse reads: "Fight against those who – from among those who were given aforetime the Book – *do not believe* either in God or the Last Day, and *do not observe what was forbidden* by God and the Conveyor of His message, and do not follow the religion of truth, till they [agree to] pay *jizya* [the exemption dues] with a willing and affording hand, and to be under [your] authority" (9:29). In other words, those from the People of the Book who are to be fought against until they paid jizya, represent a *specified and restricted subset under the general related rule* governing fighting and jizya payment. The rule cannot be generalized to include the People of the Book.

Although the prominent commentator on the Quran al-Fakhr al-Razi (d. 604 AH/ 1207 CE) considered that most People of the Book did not follow the truth, even he stressed the fact that there are restrictions and specifications for the rule of fighting and paying jizya. But more importantly, one cannot possibly accept al-Razi's judgment about the applicability of such qualities to all or most of the People of the Book all over the world during his time, let alone for all time. Even his knowledge about his time could not be so comprehensive and definite. However, his view on restricting Muslims' fighting against and taking jizya from those with the specific qualities indicated in the verse 9:29 is obviously

175

correct, and it was agreed upon by al-Shawkani (d. 1255 AH/ 1839 CE). *Tafsir al-Manar* quoted the view of al-Fakhr al-Razi about these restrictions, adding that there should be a *legal reason for fighting* such People of the Book according to Shari'a, rather than merely because they are People of the Book [7].

The "*saghar*" pictured in the verse with regard to the payment of jizya by *dhimmi*s refers to the acceptance of the authority and law of the Muslim state, according to prominent commentators and jurists, and does not indicate "humiliation" as some others perceived [8]. Furthermore, Caliph Umar accepted a suggestion that the proud Christian Arab tribe of Bani Taghlib pay charity dues, *sadaqa*, at a high rate instead of paying jizya, which they did not wish to pay because of the impression it might give of inferiority and subjugation. The Caliph made a similar offer to Jabala ibn al-Ayham after his departure to the Byzantine lands to avoid a ruling that allowed a bedouin whom he had slapped to retaliate, but the attempt was unsuccessful [9].

Therefore, the exemption of jizya payment if the *dhimmi* is to participate in defense, and the substitution of other dues in place of jizya, occurred historically at the time of Caliph Umar, a precedent that paves the way for similar flexibility in a modern Muslim state. The authenticity of what was attributed to Caliph Ali about changing such a policy towards Bani Taghlib was rejected by Ahmad ibn Hanbal and Ibn al-Qayyim; the latter did not agree that the payment of Bani Taghlib would be called jizya, for it was due to an agreement, *sulh*, and should be related only to the agreement [10]. Yet another striking precedent was Caliph Umar's giving the needy *dhimmi*s from the assets of *zakat* [11]. Along the same lines, Khalid ibn al-Walid stated in his agreement with the people of Hira that whoever is needy as a result of old age, serious illness, poverty, or any inability to work would be exempt from the payment of jizya and helped from the Muslim public treasury [12]. This practice, however, could not gain consensus from jurists, who pointed out that while helping needy *dhimmi*s was a necessity, it should be done from assets of the public treasury other than from the *zakat*. The *zakat*, they argued, is a religious obligation for Muslims, and must be given to the Muslim poor only. But in general, medical treatment was offered to *dhimmi*s in hospitals throughout Muslim history, and *dhimmi*s received the same necessary state services for economic development as Muslims did, such as paved roads and irrigation canals [13].

Security and Protection
for Possessions and Houses of Worship

In the Prophet's letter to the people of Najran about their payment of jizya in return for being in the "*dhimma*" of God and the Conveyor of His Message, he stated: "For Najran and its outskirts, God's protection and Prophet Muhammad's promise [of security and protection, *dhimma*] for their possessions and themselves and their land and their religion, for any who is present or absent, and for their acts of worship and houses of worship, and for all that is in their hands, whether much or little. No change in position would occur to any bishop, monk or priest [...]. They will not be recruited in an army, nor pay '*ushr* [tax of one tenth of their agricultural products], and no army will step on their land [...]. No one will be taken accountable for injustice committed by another [...]"[14].

Accordingly, the security and protection of *dhimma* are not only offered for persons, but for possession, faith, acts of worship, and houses of worship. No military occupation nor tax payment should occur in lieu of jizya. Justice should be strictly secured for all.

Al-Baladhuri reported from the eminent authority Ibn Shihab al-Zuhri (d. 124 AH/ 741 CE) that the first who paid jizya among the People of the Book were the people of Najran. Later, the people of 'Ayla, Adhruh, and Adhir'at paid jizya following the campaign of Tabuk [15], the last of the Prophet's campaigns in the year 9 AH/ 630 CE. If the revelation of the verse about jizya (9:29) occurred in the previous year 8 AH/ 629 CE then any earlier payment of jizya, such as that with Tayma' following the battle of Khaybar in the year 7 AH/ 628 CE, has grounds in the Sunna of the Prophet, according to a non-Quranic revelation, or to the Prophet's authority as the imam (head) of the Muslim community. Most likely, such practices of imposing a tribute as a sign of dominance were in line with widely-known tradition within Arabia and in the neighboring area [16].

The Quran states that women of the People of the Book can become wives of Muslim men (5:5). The food of the People of the Book is lawful for Muslims: the meat from their slaughtered animals (provided they are edible according to Shari'a), is a legitimate food, *halal*, for a Muslim. The exception here is in the view of Shi'is, which has been strongly criticized by the prominent Sunni jurist Ibn al-Qayyim. As for the argument that the People of the Book might not pronounce the name of God as is required by the Quran in slaughtering (6:118, 121), and that they might not know Him as He should be known, Ibn al-Qayyim responded that one can never be sure that a Muslim pronounced the name of God when he/she slaughtered an animal, or that he/she knows God as He should be known. He stated that the People of the Book "know that God is their Creator and Provider of sustenance, the One Who grants life and determines death [...] and they have this essence of knowledge. The full knowledge is difficult and thus it cannot be stipulated" [17].

Legal Capacity and Applied Laws

Moreover, in general many jurists– Ibn al-Qayyim not among them – have stated that Muslims and *dhimmi*s are equal in the area of financial transactions, *mu'amalat maliyya*, such as land lease, priority in obtaining neighbor property, *shuf'a*, partnership through work in commerce, *mudaraba*, or in farming, *muzara'a*, and other contracts of exchange and sale. Hanafi jurists elaborated that a *dhimmi* is equal to a Muslim since he/she is *subject to the Islamic law*, as one of the *people of the Muslim* land [18].

As for the applied *penal law* when a *dhimmi* commits a crime, Medina jurists, or Malikis, stated that in case of crimes punished by *hudud* (the fixed punishments for certain crimes, sing. *hadd*), the defendants should be presented to their own religious leaders to try them and apply the Islamic punishments or others according to their religion if they are convicted. These *hudud* crimes are: theft (*sariqa*), adultery and fornication (*zina*), slander through accusation of adultery or fornication (*qadhf*), and extensive disruption of public safety through murder and robbery (*hiraba*). Drinking alcohol is debatable in this context. For example, the Hanafis were of the view that a *dhimmi*, as one from a Muslim land, is committed to all Islamic laws related to worldly dealings, *mu'amalat*, including *hudud*, with the one exception of drinking alcohol, since a *dhimmi* does not believe in its prohibition. However, drunkenness and actions related to it in public among Muslims would be punished by the fixed punishment, *hadd*, or by another suitable punishment. Selling alcohol was allowed to *dhimmi*s within their communities and areas, although not openly in big Muslim cities, *amsar*, while transportation of liquor was permitted for *dhimmi*s on highways and main rivers.

A modern scholar of Shari'a, especially of Muslim-non-Muslim relations, Muhammad Hamid Allah, is of the opinion that *non-Muslims enjoy legal self-dependence* in a Muslim country, since they can rely on their own laws in settling their lawsuits, whether civil or penal. He bases his viewpoint on the verse: "It is We who brought down the Torah, wherein there is guidance and light. According to it prophets who submitted themselves to God deliver judgment unto those who follow the Jewish faith, and so do the men of God and the rabbis [. . .] and they who do not judge in accordance with what God has brought down are indeed the deniers of the truth... Let then the followers of the Gospel judge in accordance with what God has brought down in it, and they who do not judge according to what God has brought down – it is they who are truly iniquitous" (5:44, 47 respectively). They can go to their judge or to a Muslim judge as they wish. According to al-Mawardi, *dhimmi*s might have the option to go to their judges, but if they go to the Muslim judge, he has to apply the Islamic law in the cases submitted to him. Hamid Allah, on the contrary, states that even the Muslim judge may apply the law of the litigants [19].

The Shafi'i jurist al-Mawardi held *dhimmi*s responsible for six obligations even if they were not explicitly mentioned in a "*dhimma* agreement". The first three are that they should not derogate the Quran, the Prophet, or Islam. Besides this, they should not assist those who are at war with Muslims, defile a Muslim woman, or turn a Muslim away from Islam by temptation or intimidation nor cause him/her harm in his/her possessions or faith, while they should not provide any assistance to those who are at war with Muslims [20]. The Maliki jurist al-Qarafi stated that the *dhimma* agreement commits Muslims to obligations towards *dhimmi*s, for they are protected and safeguarded by Muslims, the promise of God and His

Prophet, and the religion of Islam, so any who commits any action of hostility against them even with an offending word, slander, or backbiting, he/she would be failing to observe the promise of God, His Prophet, and the religion of Islam. Furthermore, the prominent jurist Ibn Hazm wrote in his work *Maratib al-Ijma'* (Levels of Consensus) that if belligerent enemies came to attack *dhimmi*s on Muslim land (maybe refugees who have been granted *dhimma*), Muslims have to fight to the death such attackers so as to defend those who have been protected and safeguarded by them, according to the juristic consensus. A contract requiring such support and defense between Muslims and non-Muslims should be enormously weighty in its religious and legal value [21].

This status of *dhimmis* in Shari'a and in historical practice led Adam Mez to see in it an obstacle for the Muslim state in forming "a political unity", as the Jewish and Christian houses of worship and monasteries continued to be alien spots. The *dhimmi*s relied on their agreements with Muslims and the rights given to them by Muslims to keep them from integration with Muslims. I may see that Muslims also might share that attitude, and thus in Mez's view, Jews and Christians were eager to keep "*dar al-Islam/* the Muslim land" always incomplete in its formation, while Muslims might have always felt that they were victorious aliens – I may say conquerors – with regard to the indigenous people, rather than people living with their co-citizens in the homeland. Nonetheless, Mez stressed the tolerance in Muslim lands, as opposed to the situation in medieval Europe, and underscored the development of Muslim studies of religions and beliefs. He saw that the occasional public movements against the Christians among Muslim masses mainly aimed to resist the increasing authority of certain influential Christians who were able to reach distinctive positions in the government over Muslims, rather than a movement against the Christians as a whole or their faith in particular. In addition, Muslim government in general did not interfere in the religious practices of the *dhimmi*s. Some caliphs and rulers attended their parades and feast celebrations, and they ordered that such celebrations be protected. No special parts of the Muslim cities were assigned for the Jews or Christians, although some deliberately preferred to live close to each other. They were offered equal services with Muslims in governmental hospitals [22].

Gustave von Grunebaum wrote:

"It is remarkable how tenaciously these non-Muslim communities maintained themselves throughout and beyond the Middle Ages, and it is equally remarkable to observe how little the Muslim state was really hampered in its operation by the dead weight of those semi-foreign organizations within its structure [...]. The system [...] was carried to perfection by the Ottoman Turks [...]."

He emphasized that

"there was in the East during the Middle Ages less physical persecution of non-conformists than in the West [...] Individual rulers might harm the communities or some prominent members – this happened regularly after a period of conspicuous prosperity and political ascendancy – but the Muslims were equally exposed to the arbitrary and unrestrained power of the monarch."

Von Grunebaum pointed out that both Muslims and non-Muslims lived under the same basic conditions in the Islamic world, "and the eagerness to assert rank and power affected the Jew and the Christian as it did the Muslim. It would seem that outside the capital the religious groups lived fairly apart, except for their cooperation in official business.

But the yardsticks of social success, the mechanisms of social advancement or decline, appear to have been the same everywhere within dar al-Islam."

However, von Grunebaum noted that the *dhimmi* leaders' tendency "was to stimulate aloofness rather than cooperation." *Dhimmi* communities

"developed their own law and had power to enforce it within their confines [...] The positions of Jacobite Patriarch and Nestorian Catholicus were highly esteemed and apparently lucrative too, for huge sums were paid upon occasion to secure confirmation. In reading works of Christian authors of the kind of Thomas of Marga's (d. 840) *'Book of Governors'* or in following up the fate of a non-Muslim community in a provincial town, one feels very strongly how much their interests are divorced from those of the Muslim state. It is as though the author was barely touched by the events of the Islamic world despite the repercussions these must have had even on his personal fate. Muslims might scoff at or assail the influence exercised by the *dhimmi* in administration, finance or the cultural life of the Muslim community – actually a good deal if not most of the energy of a member of any subject group were spent apart from the main stream of development, devoted primarily to assuring the survival of the church or the synagogue that was source and goal of his social and spiritual existence" [23].

Differences in the Modern Stand towards Non-Conformist Minorities

The "*dhimmi status*," whatever its fair essence and rules may be, is different from the stand towards religious minorities in the modern state. In a nation-state, all belong to the state, and all are equal citizens, whatever their religious faiths or ethnic origins may be. In the middle ages, the nation-state had not yet been established, and belonging to a land was a secondary allegiance to belonging to a faith. Allegiance to a land would not deeply unite the persons of different faiths who lived on it. This explains why the medieval Islamic thought classified people according to their faith: Muslims, People of the Book, Sabians, Magians, polytheists, and deniers of the truth, *kuffar* (e.g. the Quran 2:62; 5:69; 22:17). Land might be juristically classified as "land of Islam/ *dar al-Islam*" and "land of war/ *dar al-harb*," in addition to al-Mawardi's third category of "land under a convention or treaty/ *dar-al-'ahd*." However, *dhimmis* were considered among the people of *dar al-Islam*, versus non-Muslim visitors from other lands to the Muslim land who were, upon their request, temporarily granted security and protection for a certain purpose (*musta'minin*) [24].

According to such a historical-juristic stance towards the so-called *dhimmis,* which is in its essence different from the situation of a modern state towards its citizens of different ethnicities or faiths, the "land of Islam/ *dar al-Islam*'" seemed to Adam Mez as "incomplete" in its formation, since it included within its people Muslims and *dhimmi*s, not simply equal citizens. Furthermore, its Muslims may always feel that they were victorious aliens, not people at home. Mez saw such a situation as distinct from medieval

Christian Europe, while von Grunebaum went further to state that "with the exception of the Jews, sizeable religious minorities in the West were as good as non-existent" [25].

Development of Discord and Juristic Restrictions with Regard to Dhimmis

Despite the early accord, fairness and ease in Muslim-*dhimmi* relations – in general and with Christians in particular – as reflected in the traditions and practices of the Prophet was not always maintained, and the subsequent discord was reflected in an increasingly restrictive attitude in juristic rules about *dhimmi*s.

Several reasons can be given for the discord, at the top of which was the essence of the "*conquest*" under the early Caliphs that naturally developed caution, if not outright lack of confidence and tension on both sides. From the beginning, when the Prophet's emissary Shuja' ibn Wahb al-Asadi relayed the Prophet's message about Islam to the Ghassanid prince, he was instantly furious and defiant, expressing his intention to go with his army to attack the Prophet in his land, however far it might be [26]. Later, when the Prophet heard that Christian Arabs from the tribes of Lakhm and Judham, supported by the Byzantines, were planning to attack the Muslims, he set out with a sizeable army on the campaign of Tabuk in the year 9 AH/ 630 to the northern Arabian Syrian borders to meet his opponent, a confrontation that did not materialize. Afterwards, the Byzantine Emperor Heraclius (d. 641) led a huge army to defend Syria against Muslim attack, and among his soldiers was a great number of the Christian Arabs from Lakhm and Judham led by Jabala ibn al-Ayham al-Ghassani. Jabala chose to join the Arabs, and embraced Islam, but he soon left it and went to Byzantine land after a dispute about the rights of legal retaliation for an Arab on the Ghassanid prince who had slapped him on the face [27]. Under Muslim rule, some contacts between the *dhimmi*s in Syria and the Byzantines were attributed to al-Jarajima in Lebanon and the people of Cyprus [28].

Muslim-Byzantine confrontations raised tensions and at times even caused riots among the Muslim masses, particularly in neighboring regions, and those Muslims would turn their fury against local Christians. Byzantine attempts to impose Christianity on the Muslim prisoners of war under the threat of the sword were reported, and when such news would reach Muslims, a backlash against local Christians could occur [29]. Someone asked Ibn Taymiyya about some Christian *dhimmi*s' wish to contact an emissary of a Christian kingdom or even write to the monarch to request interference to reopen churches that had been closed by Muslim authorities. In his response, the prominent jurist was furious that rulers who claimed to be Muslims allowed Christian and non-Muslim powers to take advantage of Muslims and acquire the upper hand in Muslim lands. He emphasized that such behavior should be punished and never tolerated again [30]. In addition, the Muslim masses might be provoked by certain actions of Christian tax-collectors and administrators, and would turn their fury against some Christian properties and churches. In certain limited cases, the caliph or governor might be hostile to Christians and thus make harsh decisions against them, as was the case with the Abbasid caliph al-Mutawakkil (232-47 AH/ 847-61 CE) and a few other rulers. Sometimes, the ruler might attempt to turn the public grievances and fury against some scapegoat to keep himself safe [31].

In Egypt, after the earlier accord between the Muslims and the Copts, later tension and conflicts surfaced due to several factors. The arabization of the administration led to the dismissal of some Copts, and the mass Arab immigration to Egypt and settlement of the Arab immigrants in the country led sometimes to tensions with Coptic neighbors. Increasing land-taxation raised Copts' – and Arabs' – protests. The Umayyad Arab-centrist policy also might have led to unfairness and discrimination towards the Copts, even those who had converted to Islam. Contacts between the Egyptian and Abyssinian Coptic churches aroused suspicion. Moreover, whenever a dispute within the ruling dynasty arose, such as on the occasion of the escape of the last of the Umayyad dynasty Marwan II to Egypt, or during the conflict between the Abbasid brothers al-Amin and al-Ma'mun, the Copts and their churches faced attacks [32].

Tensions between the Muslims and the *dhimmi* Christians in the Muslim lands around the Mediterranean, raised by Muslim-Byzantine confrontations and other factors, were exacerbated by the advent of the European Crusades to the Muslim East (489-690 AH/ 1098-1291 CE). As religion was what identified a person in the middle ages, the attacking European Crusaders were seen as the same as the local Christians, without any distinction or specific advantage for the latter. Jerusalem, the sacred city for Muslims as well as for Christians and Jews, was captured by the Crusaders in 493 AH/ 1099 CE and remained in their hands until it was restored to Muslim authority by Salah al-Din in 583 AH/ 1187 CE. As Ira M. Lapidus correctly indicates:

"The Crusades had origin in general European counter-attack against Muslim powers in the Mediterranean. Italian towns were pushing back Muslim pirates. The 'conquista' had begun in Spain; by 1085 Toledo was in Christian hands. In 1087 Piza and Genoa destroyed Mahdia the political and commercial capital of Muslim North Africa. The Normans conquered Sicily between 1061 and 1091, and moved on to attack the Byzantine Empire [. . .], the papacy was eager to reconcile the Greek and Western churches, and to support the Byzantine empire against the Saljuk Turks. It was eager to establish new states under its auspices in the Eastern Mediterranean to spread the influence of the Latin church among eastern Christian peoples. Alongside the political currents, ran a strong (Christian) passion for pilgrimage" [33].

"As an example, a horrible night assault of some sailors from coasts off the Italian Republics, Spain, and France attacked the African coast ruled by Muhammad ibn Ibrahim al-Aghlabi (from 226 H./841). They took the coastal villages by surprise, committed excessive killings and caught hundreds of women and children whom they sold at the ports as slaves. The Aghlabi navy retaliated in 232 H./846. It prepared for the attack in Syria, from which they crossed the Mediterranean and landed at Ostia at the mouth of the Tiber river, and those in the navy penetrated the land until they reached the area of Rome, destroying the forts and plundering the churches. They built a fort outside the city, from which they continued their raids against the city for a month. When they felt satisfied materially and psychologically, they returned on their ships to Susa. As Husayn Mu'nis has commented, "The incident raises sorrow, but this was the picture of the relations between Islam and Christianity in a period that did not know except fanaticism and violence. The Christians had never shown mercy to those who might fall in their hands from among the Muslims, as they did on the Maghribi coasts; and in the Crusades more severe and cruel actions would be seen. The priests and monks would never cease to instigate the Christian masses against Muslims" [34].

The Crusaders gave certain Christian denominations under their rule a privileged status: at the top of these were the Maronites and the Catholics, while the Greek Orthodox felt closer to the Byzantines who were hostile to the Crusaders. Other Christian denominations were legally inferior, and therefore the most antagonistic. The Orthodox patriarch of Jerusalem Symeon accompanied the first Crusade during the early part of its journey until he died in Cyprus. Certain lightly armed cavalry units, the Corps of Tuscapoles, were composed largely of native Christians, including apparently converts from Islam [35].

Such cooperation between some local Christians and the attacking Crusaders, and later the attacking Mongols or Tartars, contributed to worsening the relationship between Muslims and Christian *dhimmi*s. This might have been reflected in a juristic increase of restrictive rules against *dhimmi*s, as Subhi al-Salih accurately observed. Ibn al-Qayyim mentioned that the king "al-Salih Ayyub" (638-647 AH/ 1240 CE) had an influential Christian official named Muhadir al-Dawla abu al-Fada'il ibn Dukhan, who wrote to the Crusaders detailed information about the country, and welcomed their envoys, while Muslims were not allowed to meet him [36].

In modern times, European colonization of Muslim lands, combined with the Christian missionary activities that occurred under its auspices, maintained and even escalated the tensions and sometimes the discord that is reflected in the earlier juristic contractions towards *dhimmi*s.

The Conditions of the Covenant Attributed to Caliph Umar

The restrictive juristic attitude towards *dhimmi*s was comprehensively represented in a document attributed to Caliph Umar (13-23 AH/ 634-44 CE). Although such attribution is enormously doubtful, the document may represent in a general and condensed way some main tendencies of the numerous voluminous juristic works, as Subhi al-Salih pointed out [37]. It presents, in spite of its alleged early date, different kinds of later restrictions, suggesting that it might be a condensed collection of later juristic rules that was attributed to Caliph Umar in order to provide legal credibility and authority. Doubts were raised about some words that could not have been used by Caliph Umar or during his time, such as "*zananir* (waistband), or *qallaya* (Christian religious building).

Classical Islamic scholars of Shari'a, whenever they mention a Prophet's tradition, almost always discuss its transmitters and their credibility. However, with regard to this enormously important document Ibn al-Qayyim – with his well-known Salafi attitude and great care in examining the traditions attributed to the Prophet and his Companions, especially the early Caliphs – completely ignored the essential issue of the document's transmission chain, *isnad*, simply stating that as the document was "widely known and spread, there is no need to indicate the transmitters of these conditions!" He accepted the statement attributed to Ibn Abbas that prohibited *dhimmi*s from "building a new church, ringing a church bell, selling – or even drinking – liquor, or having the swine" in the Muslim distinguished cities, *amsar*. In so doing, he restricted what the Quran states about defending the various houses of worship in which the name of God is abundantly extolled (22:40), as well as the Quranic verses and the numerous Prophet's traditions that strictly prohibit any injustice in dealing with *dhimmi*s or their acts of worship.

Furthermore, the various versions of the claimed *"Covenant"* seem contradictory. The first stated that *the people of al-Jazira* (north Euphrates) wrote to their *governor Abd al-Rahman ibn Ghunm*, who in turn wrote to Caliph Umar. The second explained that Abd al-Rahman ibn Ghunm *initially* wrote to Caliph Umar when he made his agreement with the *Christians of Syria*, while the third declared that Abd al-Rahman *merely formulated the conditions* to which the Christians committed themselves.

The differences extend to *the text* itself. In the first version, as opposed to the other two, *the Caliph himself stipulated two conditions:* forbidding the *dhimmi*s from buying the Muslims' female slaves, and revoking the Covenant with regard to any *dhimmi* who beat a Muslim. The *city* in which the Covenant was written remained unnamed in the document, referred to as "city such-and-such" (*madina kadha*).

Moreover, we know from other sources nearer to the supposed time of the Covenant that the general leaders in the campaigns in Syria were *Khalid ibn al-Walid* and *Abu 'Ubayd 'Amir ibn al-Jarrah* successively, and each reached his agreements at his site. So what was the role of Abd al-Rahman ibn Ghunm, and why should he have a role in such a general document that dealt with the status of all Christians in all of Syria, while the area under his authority was only al-Jazira?

Furthermore, why did such a detailed form of the assumed covenant emerge only in the second century of Hijra, while it was not known in the first century? This is particularly suspect since some of its details – such as the special dress of *dhimmi*s – were never mentioned by early prominent historians like al-Baladhuri and al-Tabari, whose recorded agreements were considerably more concise and also fairer towards the *dhimmi*s.

Therefore, one is justified in seeing the alleged covenant as a mere combination of later juristic restrictions, brought together in one text that was attributed to Caliph Umar, in order to give it power and influence [38]. As Philip Hitti wrote: "The so-called 'covenant of 'Umar', implying Umar I, is recorded in several forms, mostly in later sources; and the provisions presupposed closer intercourse between Moslems and Christians than was possible in the early days of the conquest" [39].

It seems, then, that the claimed covenant was forged to combine what might have been scattered in later juristic books. Pictured in its attitude and details was a clear shift from the early rules towards *dhimmis* that had been in a concise, general, fair, and lenient form, to a formula that was more detailed, unfair and even repressive.

• *Building New Churches*

In the Prophet's covenant that offered protection and promise (*jiwar wa dhimma*) to the people of Najran, he simply stated: "To Najran and its close neighboring areas the protection and promise of Muhammad the Prophet, for their possessions, themselves, their land, their faith [...] their clan, their churches and all they have in hand whether it is little or much; and no priest would face any change in his priesthood, nor any monk in his friary" [40]. The protection and promise of security were given regarding *the churches*, without specifying the "existing" ones or excluding ones constructed in the future.

About a century and a half after that document, the prominent jurist Abu Yusuf (d. 182 AH/ 798 CE), who recorded the document in his book *al-Kharaj*, indicated that according to the agreement between the Muslims and the *dhimmi*s in the annexed lands, *no new church or house of worship* would be built, and that this applied to all of Syria/ *al-Sham*, and most of al-Hira. He attributed to Makhul (d. 113 AH/ 731 CE) an account that agreements made by Abu 'Ubayda in Syria had included such a condition, while he attributed to Muhammad ibn Ishaq (d. 51 AH/ 768 CE) an account that Khalid ibn al-Walid had secured the religious freedom and the houses of worship in his agreement with the people of Hira and villages in the lower Euphrates. *No statement prohibiting the building of new churches or houses of worship was attributed to Khalid*, yet after the narratives Abu Yusuf emphasized his opinion that all houses of worship at the time of such agreements should be secured, but building any *new* one had to be forbidden, and if it happened to be built, then it should be pulled down [41].

The covenant attributed to Caliph Umar was, according to one version, initially a set of obligations promised by the people of Jazira (Northern Euphrates) and approved by Caliph Umar. In another version, the covenant was written for Caliph Umar by Abd al-Rahman ibn Ghunm the governor of al-Jazira. The people of al-Jazira in return for security for themselves and the people of their faith, bound themselves in what was approved by Caliph Umar and became known as his covenant:

195

"not to build in our city a church, nor around it a monastery or a hermitage, and not to renew what might be disfigured of our churches, nor what might be within the bounds of Muslim [urban] areas, and never to forbid Muslims from coming to our churches day or night, and to allow the passersby and the wayfarers, and never to accommodate in them nor in our homes a spy. We would never harbor any deception for Muslims, and would ring our bells lightly inside our churches, would not let a cross appear on them, nor raise our voices in prayer or recitation whenever Muslims are there, nor show a cross or a Book in Muslims' market, nor go in a procession or raise palm branches. We would never have swine nor sell liquor in a Muslim neighborhood, nor show any sign of polytheism, nor persuade others to embrace our faith or invite any to it, nor prevent any of our relatives who would wish to embrace Islam [...] " [42].

As has been pointed out before, many questions can be raised about that claimed covenant regarding its transmission, form and content. It may just be underlined here the extent of small details and harsh restrictions that the people of al-Jazira committed themselves to observe. However, these strict obligations do not comply in form or content with the Prophet's agreement with non-Muslims, or with the Quranic verses that indicate the Muslims' attitude towards and relations with the People of the Book. Rather, they became dominant in juristic books, probably for the previously mentioned internal and external circumstances that disturbed Muslim-Christian relations in general [43].

However, the jurists allowed the *dhimmi*s in the areas that Muslims had entered as a result of a peaceful agreement, *sulh*, and the areas that were outside Muslim cities, *amsar*, to build *new* churches and *renovate* old ones. According to Abu Ubayd al Qasim ibn Sallam, the *"amsar"* comprised several kinds:

   — *first:* all cities whose people had embraced Islam, such as Mecca, Medina, and Ta'if;

   — *second:* the unpopulated land on which Muslims established cities where they settled, such as Kufa and Basra;

   — and *third:* every town or village that Muslims annexed by force and the imam/ head of the Muslim state decided not to return to its people, but instead divided among the Muslims who annexed it. This was based on what the Prophet had done in Khaybar. "These are the *'amsar'* of Muslims, in which there is no share for *dhimmi*s," as ibn Sallam concluded [44].

Muhammad ibn al-Hasan, the early pillar of the Hanafi school, considered open dealings in liquor and swine, ringing the bells of churches and raising crosses in processions to celebrate Christian feasts, as signs of *dhimmi*s' depreciation towards Muslims. Usually, outside of the *amsar, dhimmi*s were allowed to carry out all the previous activities. If a *dhimmi* city became one of the Muslims' *amsar*, then was abandoned by most of the Muslims, it would return to its previous non-*amsar* status. If the Muslims returned to it, they were not allowed to pull down any new church that might have been built during the period when the city lost its status as one of the *amsar* [45].

In Balkh, the *'ulama* forbade the above actions in the *amsar* as well as the villages, since in all of them Muslim congregations (*jama'at*) existed. However, Muhammad ibn al-Hasan stated that the *dhimmi*s could carry out these activities in *amsar* whose residents were mostly *dhimmi*s such as al-Hira, and in villages of which the *dhimmi*s were the majority of residents. Transportation of liquor and swine via large rivers such as the Tigris was allowed, even if the river passed through Muslim villages.

Muhammad ibn al-Hasan provided as evidence for such restrictions a statement attributed to Caliph Umar mentioning Khurasan, not al-Jazira as would have been expected from the content of other accounts. The statement reads: "I forbid the people of *dhimma* from building new churches in the conquered land in Khurasan and else, but I shall not pull down any of the old ones that I found before in their lands, unless I know that they built it after the place became one of the Muslim *amsar*" [46]. This statement is problematic historically for several reasons. It lacks a chain of transmitters, and so its reliability cannot even be judged. Besides, churches were not so common in Khurasan at the time of conquest. In addition, Muhammad ibn al-Hasan mentioned a Prophet's tradition on the authority of Tawba ibn Tamr al-Hadrami, stating, "No castration is allowed in Islam, nor a church," and also lacking a chain of transmitters. Abu Ubayd al-Qasim ibn Sallam mentioned the same *hadith*, indicating that he obtained it from Abd Allah ibn Salih on the authority of al-Layth ibn Sa'd. The editor of the book, Muhammad Khalil al-Harras, repeatedly discredited Abd Allah ibn Salih [47]. In any case, the tradition probably means that there is no clergy or clerical body in Islam – also reported in another hadith narrated by Ibn Hanbal: "no monkhood is ordained for us" – not that there is no building of churches in Islam.

Another tradition of the Prophet on the authority of Abd Allah ibn Abbas was also mentioned by jurists to support this restrictive attitude towards building churches. The hadith, which reads, "It is not appropriate to have two directions of prayer (*qiblas*) in one land," was reported by

Ahmad ibn Hanbal and Abu Dawud. However, some criticism was made against its transmitter Qabus ibn al-Husayn ibn Jundub, and al-Tirmidhi, one of the prominent collectors of the Prophet's traditions, mentioned that the link of the Prophet's Companions in the transmission chain was not solid, and so the hadith was lacking the direct connection with the Prophet (*hadith mursal*) [48]. Furthermore, the tradition's forbidding of two directions in prayers was probably to be taken metaphorically to mean that one should not hold two contradictory goals in life, not literally to refer to a ban on building churches.

A statement attributed to Abd Allah ibn 'Abbas was more explicit: "In whatever Arabs established as *amsar*, no *dhimmi* is allowed to build a church, sell liquor or acquire swine; no ringing of a church-bell should exist; but whatever existed before this [establishment of *amsar*], the Muslims should fulfill what they promised about it." Al-Shawkani indicated a weak link in the chain of transmitters of this statement [49], which in any case cannot be accepted as a single piece of evidence against many stronger others that supported religious freedom for *dhimmi*s, however respectable Ibn 'Abbas might be as a source. The establishment of *amsar* came after the divine revelation stopped, and mere human *ijtihad* on a subject is not permanently binding.

Moreover, making a distinction between *dhimmi*s' rights to build new churches, display crosses, deal in liquor and own swine in lands acquired by force, *'anwa*, and others acquired through a peaceful agreement, *sulh*, is arbitrary, for such actions in principle were either allowed for *dhimmi*s – as was the case – or they were not. The early sources stated the rights or privileges of *dhimmi*s in a general and simple way without such specifications or complications. The juristic specifications and restrictions came later, most likely as a reflection of hostilities against non-Muslims, because of internal or external harm caused by some of them to Muslims, or because of an increase in the Muslims' feeling of superiority. Regardless of the reason for their establishment, such later reactions should by no means represent permanent rules.

Furthermore, the juristic theoretical distinction between *'anwa* and *sulh* lands was never easy or obvious in reality. Abu Yusuf reported from an anonymous old man from al-Hira, that that person "gathered what he had known about Syria/ *al-Sham* and al-Jazira, but none of it I had in memory related to jurists or transmitted and authorized by jurists. It is simply taken from a narrative of someone who was described as knowing thus," and that narrator from al-Hira, "did not ask any about the chain of transmission" [50]. Vague, confusing, overlapping and divergent reports about *'anwa* and *sulh* lands can be found in the historical and juristic sources [51]. The Hanbali jurist Ibn Rajab (d. 795 AH/ 1393 CE) mentioned that Ahmad ibn Hanbal had been asked how *'anwa* and *sulh* lands began and where each ended, and had answered, "Who can provide such information?" Ibn Rajab presented clearly the numerous differences about that categorization [52]. A categorization and description of the ever-changing *amsar* could be difficult and controversial [53].

In view of such weakness of evidence and confusion, modern authors have chosen to follow the view of the Zaydis and the Maliki authority Ibn al-Qasim in allowing *dhimmi*s to build new churches and houses of worship by permission of the *imam*, or in other words, the state [54]. The Quran and Sunna strongly protect freedom of religion, and this freedom can never be separated from the freedom to build houses of worship. For one, constant demographic changes would inevitably require building new houses of worship in areas that may be developed or may become more populated, and bring about possible abandonment of old houses of worship in areas where the *dhimmi* population may diminish for any reason.

However, later jurists were harsh with regard to *dhimmi*s in general, whether in relation to building new churches, or other distinctive signs of their communal life such as ringing church bells, walking in processions, raising crosses during their festivals, or dealing in liquor or swine. The previously-mentioned account about the question directed to Ibn Taymiyya (d. 728 AH/ 1327 CE) about the closure of the *dhimmi*s' churches in Cairo, and Ibn Taymiyya's fury at the idea of *dhimmi*s building new churches, is an indication of that. Ibn Taymiyya was unhappy with the Isma'ilis, Nusayris, and Druzes for their relations with the Crusaders and the Mongols, both of whom had attacked Muslim lands. He emphasized that Muslims were in no need of help from non-Muslims, and non-Muslims had never offered any trade or help to Muslims unless they also had their own benefit from such a deal [55].

Nonetheless, several new churches were established in Egypt under the early Muslim rulers, and other churches were renovated there. In the period of the Coptic Patriarch Agaton (41-58 AH/ 661-677 CE), the Church of Abu Maqar was built. The Church of Saint Mark (*Murqus*) in Alexandria was established when 'Amr ibn al-'As became the governor of Egypt for the second time (38-41 AH/ 658-661 CE), was renovated under the Patriarch Ishaq, and remained in use until it was pulled down in the 12th century by Sultan al-'Adil (596-615 AH/ 1199-1218 CE), the brother of Salah al-Din. In one of the *amsar*, Fustat, the first church was built when Maslama ibn Mukhallad was governor

(47-62 AH/ 667-682 CE). Under the governor Abd al-Aziz ibn Marwan (65-86 AH/ 685-705 CE), many churches were constructed, including the Church of Mar Jirjis and the Church of Abu Qir in Babylon. Many other churches were built throughout Egypt under the Umayyads.

Under the Abbasid governor Musa ibn 'Isa (171-2 AH/ 787-8 CE), the Christians were allowed to build the churches that his predecessor Ali ibn Sulayman (169-171 AH/ 785-787 CE) who governed Egypt under al-Rashid, had torn down. They were all built with consultation from jurists al-Layth ibn Sa'd (d. 175 AH/ 791 CE) and 'Abd Allah ibn Lahi'a (d. 174 AH/ 790 CE) who approved of the construction as land development, and supported that view by indicating that most churches in Egypt were built under Islam during the time of the Prophet's Companions and their Successors. The Church of Alexandria was renovated and others were built there in the eastern and western parts of the city [56].

Occasionally, church construction was paired with church destruction, as Muslim masses, fueled by rage over some episode of Muslim-Christian tensions, unfairly attacked a church. Such was the case with the attack on a church in Tinnis in 326 AH/ 912 CE, which the Sultan helped the Christians to rebuild. As for Christian processions and feasts, they were protected and sometimes attended by the Caliphs and/or the rulers [57].

Restrictions on Dress, Mount, and Houses

After the above-mentioned rules to the people of al-Jazira about building new churches, ringing bells, raising crosses, celebrating festivals in processions, allowing

Muslims into churches, refraining from accommodating spies or harboring any deception for Muslims, displaying liquor or swine, and avoiding to take slaves from those who had been allotted to Muslims as booty, the claimed Covenant indicated commitments related to personal life: "We shall adhere to our dress wherever we may be, and we shall never dress ourselves like Muslims by wearing a cap (*qulunsuwa*), a turban, or footgear (*na'layn*), or in hair parting (*farq sha'r*), riding, speaking, or in using a surname or a nickname (*kunya*). We have to cut the hair at the front of our heads and not to part our hair there, to draw our particular belts (*zananir*) around our waists, to avoid using Arabic on our seals, putting saddles on our horses, or carrying any arms or swords" [58].

As if these restrictions indicated in the Covenant and attributed to Caliph Umar were not sufficient, more restrictions imposed on *dhimmi*s were mentioned in later juristic rules. For example, the Shafi'i jurist al-Mawardi (d. 450 AH/ 1058 CE) listed recommended conditions for the *dhimmi*s, to be practiced along with the obligations. *Dhimmi*s should not have higher buildings than the Muslims', and if their buildings were not lower than the Muslims', they should be at most equal to them. Bells, church recitations, funerals, mourning the deceased and wailing should all occur far from Muslims. *Dhimmi*s should avoid riding horses if they could ride mules or donkeys. These recommendations could not be considered implied through a *dhimmi* agreement, but should be stipulated explicitly in order to be considered binding [59].

Mez wrote that al-Mawardi was the first to describe such a restriction about the height of a *dhimmi*'s house. He added that later the Pope Innocent III (d. 1216) complained that a Jewish synagogue was built higher than a neighboring church in a certain city called Sens [60]. Abu Yusuf cited the restrictions on *dhimmi*s regarding churches, display of crosses, liquor, or swine, about dress and mounts, but mentioned nothing about the height of houses. With regard to *dhimmi*s' mounts, Abu Yusuf indicated restrictions about their saddles, but he did not remark that they were forbidden from riding horses in general [61].

No restrictions were given about dress before the Covenant attributed to Caliph Umar. Nothing also was discussed about it by early prominent historians such as al-Baladhuri and al-Tabari. These restrictions were sometimes supported by the Prophet's tradition that "one who imitates certain people becomes one of them" [reported by Abu Dawud and al-Tabarani in his collection *al-Awsat*, graded by al-Suyuti as merely good or acceptable, as opposed to authentic]. The tradition cannot be considered to provide support for imposing certain dress on non-Muslims, or making such dress a permanent obligation on them.

Ibn al-Qayyim plainly considered the restrictions about dress related to the *dhimmi* status of humiliation, *saghar*, although he stated in another place that the "*saghar*" meant in the verse 9:29 is merely the subjection to the law of Islam. He extended the restrictions to forbidding *dhimmi*s to have beards. This and other restrictions such as that of footgear (*na'layn*) and hairstyles point to how the alleged covenant had transferred its focus to small details that were insignificant in the identification of a Muslim. It was reported that the Prophet first let down his hair, then later used to part it. In addition, *dhimmi*s were not allowed to gird themselves with swords, nor to use Arabic in their speech or seals if they were not Arabs. Furthermore, they were forbidden from teaching their children the Quran! [62]

Such interference in the smallest details of *dhimmi* life is against the principles of the Quran in treating non-Muslims fairly (60:7-8), and against the general principles of justice (16:90). Even if the covenant's attribution to Caliph Umar was credible, it is important to see that Caliph Umar was a human being who was authorized to do his best in making his own judgment (*ijtihad*) under the given circumstances about any matter for which there was no direct and explicit rule in the Quran and Sunna. Ibn al-Qayyim considered the practice of Umar as something that had to be followed due to the Prophet's high recommendation of Umar. However, this point is arguable, especially when Umar's saying or practice is clearly different from the guidance of the Quran and Sunna. After all, there is no juristic agreement about giving the four early Caliphs, or Abu Bakr and Umar in particular, any special legal authority besides the Quran and Sunna [63].

What was attributed to Umar ibn al-Khattab – if its authenticity can be proven – was merely a practice of *ijtihad*. *Ijtihad* can be adjusted according to the variation of the objective social circumstances as well as the change of personal knowledge and thinking. When asked about an alteration of ruling that he had made from one year to the next, Caliph Umar was reported to have answered, "That was according to what we ruled before, and this is according to what we are ruling now!" Al-Mawardi quoted this account, but added surprisingly, "The imam (head of the Muslim state) should not reverse an *ijtihad* of his predecessor" [64]. Did al-Mawardi mean that the imam himself can change his own *ijtihad* while he was in his position, but his successor could not change the *ijtihad* of another imam who had preceded him? Or did he simply mean that the change could not affect what had been executed in the past according to the *ijtihad* of the previous imam, so as to maintain the stability and constancy of rulings and avoid the retroactivity of laws? The statement is unclear.

In Islamic jurisprudence the imam can practice judicial authority, for separation of powers might often practically exist, even though this was not pointed out in Islamic institutional history or legal thought. In the discussion of reversing one *ijtihad* by another, the juristic prohibition might be mainly referring to judicial rulings in particular cases, not with regard to general governmental and administrative decisions. In that latter case, it was clearly stated that the change should only affect what would occur after the change, not what had been executed according to the previous *ijtihad*.

The general goals, principles, and rules of Shari‘a, as well as the public interest, are always among the factors of engaging in *ijtihad* and changing a ruling based on it [65]. Ibn al-Qayyim sometimes allowed the public interest to be considered only in what might be within the judgment of the imam, such as in the case of the continuation of existence of old churches in lands acquired by force (*'anwa*) [66]. As for the dress code, Muhammad Hamid Allah has sharply emphasized: "As the Quran and Sunna have never dealt with the *dhimmi*'s dress, it had then no religious basis, but its basis was social or political, temporal and temporary" [67].

With regard to the *dhimmi*s' houses, to which there was no reference in the covenant attributed to Caliph Umar, Ibn al-Qayyim allowed *dhimmi*s to build their houses as they might wish when they had no Muslim neighbor far or close. If they had any, their houses should not exceed the height of the house of the Muslim neighbor, whether he might agree or not that his *dhimmi* neighbor's house be higher than his house. However, if a Muslim came later and built a house lower than a neighboring or previously built *dhimmi*'s house, the *dhimmi* should not be required to make his previously built house lower or equal to the Muslim's house that was later built. Nevertheless, if the *dhimmi*'s house in such a case was pulled down for any reason and was rebuilt, it should be lower than the Muslim's house! To support this view, the Prophet's tradition "Islam rises high, and is never risen above" [reported by al-Daraqutni and al-Bayhaqi in *al-Sunan*, and graded as merely "good" or "acceptable" by al-Suyuti] was cited. In my understanding, the tradition is related to the moral elevation of the teachings of Islam above any other human idea, not the material height of Muslims' houses.

Extended Emphasis
on Inferiority and Humiliation

More conditions followed in the covenant attributed to the people of al-Jazira and Caliph Umar: "[We bind ourselves] to revere Muslims in their gatherings, show them the way, stand up to allow them the place to sit down when they wish. We should never watch them in their homes, *nor teach our children the Quran* [!] None of us would be a partner with a Muslim in commerce unless the Muslim would manage it. We have to host any Muslim passer-by for three days and offer him food which we can fairly find. We guarantee [the fulfillment of] this for you from ourselves, our children, our wives, and our poor, and if we act differently from what we imposed on ourselves as conditions and received security accordingly, our status of *dhimma* would become null, and it is up to you to deal with the people of disorder and discord."

It was reported that Caliph Umar added here conditions that the *dhimmi*s should not buy female slaves who might be in Muslim hands as a result of war, and whoever from among them might beat a Muslim, he (/she) would have broken the promise of security and protection "*dhimma*" given to him(/her). In another version, the condition about female slaves was incorporated into the text itself, in addition to a commitment of refraining from raising their voices or displaying fire in case of a death [68].

Thus, in spite of what was indicated by jurists that the state of humility, *saghar*, mentioned in the verse 9:29, merely refers to subjection to Islamic law, Shari'a, we see in the claimed covenant – to which more restrictions were added through the juristic works – many aspects of imposed inferiority and humiliation on the *dhimmi*s throughout their entire lifetimes.

- ## *The Testimony and Life of the Dhimmi*

If a Muslim is beckoned by death on a journey far from home and he(/she) has to make his/her will straightaway, the Quran explicitly states that such a will can be witnessed by "two persons from [among people] other than your own" (5:106). Instead of drawing from the verse that the testimony of a non-Muslim in relation to a Muslim can be accepted in principle, and leaving to judges the evaluation of the credibility of the testimony in each case according to its merits, many jurists did not accept the *testimony of a non-Muslim* in relation to a Muslim even in case of travel or another necessity. If the non-Muslims are allowed to have transactions with Muslims that may require witnessing an event or a transaction, how could they be forbidden from being witnesses, while they enjoy with Muslims equal legal rights in general, and civil rights in particular?

In other verses, the Quran places no restriction on the background of witnesses, as a contemporary jurist, Muhammad Sallam Madkur, correctly underlined: "and have witnesses whenever you trade with one another" (2:282), "and when you hand over to them [the orphans when they reach the age of marriage] their possessions, let there be witnesses [...]" (4:6). A contemporary juristic view is that a non-Muslim's testimony – vis-à-vis a Muslim's – should be accepted in any case of necessity. Even the testimony of a non-Muslim in relation to another non-Muslim was rejected by many jurists, while accepted by some others such as Ibn Taymiyya and the Zaydis. The Hanafis stipulated in such a case that the non-Muslim witness should be credible [69], and this is naturally required for any witness. Mez determined that such a restriction about *dhimmi*s' testimony hurted them badly, making them feel as if they were slaves to the Muslims [70].

Furthermore, the *life of a dhimmi* has not been considered equal to the life of a Muslim, according to a great majority of the jurists. When a Muslim kills a non-Muslim deliberately and premeditatedly, he/she would not be punished by death. Only the Hanafis saw that a Muslim should be sentenced to death in such a case, since the Quran states the sanctity of life in principle and the retribution for murder in general (e.g. 2:178; 5:45; 17:33). According to Malik and al-Layth ibn Sa'd, a Muslim could be punished by death if he/she assassinated the non-Muslim through a deception that had made the victim trust his/her murderer, and the death punishment would be inflicted for committing evildoing on earth (*fasad fi al-ard*) and not as a retribution for the life of a non-Muslim. Imami Shi'is held that the death sentence only applied if a Muslim killed *dhimmi*s in general, and some of them saw that the death punishment would be for evildoing, not in retribution for the *dhimmi*'s life. In case of accidental homicide or manslaughter (4:92), and when compensation for the deliberate murder or blood money (*diya*) is accepted (2:178), the juristic opinion, with the exception of the Hanafis, was that the compensation for the life of a *dhimmi* victim would be half or less of the "*diya*" for the life of a Muslim victim [71].

It is obvious then that most of the Muslim jurists believed that the *dhimmi*'s life is not equal to the Muslim's, although the teachings of Islam emphasize the sanctity of human life in principle, the equality of all human beings, and the dignity conferred by God on all the Children of Adam

(17:70). It was reported that Caliph Ali ibn Abi Talib said: "They [the *dhimmi*s] did accept the agreement of *dhimma* in order to see their possessions dealt with as our possessions, and their blood dealt with as our blood." In the commentary of al-Sarakhsi on *al-Siyar al Kabir* by Muhammad ibn al-Hasan al-Shaybani, he indicated "they accepted the agreement of *dhimma*, in order that their possessions and rights be dealt with as the possessions and rights of Muslims" [72].

A Prophet's tradition was mentioned as support for that inequality of Muslim and non-Muslim lives: "No Muslim should be killed for an infidel, *kafir* [reported by Ibn Hanbal, al-Tirmidhi and Ibn Majah; graded by al-Suyuti as "good" or "acceptable," one lower than authentic]. We have previously pointed out that neither a Jew nor a Christian is a "*kafir*" in the general sense of the word, as neither denies the One God nor the afterlife. Besides, the Hanafis believed that the "*kafir*" referred to in the Prophet's tradition was the "*kafir combatant*," since another Prophet's tradition stated: "No Muslim should be killed for a *kafir*, and a *dhimmi* as well [should not also be killed]." Thus the intended "*kafir*" in the tradition is the one who has no promise of protection *dhimma*, and a *dhimmi* is equal to the Muslim in not being killed for a *kafir* combatant [73]. In this way, the sanctity of life should be secured and sanctioned by Shari'a for all peaceful human beings who abide by the law.

• *No State Positions of Authority*

Even in the covenant attributed to Caliph Umar, there was no reference to forbidding the employment of a non-Muslim in state positions of authority over Muslims. The verses 4:144 and 5:51, as previously mentioned, cannot give grounds for forbidding Jewish or Christian *dhimmi*s from

211

positions of authority in the Muslim state. The first verse (4:144) forbids those who have attained to faith from taking the "*kafirin/ kuffar*" as supporters, or even upholders and patrons, *awliya'*, in preference to the believers. The same verse, along with 5:51, indicates a basic requirement for such avoidance that does not apply in most contemporary cases, since we do not deal with or choose as *awliya'* the *kafirin* or *kuffar* with whom Muslims were persistently fighting at the time of the Prophet.

The verse 5:51 warns against taking the Jews and Christians as upholders and patrons/ *awliya'*, as they only "uphold one another." However, if employed in the Muslim state apparatus, they would work under the authority of the entire Muslim state as a legal personality, ruled and controlled by the Islamic law and conducted by the ruling bodies of the Muslim state. A subsequent verse adds that those whom the Muslims should not take as upholders "*mock of your faith and make jest of it, and when you call to prayer they mock at it and make a jest of it*" (5:57). This can never be the case with regard to Christians and Jews, who are a part of the people of the Muslim country. A third verse reads: "Do not take as close entourage people who are not of your kind; they spare no effort to cause you trouble; they would love to see you in distress; vehement hatred has already come openly from their mouths and what their hearts conceal is yet worse [...]; and when they meet you, they assent, 'We believe [in what you believe], but when they find themselves alone they gnaw their fingers in rage against you [...]" (3:118-9). Such a description cannot apply to non-Muslims within a Muslim state.

The Shafi'i jurist al-Mawardi (d. 450 AH/ 1058 CE) allowed *dhimmi*s state offices as high as executive minister, including executive chief of *zakat*, *fay'*, or *kharaj*, in addition to any work below leadership in the military or civil service [74]. Until the state administration was Arabized under Abd al-Malik ibn Marwan of the Umayyad dynasty (65-86 AH/ 685-705 CE), the Muslim state bureaucracy in Iraq, Syria, and Egypt consisted of non-Muslims [75]. Muhammad ibn al-Hasan al-Shaybani allowed Muslims to be helped militarily by non-Muslims, and even the reversed case could have been accepted by him in certain circumstances [76].

However, Ibn al-Qayyim (d. 751 AH/ 1350 CE) wrote a long chapter on "Forbidding Jews and Christians from positions of authority over Muslims and their affairs." He supported this argument with a Prophet's tradition: "We do not take help from a polytheist *mushrik*" [reported by Ibn Hanbal, Abu Dawud, and Ibn Majah]. But the language and historical context of the tradition can not support Ibn al-Qayyim's argument. It was said when an Arab polytheist asked the Prophet to join the Muslims in the battle of Badr against the polytheists of Quraysh, in return for spoils of war. The man was a polytheist and could not be trusted in fighting against other polytheists who might easily have been able to lure him to their side. Similarly, another tradition of the Prophet that states "We do not obtain help from a polytheist to fight polytheists" refers to a situation that is completely different from the employment of Jews and Christians in state positions of authority. Employing Jews and Christians occurs in times of peace, and they are *dhimmi*s included juristically in the people of the Muslim land, *ahl dar al-Islam*, not polytheists.

Ibn al-Qayyim quoted Caliph Umar in certain incidents, when he disagreed about the employment of Jews and Christians by his provincial governors, saying that neither the Prophet nor Caliph Abu Bakr had ever directed that *mushriks* be employed. However, on the other hand, the Prophet did not prohibit the employment of Jews in the state administration during times of peace when they were among the people of the Muslim land and enjoyed its protection as *dhimmi*s. On the contrary, the document written by the Prophet in Medina, gave the Jews significant self-rule responsibilities, and even some autonomy in a type of federation. Even the covenant attributed to Caliph Umar did not include such a prohibition, although it comprised far less serious conditions.

As for the other tradition that reads: "Do not get light from the light of *mushriks*" [reported by Ibn Hanbal and al-Nisa'i], this can be also understood in the context of making all efforts to build a distinctive identity among Muslims at a time of confrontation with all *mushriks* in Arabia. Furthermore, the tradition might be taken as an allegorical warning against following the beliefs of the mushriks. However, Ibn al-Qayyim went on to record precedents from Umar ibn Abd al-Aziz (99-101 AH/ 717-20 CE) and some Abbasids, regarding contradicting the following of the actions, rather than the beliefs, of the *mushriks*, and explaining that these precedents enjoyed "praise among the umma" [77]. Moreover, the tradition cannot be taken as a general and permanent rule in dealing with the Jewish and Christian *dhimmi*s, who are not *mushriks* and constitute a part of the Muslim state.

Despite the juristic discussions, *dhimmi*s did not suffer in general such a state of humiliation in real life, as von Grunebaum and others correctly pointed out. [78]. Mez accurately indicated that the large number of non-Muslim officials, many in influential positions, was remarkable in Iraq, Syria, Egypt and other Muslim regions. Mass movements against Christians – in Mez's view – were in fact rebellions against the domination of *dhimmi*s in important administrative positions over Muslims. Such uprisings were not frequently mentioned in historical works, even those written by Christians. Jews had influence in the court of the Fatimid Caliph al-Mu'izz (341-365 AH/ 952-75 CE), and the Christians under al-'Aziz (365-86 AH/ 975-96 CE). That was reversed under al-Hakim (386-411 AH/ 996-1030 CE), but the situation returned to normal under his successor al-Zahir (411-27 AH/ 1020-1035 CE) [79].

- **Transactions**

In the attributed covenant, the people of al-Jazira bound themselves that "no one from among us would be a *partner with a Muslim* in commerce unless it is conducted by Muslims." Ibn al-Qayyim justified the condition by saying that the non-Muslim does not observe in his dealings what the Muslim observes with regard to lawfulness according to Shari'a, and mentioned that the non-Muslim might deal in liquor and swine, and engage in usury [80]. Would it not be sufficient to stipulate that such a mixed partnership has to adhere in its dealings to what is lawful in the Shari'a? Is not Shari'a the law of the land that is to be observed in all transactions? If non-Muslims are allowed certain exceptions in their dealings in liquor or swine within themselves, wouldn't such a particularity actually have its limits and never affect the general rule of the legal authority of Shari'a over all the people of the Muslim state?

Furthermore, Ibn al-Qayyim mentioned that the Prophet bought from a Jew a commodity for a delayed price payment, and bought barley providing his shield as a pawn. In addition, the Prophet ate from the food of the People of the Book, and all those actions implied accepting their statements and their dealings with Muslims. However, Ibn al-Qayyim insisted that in the case of a Muslim's partnership with a *dhimmi* in commerce, the Muslim should be in charge of buying and selling to observe the rules of Shariʿa. Moreover, the author mentioned that the partnership with *dhimmi*s would lead to *mixing with them and thus developing affection and amicability*, and therefore al-Shafiʿi discouraged any partnership between Muslims and *dhimmi*s!

Are *dhimmi*s, then, supposed to live separately from Muslims and refrain from having relations with them? Does this not contradict the Quranic teachings of congeniality and kindness (*birr*) and justice that should be observed in relations with those who differ from Muslims in their faith but have never fought or helped in fighting against Muslims (60:08)? Moreover, while even those who might fight the Muslims and draw them out of their lands or support this aggression should not be taken as upholders, kindness and justice towards any human being can never be prohibited. Human relations ought always to be maintained, and hope for future peacefulness and affection should never be lost: "It may well be that God will bring about affection between you [O believers] and those from among them [the unbelievers] whom you [now] face as enemies; and God is All-Powerful, and God is Much-Forgiving, Mercy-Giving" (60:7); "And good and evil cannot be equal, repel you [evil] with what is better, and thus the one between whom and yourself was enmity [may then become] as though he [/she] had [always] been a close and true friend. Yet, [to achieve] this is not given to any but those who used to be patient, it is not given to any but those endowed with good part in life" (41:34-5).

As for a *Muslim hiring a non-Muslim to work for him/ her*, the historical precedents indicate that the Prophet had a non-Muslim guide to show him the way in his migration from Mecca to Medina. With regard to the reverse situation, a young Ali ibn Abi Talib worked for a Jew, bringing water to him. However, labor for non-Muslims should never be considered a service that implies humiliation, nor work that may support a non-Muslim's faith and worship. In addition, a sale or lease of a Muslim's house to a *dhimmi* was hated by jurists, and if the Muslim mostly thought that the house would be used in something unlawful according to the Shari'a, then the deal itself would be unlawful. It is noticeable that the jurists used to refer to Jews and Christians as *"kuffar,"* something that has probably had its impact on Muslims until today, and this cannot be seen as accurate or fair from the Islamic perspective as has been explained before.

Ibn al-Qayyim concisely stated: "The fact of the matter is that the *kuffar* are forbidden to receive whatever the Muslims have a right in, be it land, a slave, a Muslim wife, reclamation of land, or acquiring ownership from a Muslim by the right of preemption, *shuf'a, for the goal of the entire message [of Islam] is that God's cause should always be supreme, and their concession with the payment of jizya was for a casual necessity, and the necessity has to be assessed only within its limits.*" This way of viewing Islam in its relation with *others throughout the entire world* is very serious in its implications and consequences, past and present, and is absolutely different from the Islamic world view or Weltanschauung, and from contemporary globalization. We must face this difference courageously and profoundly, without engaging in more unproductive apologetics or superficial adjustments.

We understand now the *"supremacy of God's cause"* (9:40) to be epistemological and conceptual, not material and physical, and today it is in this way that we understand the verse: *"It is He who has sent forth the Conveyor of His Message with the [mission of spreading] guidance and the religion of truth, to the end that He makes it prevail over*

217

all religion" (9:33, 45:28). There are also other verses that might be understood mistakenly through the same attitude of supremacy such as 4:141, 2:193, and 8:39. I can never think that the supremacy of God's cause and word (9:40) and the prevalence of His message over all others (9:33, 48:28) would be in humiliating other human beings in any way. It is certainly in working persistently together for the intellectual and behavioral supremacy and prevalence of the values and principles of God's message, such as: *"No coercion should ever be in matters of faith"* (2:256), that *the way between every human being and the Lord should always be open* for everyone to follow his/her own conviction, free from any kind of imposition (2:193, 8:39). *Dignity is conferred by the Lord Creator on all children of Adam*, whatever their inborn and acquired differences may be (17:70).

Yet, Ibn al-Qayyim quoted the verse: "And We laid it down in the *zabur* [book of wisdom in general, or book revealed to Dawud/ David in particular] that my righteous worshippers [or servants] shall *inherit* the earth" (21:15), commenting: "God's righteous worshippers [or servants] are the inheritors of the earth and they are *in reality who own it*, and the *'kuffar'* are merely a supplementation to them, benefiting from it by remaining on it in return for paying jizya, and thus they cannot be equal to those who own it in reality*" (81).

This viewpoint is fundamental in underlining the sharp difference between traditional juristic thought and our contemporary Muslim thinking. This difference should be stressed and clarified, not confused, nor garnished or apologized for in order to be obscured. It is obvious that later juristic views after the early Islamic period were under a certain conception and a world-view of supremacy over all non-Muslims, believing that they would survive and exist

218

only under *saghar*, not in the theoretical or moral sense of acceptance of the rule of Shari'a as some jurists indicate, but in the sense of subjection and humiliation, as Ibn al-Qayyim explicitly spelled out. Such a view might have been developed, not from the divine sources, but from the previously-mentioned *socio-cultural internal and external circumstances*, especially the heavy burden of the two centuries of the Crusades (490-690 AH/ 1096-1291 CE), followed by the heavier and longer burden of European colonization, with a destructive Mongol occupation in between.

Muslim contemporary thinking is trying to break free from these historical complexes. It attempts to understand the divine sources in the light of the continuous developments through an era of intellectual and practical experiences of human rights and democracy, especially the world-view about *"the other,"* as represented in pluralism and globalization. Human intellect is the distinctive divine gift to *homosapiens*, which has to interact and cooperate with the other divine gifts to humankind, as well as with the divine guidance, in order to develop the human life and the world.

What may prove that the Muslim juristic views in that respect represented merely human reactions, not facts derived from the divine sources, is that the Hanafi jurists differed sometimes from the prevalent juristic trend. They emphasized that the *dhimmi* is like the Muslim as soon as he/she accepts the laws of Islam, and *dhimmi*s comprise an equal part of the people of the Muslim land. They clearly indicated in the chapters on lease the right of *dhimmi*s in pre-emption (*shuf'a'*) and in partnership by work in trade (*mudaraba*) or land cultivation (*muzara'a*). They stressed that being a Muslim is not at all a condition for the party in the contract, and that the non-Muslim has the right to make any contract of parallel equivalent exchange and of all other forms of sale. Shafi'is agreed with the Hanafis with regard to some transactions, as Subhi al-Salih has stated [82].

• *More Suggested Signs of Humiliation*

As has been repeatedly emphasized, there have been clear principles in the Quran and Sunna about fairness, congeniality and kindness in dealing with "the other" in general (60:7-8), and with the "People of the Book" in particular (3:113-5; 5:44-8, 29:46; 42:15). Besides, there have been clear indications in the early documents related to the Prophet and the early Caliphs about securing and practicing freedom of faith [83]. Any presentation of Islam or discussion of religion should be conducted with wisdom and good exhortation and through the best constructive way logically and morally (16:125; 29:46). Nevertheless, the restrictions on non-Muslims who lived under the Muslim promise of protection, *dhimmis*, increased in time [84].

Serious differences have been expressed by jurists between the status of non-Muslims in the lands that were annexed by force, *'anwa*, and those annexed by peaceful agreement, *sulh* [85], although there was no clear evidence or agreement about which land had been historically annexed via which method [86]. The Arabic expression "*an yad*" (from the hand) in the Quranic verse about payment of jizya by *dhimmi*s (9:29) was interpreted by some as an indication of subjection to the Muslim power and superiority over them, while some considered the verse merely to be referring to the financial ability of the payer. The Arabic word "*saghar*" in the verse was assumed by many to mean humiliation, while some others understood it as a mere indication of the *dhimmi*s' acceptance of Islamic law and Muslim rule. The prominent jurist al-Mawardi stated that restriction about dress, mount, and houses, displaying liquor and swine, and ringing church bells and reciting religious incantations loudly could not be presumed nor implied through the agreement of *dhimma*,

221

but should be explicitly documented. In addition, violating such extra restrictions, even if they were documented, would by no means be considered a revocation of *dhimma* [87]. However, strictness and harshness on *dhimmi*s, and stressing their humiliation increased in juristic works – independent of the actual reality of the *dhimmi*s' status in a Muslim land – as the internal and external hostilities with non-Muslims accelerated.

□ *A Contradictory Combination of Kindness and Exhaustion Infliction in Jizya Collection*

While Ibn Sallam assigned a chapter in his book *Al-Amwal* to: "The collection of jizya and *kharaj*, and the commanded kindness to its payers and the forbidden harshness with them," he later presented a chapter with the title: "How jizya should be collected, the dress they should observe, and the marking of the necks"! In the latter, the author mentioned that a *dhimmi*'s hair might be shaved if he did not pay the jizya. Furthermore, he quoted some who recommended that *dhimmi*s be tired out while paying the jizya, but Ibn Sallam commented that this should not mean torturing or overburdening them, but only that they should not be treated with honor. He mentioned that some understood the verse 9:29 as an indication for requiring the payers of jizya to walk to the collector to pay it, or to stand while the collector sits [88].

Ibn al-Qayyim, despite understanding the *"saghar"* in the verse as submission to the laws of Islam not as any physical debasement, still considered the payment of jizya as a punishment and sign of humiliation. He did not reject the views of tiring the payers of jizya, belittling them and observing that the payer's hand should be lower than the receiver's [89]. Ibn al-Qayyim referred to distinguished caliphs from Umar ibn al-Khattab, followed by Umar ibn Abd al-Aziz, and up to the Abbasids al-Rashid (170-193 AH/ 786-809 CE), al-Ma'mum (198-218 AH/ 813-833 CE), al-Mutawakkil (232-247 AH/ 847-61 CE), al-Muqtadir (295-320 AH/ 908-32 CE), and the Fatimid al-'Amer (495-524 AH/ 1101-1130 CE), pointing out how they were all keen to have *dhimmi*s maintain their lower place, as if the Abbasids and Fatimids as a whole had been Muslim models of observing the teachings of Islam and securing justice! The author made the reason for his bitterness towards *dhimmi*s clear by indicating their collaboration with the Crusaders while they were working for the Muslim monarchs, and such treason was reportedly repeated during the attack of the Mongols or Tartars [90].

In addition to making *dhimmi*s distinctive from others in dress, mount and houses, their necks had to be marked to display their identity. Such neck marking was obviously humiliating, and indicated with other signs that *dhimmi*s were not actually considered an equal group with the people of the land of Islam, as might have been theoretically and juristically stated. Adam Mez stressed that such marking had been known in history before the Muslims, but also pointed out that it had always been a sign of slavery or inferiority in general [91]. However, it seems from what Abu Yusuf stated that the marks were made by a solid matter held around the neck and were temporary until the *dhimmi* paid his jizya, after which it could be removed if he so wished [92].

□ *Extra Levies besides Jizya*

The payment of jizya was only an obligation for the free, sane and healthy men who were able to fight, as it was taken in return for the duty of defense from which the *dhimmi* was exempted. Therefore, women, children, the elderly, monks, and peasants did not pay jizya. Any *dhimmi* who participated in defense services was excused from paying jizya, as was the poor man who could not afford the payment. The due amount of jizya was fixed by the Hanafi jurists into three tiers for the wealthy, the middle group, and those below them, and in their view no *ijtihad* should be practiced in this matter. The Maliki jurists left the assessment of the due amount in its maximum or minimum for all ranks of people up to the *ijtihad* of the rulers, who would choose whether to make it a uniform equal payment for all who ought legally to pay jizya, or to vary it according to wealth. As for the Shafi'is, the minimum was fixed but the maximum was left to the *ijtihad* of the rulers, whether uniform or varied [93]. Some jurists saw that the amount of jizya should not exceed what Caliph Umar ibn al-Khattab had imposed, even if a person was able to pay more, but it could be reduced if anyone was not able to pay what had been assessed. Others saw that the payment could either be increased or reduced by the decisions of the rulers according to the changing circumstances [94].

An extra obligation of offering hospitality to Muslim passers-by for three days was imposed on *dhimmi*s. Another narration required offering fodder to the Muslims' mounts. Muslims could share a ride with a *dhimmi* if the destination was the same, and could require *dhimmi*s to guide them in their way. They might also require them to repair a bridge. *Dhimmi*s had to clean without payment the city of Jerusalem from the amassed waste there.

When Imam Malik stated that nothing should be taken from a *dhimmi* without his/her consent, he was asked about the obligation of offering hospitality to Muslims.

His answer was that they had been *released from some due payment in return* [(95)]. Malik did not support his view with any historical evidence, and thus it seemed as wishful thinking or an apologetic attempt. Al-Mawardi stated that offering hospitality could not be an obligation unless it was explicitly stipulated in the Muslims' agreement with the non-Muslim people, as Caliph Umar had done in his agreement with the Christians in Syria. In such a case they had to offer the food that they were eating, and could not be charged with slaughtering a sheep or a chicken. As for the animals that might be with the Muslim passers-by, they should be merely offered shelter, but not food.

These conditions were assumed to have been imposed on the people not of the cities but of the country-side [(96)], where Muslim passers-by might not know the people of the area, and thus it would not be easy for them to find a place to spend the night. Ibn al-Qayyim stated that offering hospitality should be explicitly stipulated in Muslims' agreement with non-Muslims, also pointing out that offering hospitality to the stranger is religiously required of a Muslim for a day and a night as an obligation, and for three days as a recommendation [(97)]. One may not forget that offering hospitality to the stranger had even been part of pre-Islamic Arab tradition, as necessitated by the desert nature of Arabia. Taking care of the stranger was also stressed in the Torah (Exodus 22:21, 23:9, Deuteronomy 10:19, 24:17-21).

□ *Overt Offensive Terms*

One of the conditions to which the people of al-Jazira committed themselves to in the attributed document, was that they should *not speak Arabic, engrave their names on seals in Arabic, nor use an Arabic title or epithet, kunya.*

225

Ibn al-Qayyim commented that these conditions aimed to forbid those whose language was not Arabic from acting like Arabs in their speech, just as they were forbidden from imitating Arabs in their dress, mount, headgear, and even hair shape and beards! Ibn al-Qayyim stated that *dhimmi*s were *forbidden from some clothing because it was prestigious, and from others to distinguish them from Muslims.*

Moreover, Ibn al-Qayyim thought that requiring non-Arabs to speak in their own language would make them realize that they were fully different from the Arabs whom and whose language they should regard very highly, and that they were non-Muslims, and even in his words, *"kuffar."* He also believed that *dhimmi*s should not have characteristic Muslim names such as Muhammad, Ahmad, Abu Bakr, Umar, Uthman, and Ali, but they could have common names shared by Muslims and non-Muslims such as Ibrahim, Yahya, Ya'qub, Yusuf, and 'Isa. While the document stated that *dhimmi*s' children *should not be taught the Quran*, Ibn al-Qayyim held the view – inconsistently – that *dhimmi*s could hear the Quran from a Muslim at their request [98]. It seems strange how such persistent cultural separation or segregation developed, in contradiction to the guidance of Islam and the sensible and historical trend of Arabization. This is particularly remarkable in the modern world, where the common interest of nations is to spread their culture, not isolate it in this manner.

What may seem more shocking, according to this alleged covenant, is that *dhimmi*s were to hang bells around their necks when they went to public baths so as to be distinctive from Muslims. Mixing between naked Muslim and non-Muslim women in public baths was not allowed. The claimed document required *dhimmi*s to wear shoes that were different from the Muslims'. According to a juristic view, *dhimmi*s had to be forbidden from wearing yellow clothes, since they had been worn by the Prophet and many of his Companions. A *dhimmi* woman was to wear one red shoe when she went out, and should never let her hair braids down [(99)].

Such strange restrictions may or may not have actually been observed, or may have reflected social traditions, not legal obligations. What is of concern here is the juristic statement of the matter that was supposed to represent Islamic law. The jurists clearly felt strongly about keeping a *sharp distinction between Muslims and non-Muslims in every possible aspect of life*, even in realms that do not relate directly or even indirectly to faith, worship or other basics of religion. They over generalized the significance of the Prophet's tradition "Whoever imitates some people, he [/she] becomes a part of them" [reported by Abu Dawud and al-Tabarani]. Whether one chooses to accept the attribution of conditions of *dhimmi* dress to Caliph Umar ibn al-Khattab, or even to the Umayyad Umar ibn Abd al-Aziz, it is clear that such ideas were never mentioned at the time of the Prophet, as Ibn al-Qayyim himself pointed out. Therefore, he saw that the principle of observing a distinction in *dhimmi*s' dress should be maintained, but the details had to be left to the "*imam*" or the Muslim state authorities, according to the given circumstances of time and place.

Such a strong feeling of "distinction" was nurtured by a certain understanding of "*saghar*" (9:29) as inferiority and subjection. Again in spite of Ibn al-Qayyim's considering it as merely the acceptance of the rule of Islamic law, his work was full of references to the due inferiority or subjection that *dhimmi*s always ought to be made to feel. Considering Jews, Christians, and all *dhimmi*s in general as simply "*kuffar*," instead of keeping in mind precisely the difference between

227

the categories, probably also contributed to the juristic persistence about the essential distinction of *dhimmi*s from Muslims and the prevention of any equality or assimilation. The external attacks of the Crusaders, and some internal cases of *dhimmi*s' collaboration with them helped to nurture this attitude. Thus the distinction of non-Muslims as a result of "*saghar*" and of being "*kuffar*" was stressed by jurists as an essential Islamic principle, and so viewed as a matter of faith and one of the permanent basics of the Quran and Sunna, not merely a historical practice related to some circumstantial occasions [100].

Increasingly peculiar is that some jurists saw that *such restrictions and humiliation might lead the dhimmis to convert to Islam*! [101] I can not imagine how such a thought entered their minds, for oppression naturally alienates the oppressed from the oppressor, making the former bitter and hostile towards the latter. Even if any opportunist or hypocrite might embrace Islam under such pressures, this is not the true belief without compulsion that Islam mandates (2:256), nor the proper climate that Islam demands and develops among Muslims in their relations with all children of Adam (17:70). How can a juristic mind tolerate pressure as a way of spreading God's message of justice and mercy, while any coercion in matters of faith is absolutely prohibited? Historically, Islam spread among the *dhimmi*s, but I do not think that this was because of the restrictions that the jurists wished to impose on them, which fortunately mostly did not materialize.

□ *Unfriendly Personal Relations*

A Prophet's tradition forbade initiating a greeting of peace to Jews and Christians, and suggested that if they were met on a road they should be left to pass on the narrowest part of it [reported by al-Bukhari and Muslim]. Another tradition stated that if the People of the Book initiated a greeting of peace to a Muslim "*al-salam alaykum*", his (/her) response should simply be "and to you, *wa alaykum*" [reported by al-Bukhari and Muslim]. It was reported that some Jews deliberately distorted the pronunciation of the Arabic word "*salam*" which means "peace," to "*sam*," which means in Arabic "death." Such traditions can be properly understood within the historical hostile climate between the Muslims and the Jews in Medina (e.g. 2:40-44, 58-9, 61, 63-6, 74-9, 83-101, 105, 109, 113, 120, 139-40, 145, 210-11, 3:65-78, 98-100, 111-2, 181- 4, 186; 4:44-7, 51-2, 60-3, 153-61; 5:41-2, 59-64, 68, 71, 82). They emerged as a reaction to the Jewish feeling of religious superiority that was pictured in the Quran (e.g. 2:80-2, 94, 111-2, 135-7; 4:49-50, 5:18).

Such an occasional historical tension cannot establish a permanent law. And if the hostility was with the Jews, why were the Christians included and thus the rule was given a religious dimension? The Quran, as has been stressed before, teaches due fairness in judgment by stressing that generalization has to be avoided and each case has to be judged according to its own merits: "*They are not all alike; among the People of the Book there are those who are upright, who recite God's messages throughout the night and prostrate themselves [before Him]. They believe in God and the Last Day and enjoin what is right and good and forbid what is wrong and evil, and vie with one another in doing good works, and these are among the righteous. And whatever good they do, they shall never be denied the reward thereof; and God has full-knowledge of those who are conscious of Him*" (3:113-5). With such peaceful good people, fairness, kindness, and good relations have to be developed, "and verily, God loves those who act equitably"

(60:8). And even with those who might "fight against you because of [your] faith and drive you forth from your homes, or aid [others] in driving you forth," what should be avoided is "being their upholders," not simply being fair or congenial to them (60:9). The Islamic principle in human relations is to always look for the potential in every individual: "*It may well be that God will bring about [mutual] affection between you and those from the others whom you [now] face as enemies*" (60:7).

Some jurists allowed the Muslims to initiate greetings of "*salam*" to Jews and Christians, according to the general teaching of extending "*salam*" in several other traditions. The dominant juristic view is that the *specifying text ought to have priority over the general one*. I do not understand such limitation of the general text, which represents an essential rule, and why a *reversed approach may not be suggested*. We should try to understand the particular circumstances and reasons due to which the specific rule emerged and thus limit it to those circumstances, while applying the general rule to other cases as a broad principle. In this way we keep both of the general and specific legal texts, each working within its context.

Some other jurists understood the interdiction against initiating the greeting of "*salam*" to Jews and Christians as merely a discouragement, not a prohibition, while yet others saw that "*salam*" can be initiated only when it is necessary! However, a Muslim has to respond somehow when a Jew or a Christian initially greets him/her with "*salam*." The prominent jurist al-Awza'i reportedly said: "If I initially greet with *salam* (in that given case) some righteous and virtuous persons did so before; and if I do not, some other righteous and virtuous persons also did not." As for letting the Jew or Christian walk through the narrowest part of the road upon passing a Muslim, this was explained by the jurists as a sign of the due inferiority *"saghar"* with which the People of the Book should be treated. However, they warned that this should not in any way lead to the Jew or Christian's falling in a ditch or colliding with a wall! [102]

Another element in the inhospitable relations with the People of the Book was regarding visiting their sick. Such a visit was advised by the Prophet. When a young Jew who was serving him fell ill, the Prophet visited him, and advised him to embrace Islam, which the young Jew did after consulting his father [reported by al-Bukhari, Ibn Hanbal, and Abu Dawud]. The two events became connected in the jurists' view, and so some of them held that unless there is hope that the sick *dhimmi* would embrace Islam, there is no requirement to visit him/her! However, some were of the opinion that such a visit may be a good deed in itself if the sick person is a neighbor or a relative, while others generalized this to say that there was reward in accomplishing any legitimate good when dealing with Jews and Christians [103].

With regard to the various life occasions, jurists allowed a Muslim to attend the funeral of a Jew or a Christian, but stipulated that he walk in front or at a corner, but not behind the coffin. Condolences may be given to a *dhimmi* whose relative has died. Congratulations can be also offered to a *dhimmi* for a family or worldly occasion, but not for a religious one. In all cases, the words said to a *dhimmi* should be accurately chosen, so that any praise of his/her religion would be avoided [104].

Apparently, the contradictory approaches of both dealing nicely with *dhimmi*s and at the same time assuring their inferiority, *saghar*, could co-exist in the juristic mind. To clarify such a complexity, the prominent Maliki jurist al-Qarafi pointed out that dealing with *dhimmi*s fairly as indicated in the Quranic verse 60:8 is *different from being affectionate towards them*. The latter was warned against, in al-Qurafi's view, at the beginning of the same sura (60:1). The jurist went on to argue that the agreement of "*dhimma*" imposes on the Muslims certain obligations towards *dhimmi*s, as they are under their protection and are secured by the guarantee of God, the Conveyor of His message and the religion of Islam. Any Muslim who commits aggression against a *dhimmi* even with an offensive word, backbiting or any harmful action, or helps in this, breaks what has been promised and secured for the *dhimmi* by God, the Conveyor of His message and the religion of Islam. Whenever the *dhimmi* may be attacked, Muslims have to defend them with whatever forces they may have, as it has been consensually agreed upon.

But such congeniality should not show a *sign of the hearts' affection or respect for symbols of "kufr"*. Therefore, clearing the place for *dhimmi*s when they approach Muslims, standing for them, calling them by honorific titles, allowing them the most convenient parts of the road when they pass by Muslims – all such behavior is, in al-Qarafi's view, absolutely prohibited. Similarly, allowing *dhimmi*s to exert authority or superiority over Muslims should never occur, even if it is practiced with gentleness, since such *gentleness in practicing authority is also a kind of superiority,* distinction and highness of rank. On the other hand, being kind to the weak among them, helping the poor and the needy, speaking to them gently on the grounds of kindness, dealing with them as neighbors in the same area, offering them advice, praying for them to reach guidance and real happiness, defending them whenever their lives, families, property, or honor may be threatened, and supporting them against any injustice and in securing their rights – all such good deeds are encouraged.

In conclusion, al-Qarafi concisely and significantly added to the permitted or encouraged deeds from a Muslim to a *dhimmi*: "*whatever good that is praised from the superior to the inferior, or between two enemies*, since this is a part of the due morality and nobility." Nevertheless, according to the jurist's advice, Muslims have to keep always in their minds and hearts "how Jews and Christians hate Muslims, and give the lie to their Prophet, and that if they have power over Muslims they would attack their lives and properties [...] *But we ought not allow any signs of what we feel to appear*, according to the agreement of *dhimma*, and merely remember those [feelings] to prevent any heart's affection towards them, while we follow the commands of our Lord and our Prophet in dealing nicely and kindly with them, not because we feel deep affection towards them" [105]. What a laborious intellectual and psychological exercise, made by the jurists, and required of all Muslims!

The Quranic verse 60:1 that al-Qarafi made the basis for the prohibition of affection, *mawadda*, in dealing with the non-Muslims in general, indicates that those to whom the verse refers are "the enemies of God and the Muslims," and that "they have driven the Conveyor of [God's] message and yourselves away, [only] because you believe in God your Lord." Thus, denying stubbornly God's message was not the only reason for forbidding Muslims from dealing with them affectionately. Later verses in the same sura remove obstacles from fair and kind dealings with the unbelievers who "do not fight against you on account of [your] faith, nor drive you away from your homes" (60:8). Righteous, virtuous, and kind behavior, *birr*, has broad range and depth.

It cannot be merely limited to physical actions, nor restricted to visible congeniality with concealed hatred that cannot be considered justice and fairness, let alone *birr*. Such good and constructive relations are urged on two grounds: *first*, that acting with justice and fairness is in itself loved by God, and *second*, that such fair and kind dealings with the peaceful unbelievers might even let the hostile and belligerent ones begin to feel better and more open and even affectionate towards Muslims and probably towards Islam: "It may well be that God will bring about [mutual] affection between you [O believers] and those from among them [the unbelievers] whom you [now] face as enemies" (60:7).

However, all such obvious Quranic indications and distinctions were overshadowed in the jurists' views by the hostile climate of inter-faith relations. As for taking the non-Muslims as supporters or even patrons, the Quran indicates that the unacceptable dealing with them in this way has to be done "in preference to the Muslim" who should be the natural supporter, or done while ignoring Muslims and their interests, as several verses clearly indicate (3:28; 4:139, 144).

Furthermore, taking those who stubbornly denied the truth as supporters or patrons might be motivated by gaining honor, power, and prestige, a motive that true believers should never hold: "do they hope to be honored through [such a relation with] them, [they then have to realize that] all honor belongs to God [alone]" (4:139). "And you can see how those in whose hearts there is disease vie with one another in [taking the Jews and Christians as supporters [and] turning to them], [making alliances with the Christians and Jews] saying: 'We fear lest an adversity should befall us'. But God may well bring about good happenings [for the believers], or any event of His own devising, whereupon those will

234

be smitten with remorse for the thoughts which they had secretly harbored within themselves" (5:52). Muslims have been repeatedly taught to rely on God and on their own efforts, and not just be dependent on others (e.g. 2:257; 3:68; 5:56; 9:71). In addition, it was already mentioned that those whom the Muslims were forbidden from taking as supporters and upholders from the People of the Book or from those who stubbornly denied the truth, "*kuffar*," were explicitly described in a verse as "mocking at your faith and making a jest of it [...] and when you call to prayer, they mock at it and make a jest of it" (4:47-58). It is obvious from such a comprehensive picture, that the prohibition was historically related to given circumstances of time and place, and does not establish a permanent law for all Muslim generations.

It seems that the Islamic intellectual heritage *could not transcend the historical circumstances* of the given times and places in the past: the Jewish tribes in Arabia in early times, the Crusaders, the European colonists, and the internal unjust *dhimmi* officials or collaborators with the foreign invaders or occupiers. No line was drawn between the *universal permanent principles* and laws that address the entire humanity in all times, and the *confined transient stances* that addressed only certain historical socio-cultural circumstances. Furthermore, the classical view saw in all human beings through all times and places – according to what was dominant in the Middle Ages among Muslims and among believers of other faiths as well – either believers, *mu'minin*, or unbelievers, *kuffar*. Within the Muslim land, an additional distinction existed consciously or subconsciously between "the conquerors" and "the conquered."

Romans divided humanity into those who lived under the Roman Empire and its civilization, and "the barbarians," who were all the others. While Muslims in their contact with non-Muslims might have been in general – both in their juristic views and in practice – far better than the Roman authorities or the European Christian colonists in how they dealt with "others," their behavior was still inferior to what should have been inspired by a belief in the One Lord and Creator who created all humans as equal, and by His message of justice and mercy to all of humanity. Their behavior in Muslim countries is particularly inferior in today's era of globalization where human rights have been widely recognized.

A belief in the supremacy of God and His message has developed a mistaken feeling of superiority among Muslims, and thus a due moral and even physical separation of them from all other humans, a feeling that might have existed before among the Jews as "the chosen people," or among many Christians as "the saved people." The rigid Jewish exclusiveness was strengthened after the Babylonian captivity, as the "stranger" became one living "within your gates," as opposed to "the foreigner." The view about the resident "stranger" among the Jews might have "evolved from an ethnic concept into a religious attitude based on a rejection of idolatry." Something similar might have happened among Muslims in their latent feelings towards the "*kuffar*." In rabbinic law, the stranger, in order to qualify for the protection provided by Jewish law, was expected to adhere to the seven "Noachic laws," and not infringe upon any of the fundamental laws of the Israelite state. The Israelites were prohibited from marrying Canaanites on the grounds that such a marriage would lead them to idolatry (Exodus 34:16, Deuteronomy 7:3-4). As for the Moabites and Ammonites, there was a general legal barrier against having other strangers in the Israelite state (Deuteronomy 23:3) [106].

The founders of *apartheid* in South Africa summed up their system as "*segregation with equality.*" One may see in the Islamic juristic heritage – fortunately neither the divine sources nor the practical reality – the status of "*dhimmis*" on Muslim land as "segregation with congeniality." Each of the two precepts comprises a sharp contradiction, since neither equality nor congeniality can go in accordance with segregation. Contacts between Muslims and non-Muslims in the Muslim lands and abroad actually existed, and congeniality was always urged, but equality in rights and obligations between Muslims and *dhimmis* in a Muslim land was never considered. *Dhimmis* should always be made to feel inferiority, *saghar*, since they are "*kuffar*" and "conquered". How would a society enjoy a unity and solidarity under such a situation, especially when it met a foreign attack? And how would those who were looked upon as "*kuffar*" and conquered in their native homeland, be expected to side with the Muslim "conquerors" against any external attack?

In fact, congeniality is not enough to develop such social unity and solidarity, if a part of the people is always experiencing inequality and inferiority. Unfortunately and ironically, such behavior in human relations was conducted in the name of God and His message of justice and mercy. And how might this create a climate under which "*dhimmis*" would know about Islam through their shared life and mutual relations with Muslims?

It could not be unexpected then, as Adam Mez rightfully indicated, that such a status and situation made the *dhimmis* primarily an obstacle for developing "a political unity" among the Muslim peoples and on Muslim land, "and the worship houses of the Jews and Christians and the monasteries continued to be alien parts." Historical documents and legal records showed that *dhimmi*s on their side did not like to integrate with Muslims. Thus Jews and Christians – throughout the earlier centuries at least – were keen that *dar al-Islam* never actually be completely formed as one united country and people, while Muslims always felt that they were victorious aliens rather than people of the land. However, Mez pointed out the development of religious tolerance, and the emergence of works on "comparative religion" in Muslim medieval societies and civilization [107].

We may quote here what Gustave von Grunebaum significantly wrote: "It is true that with all those restrictions, non-Muslims frequently became influential in the government. But it is equally true that appointments to executive posts of non-Muslims were, strictly speaking illegal, that the appointees held their places on sufferance, and that pious circles always fought such laxity of practice on the part of certain rulers."

He continued,

"This is not, of course, to deny there *was in the East during the Middle Ages less physical persecutions of non-conformists than in the West,* where by the way, with the exception of the Jews, sizable religious minorities were as good as non-existent. The minority situation within the world of Islam is, however, portrayed most clearly by saying that the minority bought their safety at the price of *Geschichtslosigkeit,* at the price of more or less the status of the crown colonies in our days: no influence or taxation, and no influence on the foreign policy of the sovereign body to which they belonged. Within this framework, their economic life suffered comparatively little interference" [108].

Fortunately, modern Muslim jurists believe that non-Muslim citizens in a Muslim country have full rights and responsibilities equal to Muslims, except in what is absolutely related to the faith and worship and to some extent to family matters, in which each religious group follows its beliefs as a fulfillment of religious freedom. The late Shaykh Khalid Muhammad Khalid pioneered this direction in his 1950s book that boasted the significant title *Muwatinun la Ra'aya* (*Citizens not Subjects*) [(109)].

• *Restricted Places for non-Muslims: Hijaz, especially the* Haram

When Ibn Sallam quoted the statement of Ibn Abbas that in all the areas given *"amsar"* status by the Muslim Arabs, no *dhimmi* could build a church, sell liquor, or own swine, and no church bell could be rung, he listed the types of *amsar*. They included areas whose population embraced Islam such as Medina, Ta'if, and Yemen, unpopulated areas that were initially developed by Muslims such as al-Kufa, al-Basra, the border towns, *al-thughur*, and every area seized by force (*'anwa*) that the imam decided that Muslims would keep and not return to the people from whom it was taken. In areas that had existed before the Muslim Arabs, people could maintain what they used to have before. The statement of Ibn Abbas became a rule that jurists observed, without discussing its legal evidence in the Quran and Sunna or in the practice of the early four caliphs, or considering if it might be merely a view of Ibn Abbas according to his own personal *ijtihad*.

However, Ibn Sallam instituted the rule related by Ibn Abbas based on the Prophet's tradition that commanded expelling the polytheists, *"al-mushrikin"* – or Jews and

239

Christians in other verses – from the Arabian Peninsula (*Jazira-t al-Arab*) [reported by al-Bukhari, Muslim, Abu Dawud, al-Tirmidhi, and al-Nisai'i]. *Jazira-t al-Arab* was defined in Arab sources as extending from the Red Sea (*Qalzam*) coast to the Gulf and the Arabian Sea, and from the borders of Iraq to the valley that penetrates throughout the mountains of Hijaz southward to the end of Yemen. Since the people of Najran had been dealt with through a peaceful agreement, *sulh*, and their land had not been seized by force and thus could not be included in the *amsar*, Ibn Sallam justified expelling the Christians there by assuming that they might have breached the agreement, and provided as a support for his assumption a letter from Caliph Umar, who carried out the evacuation of the Jews and the Christians from Arabia [110]. The Jews of Khaybar had also an agreement with the Prophet that was effective until he died. The Prophet had kept the right to terminate the agreement, and therefore some jurists came to argue for the evacuation of the Jews by Umar.

Primarily, the version of the tradition referring to expelling the *mushrikin* from *Jazira-t al-Arab* [reported by al-Bukhari and Muslim] could be understood within the historical circumstances of the Prophet's time, even if the Jews and Christians cannot be included in the category of *mushrikin*. Yet, a certain reported Prophet's tradition spoke specifically about expelling the Jews of Hijaz and the Christians of Najran from *Jazira-t al-Arab*. Most jurists saw that the restriction about the stay of the *dhimmi*s or the *mushrikin* was meant only within the Hijaz, since even Najran – despite its location in the South of *Jazira-t al-'Arab* – was not considered part of Yemen, but was rather seen to be closer to Hijaz. However, other jurists preferred to go with the general indication of *Jazira-t al-Arab*, including the southern part of Yemen [111].

Yet, there should be no relation between the restriction imposed on the *dhimmi*s in the *amsar*, and the evacuation of Jews and Christians from the Arabian Peninsula or from at least the Hijaz. *Amsar* – according to Ibn Sallam – may comprise areas whose population embraced Islam in Arabia such as Mecca, Medina, Ta'if and Yemen, as well as areas outside Arabia like the cities initially established and populated by Muslims such as al-Kufa and al-Basra, in addition to areas seized by force, *'anwa*. Therefore, the relation suggested by Ibn Sallam to support the rule of Ibn Abbas does not seem convincing.

The Prophet's tradition about expelling the *mushrikin* from *Jazira-t al-Arab* was transmitted by Ibn Abbas as a testament of the Prophet before his death. Could this be considered a permanent religious decision from the Prophet in his capacity as the Conveyor of God's message, or a *discretionary decision, ijtihad, from him as "the imam"* or head of the Islamic state? The tradition was taken as a religious rule, especially after it became effective under Caliph Umar, but this important matter has to be properly settled.

The Prophet's tradition "Two religions should not be together in *Jazira-t al-Arab*" [reported by Ibn Hanbal] can be understood as forbidding domination and control of two faiths, not the mere existence of the followers of various religions. However, Caliph Umar reportedly evacuated the *dhimmi*s from Hijaz, and gave non-Muslims coming to the area for trade or commerce a period of three days to finish their business, an approach that was later supported by Abu Hanifa.

241

As for the "Inviolable House of Worship/ *al-Masjid al-Haram*," according to al-Shafi'i and most jurists, no non-Muslim should be allowed in it. Abu Hanifa, however, considered this possible if such a non-Muslim would not reside permanently there. Malik allowed non-Muslims to come to the *Haram* for trade, but al-Shafi'i did not allow them to enter the *Haram* except by permission of the imam, and only if it would benefit the Muslims [112]. Muhammad ibn al-Hasan, a known pillar of the Hanafi school, mentioned that the distinguished scholar al-Zuhri reportedly said that Abu Sufyan ibn Harb entered the Medina Mosque while he was a *kafir* in order to renew the agreement of Hudaybiya after it had been violated on Quraysh's side. While al-Zuhri himself prevented the visit of a non-Muslim to "*al-Masjid al-Haram*," that precedent of Abu Sufyan is evidence against Malik's view forbidding the *mushriks* from entering any mosque. Moreover, when the delegation of Thaqif came to the Prophet, he ordered them to camp out at the mosque. Clearly, he did not believe that they were impure, as a superficial reading of the verse "Those who associate others with God are nothing but impure, and so they should not approach the Inviolable House of Worship after this year, and should you fear poverty, then [know that] in time God will enrich you out of His bounty if He so wills" (9:28) might indicate. *The Hanafis did not forbid non-Muslims,* whether *dhimmi*s or belligerent, from entering *"al-Masjid al-Haram"* or any mosque, but simply forbade the Arab *mushriks*' pre-Islamic custom of going around *al-Bayt al-Haram* in the nude [113].

242

Revocation of Dhimmi Status

In the document attributed to Caliph Umar, the signatories – claimed to be the people of al-Jazira – stated that if they broke any of the terms to which they had committed, "the agreement of protection and security offered to them, *dhimma*, would be annulled, and it would be legitimate for Muslims to deal with them as they are allowed to deal with people of intransigence and dissension." A further addition allegedly by Caliph Umar was made: "and whoever deliberately beat a Muslim, he would be casting off his commitment." Ibn al-Qayyim commented on this addition: "That is because the agreement of *dhimma* required that *dhimmi*s would be under humiliation and subjugation, *saghar*, and that Muslims would be dominant over them, and so if they beat Muslims their action would contradict the agreement of *dhimma* that we had made with them." Ibn al-Qayyim indicated that the Byzantine residents, "*al-Rum*," in the cities of Syria agreed to that condition.

The author held that the same rule should apply *a priori* to committing adultery with a Muslim woman. According to the Hanbali school, talking insultingly about the Prophet or about God would also revoke the agreement of *dhimma*. Similar would be the result in their opinion if the *dhimmi* goes to a belligerent country for permanent residence, refrains from fulfilling his/her obligations or compliance with the Islamic law, fights against Muslims, murders a Muslim, commits a highway robbery against him/her, spies for the *kuffar*, or accommodates a spy for them. Shafi'i jurists were almost in line with the Hanbalis about this, while Malikis decided that one who breaches the agreement of *dhimma* deserves the death punishment. On the other hand, Hanafis did not consider the agreement of *dhimma* annulled unless the violators enjoyed power that made them unreachable by the Muslim authorities and led them to refrain from paying jizya, and they could not be dealt with by Islamic law due to particular circumstances [114].

Ibn al-Qayyim considered the agreement of *dhimma* as any agreement, where a violation meant that the agreement was revoked. In many cases, many jurists held that the *dhimmi* violator might be punished, but his status as a *dhimmi* would not be revoked [115]. Muhammad ibn al-Hasan al-Shaybani discussed the ramifications of a crime carried out by a non-Muslim seeker of temporary security from the Muslims, *al-musta'min*, whose status was less strong than that of the *dhimmi*, as the latter was considered by some such as al-Shaybani to be among the people of the land of Islam, *ahl dar al-Islam*. If the *musta'min* killed a Muslim, spied on a Muslim and sent the information to their enemies, raped a Muslim or a *dhimmi* woman or committed theft, he would not be breaching his agreement with the Muslims. Muhammad ibn al-Hasan argued for his opinion – which differed from others' such as Malik – by saying that as any of those violations from a Muslim would not revoke his/her faith, *iman*, it would not revoke the agreement of temporary security given to the non-Muslim comer to the Muslim land, but that he/she would be punished for any assault on the human life or honor. Why then would such crimes contradict the *dhimma*, if they would not hurt the faith, *iman*, of a Muslim, or the agreement of a *musta'min*?

As for the crimes with fixed punishments, *hudud*, the jurists of Medina held that *dhimmi*s who committed any of these crimes should be turned to their judge. This again differed from the view of Muhammad ibn al-Hasan, who argued that the Prophet had punished a Jewish adulterer, and so *dhimmi*s were bound to all *hudud* except that of drinking liquor because they believed that it was not prohibited in their religion. Yet, he – in accordance with Abu Hanifa – held that the *hudud* do not apply to *musta'min*s, since they were not included in *dar al-Islam* nor bound by its laws. However, the *musta'min* may be punished for *hudud* crimes with other discretionary punishments, *ta'zir*, such as imprisonment, and should give back all others' possessions that he/she might have illegally obtained [116].

The distinguished Shafi'i jurist al-Mawardi indicated that in case of revocation of the *dhimma* agreement, those who lost their status could not be killed nor their possessions seized as booty unless they fought against Muslims and their authorities. Significantly, al-Mawardi stated that those whose *dhimma* was revoked had to be expelled from the Muslim land and go safely to the nearest land of unbelievers or polytheists, *shirk*. If unwilling to go voluntarily, they had to be forced to do so! [117] It is obvious from such an opinion that the Muslim comers to the land considered themselves as legitimately belonging to it, while its native or indigenous people who had been living for centuries there were considered aliens, and could be expelled to a place about which they had never known, in which they had no relatives, only because it was a land of *"shirk"*!

Might we then agree with Adam Mez that "Muslims continued to feel that they were victorious aliens [or even conquerors] not native or indigenous people of a homeland," while the native people were considered favored by being allowed to stay on the land, where they were reminded always of their obligations and inferiority? Thus they on their side in such a climate could not think of integration with Muslims [118]. Indeed, in the middle ages, it was religion that was the determining factor in the identity of the person, the land, the human folk, and international relations as a

245

whole. Through such an attitude, in many ways Muslims demonstrated the norms of the dominant earthly environment, rather than the values of the divine universal message.

In conclusion

What we read in our juristic heritage about *dhimmis*, or the non-Muslim citizens of the Muslim state, is a *part of history developed under particular circumstances of time and place, not a permanent law of God*. Most Muslims and Islamists look at Shari'a, without distinguishing between what is universal and permanent and what was particular and transient, or what is divine and what is human. The moral essence of *dhimma* is dealing with "*others*" through justice and kindness, *birr*, caring about them, and observing the teachings and requirements of security and care given by God and the Conveyor of His message to the non-Muslims who live with the Muslims. The observance and fulfillment of this moral essence is ever inspiring, but many historical and juristic elements in our heritage represented the outcome of certain given circumstances of time and place, and thus could not be a part of the eternal universal message of God. "*Dhimma" as a moral inspiration should be always with us, yet "dhimma status" for non-Muslim citizens of a Muslim state and the legal rules related to it are outdated*. We can study and benefit from them, as we study and benefit from any human experience of the past, keeping always in mind that it was history and was related to circumstances qualitatively different from those of Muslims in contemporary times.

Notes

(1)   Mustafa, Ibrahim, et al. "Dhimma," "Ahl al-Dhimma," "al-Dhimmi," *al-Qamus al-Wasit*, Istanbul: Dar al-Da'wa, 1980, p. 315; Abu Yusuf, *al-Kharaj*, p. 78; al-Baladhuri, *Futuh al-Buldan*, pp. 75-6; al-Mawardi, *al-Ahkam al-Sultaniyya*, p. 143; Zaydan, Abd al-Karim, *Ahkam al-Dhimmiyya wa al-Musta'minin*, Beirut: Mu'assasa al-Risala, n.d., pp. 20-36, 53-55; 61, 68-71; Mez, Adam, *Renaissance Der Islam*, translated into Arabic by Abu Rida, Muhammad 'Abd-al-Hadi, under the title "*al-Hadara al-Islamiyya fi al-Qarn al-Rabi' al-Hijri*,", Cairo: Maktaba al-Khanji & Beirut: Dar al-Kitab al-'Arabi, 1967, vol. 1, pp. 105-6.

(2)   Abu Yusuf, *al-Kharaj*, pp. 135, 149.

(3)   al-Baladhuri, *Futuh al-Buldan*, pp. 166-7; Ibn Sallam, *al-Amwal*, pp. 221-3.

(4)   al-Mawardi, *al-Ahkam al-Sultaniyya*, pp. 27, 60, 116, 130, 152, 209.

(5)   Zaydan, *Ahkbam al-Dhimmiyin wa al-Musta'minin*, p. 482; Mez, *al-Hadara al-Islamiyya*, pp. 93-5.

(6)   al-Baladhuri, *Futuh al-Buldan*, pp. 143, 162, 164; see also, al-Tabari, *Tarikh al-Umam wa al-Muluk*, vol. 4, pp. 16, 195, vol. 5 pp. 254; Abu Yusuf, *al-Kharaj*, pp. 131-2, 150-55; Ibn Sallam, *al-Amwal*, pp. 45-6; al-Mawardi, *al Ahkam*, p. 144; Ibn al-Qayyim, *Ahkam Ahl al-Dhimma*, vol. 1, pp. 42-45, 48, 51; also: Zaydan, *Ahkam al-Dhimmiyyin wa al-Musta'minin*, pp. 121-2, 129-31.

(7)   Fakhr al-Din al-Razi, *al-Tafsir al-Kabir/ Mafatih al-Ghayb*, Beirut: Dar al-Kutub al-'Ilmiyya, 1990, vol. 16, pp. 23-25; al-Shawkani, Muhammad ibn Ali, *Fath al-Qadir*, Beirut: Dar al-Fikr, n.d., vol. 2, p. 350; Rida, Muhammad Rashid, *Tafsir al-Manar,* Maktaba al-Qahira, n.d., pp. 332-342.

(8)   al-Mawardi, *al-Ahkam al-Sultaniyya,* p. 143; Ibn al-Qayyim, *Ahkam Ahl al-Dhimma*, Introduction by Subhi al-Salih, vol. 1, pp. 24, 33; Rida, *Tafsir al-Manar,* vol. 10, p. 342.

(9)   al-Baladhuri, *Futuh al-Buldan*, pp. 142, 168, 185-7; Ibn Sallam, *al-Amwal*; pp. 37-8, 649-652; see also Abu Yusuf, *al-Kharaj,* pp. 129-130; al-Mawardi; *al-Ahkam al-Sultaniyya,* p. 144.

(10)   Ibn al-Qayyim, *Ahkam Ahl al-Dhimma*, vol. 1: Introduction by Subhi al-Salih, pp. 9-10, the text pp. 75-81. For the rejection of Ibn al-Qayyim's generalization of the rule of Bani Taghlib through analogy see pp. 84-6.

(11)   Abu Yusuf, *al-Kharaj*, p. 136; also: Ibn Sallam, *al-Amwal*, p. 57; Ibn al-Qayyim, *Ahkam Ahl al-Dhimma*, p. 38.

(12)   For different views on giving needy *dhimmi*s from *zakat* assets see: Ibn Sallam, *al-Amwal,* pp. 727-9; Zaydan, *Ahkam al-Dhimiyyin wa al-Musta'minin*, pp. 87-92. For Khalid ibn al-Walid's document to the people of Hira see Abu Yusuf, *al-Kharaj,* pp. 155-6.

(13)   Mez, *al-Hadara al-Islamiyya,* vol.1, p. 92; al-Baladhuri, *Futuh al-Buldan*, p. 273; Abu Yusuf, *al-Kharaj*, pp. 105-6, 107.

(14)   Abu Yusuf, al-*Kharaj,* p. 78; al-Baladhuri, *Futuh al-Buldan,* p. 76.

(15)   al-Baladhuri, *Futuh al-Buldan,* p. 79.

(16)   For the difference on the date of the Prophet's application of jizya see: al-Baladhuri, *Futuh al-Buldan,* pp. 48, 79; Ibn Kathir, *al-Bidaya wa al-Nihaya,* vol. 4, p. 219, Ibn al-Qayyim, *Ahkam Ahl al-Dhimma,* vol. 1, pp. 3, 7, 9, 30, 52-53; Abu Zahra, Muhammad, *Khatam al-Nabiyyin,* Cairo: Dar al-Fikr al-Arabi, 1973, vol. 3, pp. 74-6.

(17)   Ibn al-Qayyim, *Ahkam Ahl al-Dhimma,* vol. 1, pp. 11-12, 244-8.

(18)   Subhi al-Salih's Introduction to Ibn al-Qayyim, *Ahkam Ahl al-Dhimma,* vol. 1, pp. 12-13.

(19)   al-Shaybani, *al-Siyar al-Kabir,* dictated and expanded upon by al-Sarakhsi, vol. 1 ed. Salah al-Din al-Munajjid, Cairo: Ma'had al-Makhtutat al-'Arabiyya, 1971, p. 306, vol. 4 ed. Abd al-Aziz Ahmed, pp. 1532, 1545, vol. 5, p. 1854; Ibn Taymiyya, Ahmad ibn Abd-al-Halim, *Majmu' Fatawa Shaykh al-Islam Ahmad ibn Taymiyya,* collected and organized by Ibn Qasim al-'Asimi, Abd al-Rahman ibn Muhammad and his son Muhammad, Mecca: al-Ri'asa al-'Amma li al-Haramayn, n.d., vol. 28, pp. 665-6; Zaydan, *Ahkam al-Dhimmiyin wa al-Musta'minin,* pp. 171-2, 251-2; Hamid Allah, Muhammad, *Muqaddima fi 'Ilm al-Siyar,* Introduction to *Ahkam Ahl al-Dhimma,* vol. 1, pp. 89-90; cf. al-Mawardi, *al-Ahkam al-Sultaniyya,* pp. 145-6.

(20)   al-Mawardi, *al-Ahkam al-Sultaniyya,* p. 145.

(21)   al-Qarafi, Ahmad ibn Idris ibn Abd al-Rahman, *al-Furuq,* Beirut: 'Alam al-Kutub, n.d., vol. 3, pp. 14-15.

(22)   Mez, *al-Hadara al-Islamiyya*, vol.1, pp.75, 87-8, 92-3, 105, 115, 117-8.

(23)   von Grunebaum, *Medieval Islam*, pp. 173, 180, 184.

(24)   Zaydan, *Ahkam al-Dhimmiyin wa al-Musta'minin*, pp. 10-19; see also al-Mawardi, *al-Ahkam al-Sultaniyya*, pp. 138, 146.

(25)   Mez, *al-Hadara al-Islamiyya*, vol. 1, p. 75; von Grunebaum, *Medieval Islam,* p. 180.

(26)   Ibn Sa'd, *al-Tabaqat al-Kubra,* vol. 1, p. 26.

(27)   al-Baladhuri, *Futuh al-Buldan*, pp. 71, 140-2.

(28)   *Ibid.,* pp. 159-162, 164-5.

(29)   Uthman (Osman), Fathi, *al-Hudud al-Islamiyya al-Byzantiyya*, Cairo: Dar al-Katib al-Arabi, 1965, vol. 3, pp. 322-4.

(30)   Ibn Taymiyya, *Majmu' Fatawa Shaykh al-Islam*, vol. 28, pp. 631-2, 636-7, 641-6.

(31)   Mez, *al-Hadara al-Islamiyya*, vol. 1, pp. 106-112, 114-6.

(32)   Kashif, Sayyida Isma'il, *Misr fi Fajr al-Islam*, Cairo: Dar al-Fikr al-'Arabi, 1947, pp. 198, 203, 216, 222-240, 252-7.

(33)   Mu'nis, Husayn, *Tarikh al-Maghrib wa Hadaratuh*, Beirut: al-'Asr al-Hadith, 1991, vol.1, pp. 282-3.

(34)   Lapidus, *A History of Islamic Societies*, p. 349.

(35)   Riley-Smith, Jonathan, *The Crusades: A Short History*, New Haven & London: Yale University Press, 1987, pp.46, 51; Boas, Adrian J., *Jerusalem in the Time of the Crusades,* London & New York: Routledge, 2001; Article "Crusades", *The New*

Encyclopaedia Britannica, Chicago & London: Macropedias Ency. Britannica Inc, 1975, vol. 5, p. 304.

(36) Ibn al-Qayyim, *Ahkam Ahl al-Dhimma*, vol. 1, Introduction by Subhi al-Salih, pp. 71-2, the text, pp. 242-3.

(37) al-Salih, Subhi, Introduction to Ibn al-Qayyim, *Ahkam Ahl al-Dhimma*, pp. 14-15.

(38) al-Salih, Subhi, Introduction to Ibn al-Qayyim, *Ahkam Ahl al-Dhimma*, pp. 15-16, 20-1, 42-6. As for examples of conquest agreements that seem quite different from the covenant attributed to Caliph Umar see al-Baladhuri, *Futuh al-Buldan*, pp. 122, 128-9; Ibn 'Asakir, 'Ali ibn al-Hasan, *Tarikh Madina Dimishq*, Damascus: al-Majma' al-'Ilmi al-'Arabi, 1951, vol.1, pp. 149-178.

(39) Hitti, Philip K., *History of the Arabs*, p. 234; see also al-Salih, Subhi, Introduction to Ibn al-Qayyim, *Ahkam Ahl al-Dhimma*, vol. 1, p. 30.

(40) Abu Yusuf, *al-Kharaj*, p. 78; al-Baladhuri, *Futuh al-Buldan*, p. 76.

(41) Abu Yusuf, *al-Kharaj*, pp. 148-159.

(42) Ibn al-Qayyim, *Ahkam Ahl al-Dhimma,* vol. 2, pp. 658-9; also: Harras, in editing Ibn Sallam, *al-Amwal*, footnote 1, p. 68 quoting Ibn Kathir in his commentary *Tafsir al-Quran al-'Azim*.

(43) See for example Ibn Sallam, *al-Amwal*, pp.123-5; in addition to the previously mentioned references in note 39; Ibn al-Qayyim, *Ahkam Ahl al-Dhimma,* vol. 2, pp. 666-713.

(44) Ibn Sallam, *al-Amwal*, pp. 126-7.

(45)   Ibn al-Hasan, Muhammad, *al-Siyar al-Kabir,* dictated and elaborated on by al-Sarakhsi, vol. 4, pp. 1532-1550.

(46)   al-Shaybani, Muhammad ibn al-Hasan, *al-Siyar al-Kabir,* dictated and elaborated on by al-Sarakhsi, vol. 4, pp. 153-4.

(47)   Ibn Sallam, *al-Amwal*, footnotes of the editor Harras, Muhammad Khalil, p. 15 n.3, p. 123 n.1.

(48)   al-Shawkani, Muhammad ibn Ali, *Nayl al-Awtar*, commentary on *Muntaqa al-Akhbar* by Ibn Taymiyya, Abd al-Salam, Beirut: Dar al-Fikr, 1973, vol. 8, p. 219.

(49)   Ibn Sallam, *al-Amwal*, p. 126; al-Shawkani, *Nayl al-Awtar,* a commentary on *Muntaqa al-Akhbar* by Ibn Taymiyya, Abd al-Salam, vol. 8, p. 221. Al-Shawkani mentioned that in the chain of transmission of the statement of Ibn Abbas as reported by al-Bayhaqi there was one transmitter, "Hanash," who was considered weak.

(50)   Abu Yusuf, *al-Kharaj,* p. 42; see also: pp.30, 42-4.

(51)   See for example Ibn Sallam, *al-Amwal*, pp. 131-3; al-Baladhuri, *Futuh al-Buldan*, pp. 119-120, 122-4, 127-130, 132-3, 136-7, 144-8, 154-5, 162, 164, 176-183, 215-219, 223, 244, 246, 266.

(52)   Ibn Rajab, Abd al-Rahman ibn Ahmad, *al-Istikhraj fi Ahkam al-Kharaj*, in *Mawsu'a al-Kharaj*, Beirut: Dar al-Ma'rifa, 1979, pp. 41, 40-44.

(53)   al-Shaybani, Muhammad ibn al Hasan, *al-Siyar al-Kabir*, vol. 4, pp. 1549-1550.

(54)   Zaydan, *Ahkam al-Dhimmiyin wa al-Musta'minin*, p. 84.

(55) Ibn Taymiyya, *Majmu' Fatawa Shaykh al-Islam*, vol. 28, pp. 632-646.

(56) Kashif, Sayyida Isma'il, *Misr fi Fajr al-Islam*, pp.191-3.

(57) Mez, *al-Hadara al-Isamiyya*, vol. 1, pp. 91, 87-8.

(58) Ibn al-Qayyim, *Ahkam Ahl al-Dhimma,* vol. 2, pp. 658-662.

(59) al-Mawardi, *al-Ahkam al-Sultaniyya*, p. 145.

(60) Mez, *al-Hadara al-Islamiyya*, vol. 1, p. 104.

(61) Abu Yusuf, *al-Kharaj,* p.137.

(62) Ibn al-Qayyim, *Ahkam Ahl al-Dhimma,* vol. 2, pp. 735-775; cf. vol. 1, pp. 23-4.

(63) See as an example of the juristic discussion about how binding are the sayings and practices of the Prophet's Companions in general, and the early four Caliphs and among them Abu Bakr and Umar in particular; Ibn al-Qayyim, *Ahkam Ahl al-Dhimma,* vol. 2, pp. 735, 786-7, al-Juwayni, Abd al-Malik ibn Abd Allah, *al-Burhan*, ed. al-Dib, Abd al-Azim, Cairo: Dar al-Ansar, 1400 AH (1980), vol. 2, pp. 1358-1362; Ibn Hazm, Muhammad ibn Ali, *al-Ihkam fi' Usul al-Ahkam,* Cairo: Dar al-Hadith, 1984, vol. 6, pp. 237-250, 258-260.

(64) al-Mawardi, *al-Ahkam al-Sultaniyya*, pp. 68, 176.

(65) Twana, Muhammad Musa, *al-Ijtihad,* Cairo: Dar al-Kutub al-Haditha, 1972, pp. 429-449.

(66) Ibn al-Qayyim, *Ahkam Ahl al-Dhimma,* vol. 2, pp. 690-1.

(67)   Hamid Allah, Muhammad, *Muqaddima fi 'Ilm al-Siyar*, Introduction to Ibn al-Qayyim, *Ahkam Ahl al-Dhimma*, vol. 1, p. 94.

(68)   Ibn al-Qayyim, *Ahkam Ahl al-Dhimma*, vol. 2, pp. 660-62.

(69)   Zaydan, *Ahkam al-Dhimmiyin wa al-Musta'minin*, pp. 467-471.

(70)   Mez, *al-Hadara al-Islamiyya*, vol. 1, p. 95.

(71)   Zaydan, *Ahkam al-Dhimmiyin wa al-Musta'minin*, pp. 208-230.

(72)   *Ibid.*, pp. 61; see also: al-Shaybani, *al-Siyar al-Kabir*, dictated and commented on by al-Sarakhsi, vol. 1, p. 306, vol. 4, p. 299, vol. 5, p. 1854.

(73)   Zaydan, *Ahkam al-Dhimmiyin wa al-Musta'minin*, p. 210.

(74)   al-Mawardi, *al-Ahkam al-Sultaniyya*, pp. 27, 60, 116, 130, 152, 209.

(75)   al-Baladhuri, *Futuh al-Buldan*, pp. 196-7, 298; Kashif, Sayyida Isma'il, *Misr fi Fajr al-Islam*, pp. 189-190.

(76)   al-Shaybani, *al-Siyar al-Kabir*, vol. 4, pp. 1422-4.

(77)   Ibn al-Qayyim, *Ahkam Ahl al-Dhimma*, vol. 2, pp. 208-236.

(78)   von Grunebaum, *Medieval Islam*, p. 180.

(79)   Mez, *al-Hadara al-Islamiyya*, vol. 1, pp 105-118; see also Kashif, Sayyida Isma'il, *Misr fi Fajr al-Islam*, Cairo: Dar al-Fikr al'Arabi, 1947, pp. 189-191, 198-203, 259-60.

(80) Ibn al-Qayyim, *Ahkam Ahl al-Dhimma*, vol. 2, pp. 776-8.

(81) Ibn al-Qayyim, *Ahkam Ahl al-Dhimma*, vol. 1, pp. 269-294.

(82) al-Salih, Subhi, Introduction to Ibn al-Qayyim, *Ahkam Ahl al-Dhimma*, vol. 1, pp. 12-13.

(83) See for example: Ibn Sallam, *al-Amwal*, pp. 244-9, 258, 263-4, 266-270; Abu Yusuf, *al-Kharaj*, pp. 42, 77-81, 135-6, 149, 152-6, 158-9.

(84) al-Salih, Subhi, Introduction to Ibn al-Qayyim, *Ahkam Ahl al-Dhimma*, vol. 1, p. 46.

(85) See for example: Ibn Sallam, *al-Amwal*, pp. 69-83, 123-134, 149-162, 165-203; al-Mawardi, *al-Ahkam al-Sultaniyya*, pp. 137-8, 144-5, 146-8.

(86) See for example: Abu Yusuf, *al-Kharaj*, pp. 30, 42-44, 64-5, 75, 148-152, 158-9; Ibn Sallam, al-Amwal, pp. 94-5, 103-7, 185-8; al-Baladhuri, *Futuh al-Buldan*, pp. 117-124, 127-134, 136-7, 143-7, 152, 156-7, 162, 163-4, 176-9, 181, 204-5, 216-221, 223-7, 244, 246, 250, 265-6; Ibn Jama'a, Muhammad ibn Ibrahim, *Tahrir al-Ahkam fi Tadbir Ahl al-Islam,* ed. Ahmad, Fu'ad Abd al-Mun'im, Doha, Qatar: Ri'asa al-Mahakim al-Shar'iyya, 1985, pp. 204-6.

(87) al-Mawardi, *al-Ahkam al-Sultaniyya*, pp. 143, 145; see Ibn al-Qayyim, *Ahkam Ahl al-Dhimma*, vol. 1, pp. 25, 126.

(88) Ibn Sallam, *al-Amwal*, pp. 53-8, 65-8; see also Abu Yusuf, *al-Kharaj*, pp. 131-8.

(89) Ibn al-Qayyim, *Ahkam Ahl al-Dhimma*, vol. 1, pp. 15, 23-5, 34-9, 234-5.

(90)   Ibid., vol. 1, pp. 210-235, 242-4; see also the Introduction of Subhi al-Salih to Ibn al-Qayyim, *Ahkam Ahl al-Dhimma*, vol. 1, pp. 71-2.

(91)   Mez, *al-Hadara al-Islamiyya*, vol. 1, pp. 99-100.

(92)   Abu Yusuf, *al-Kharaj,* p. 137.

(93)   al-Mawardi, *al-Ahkam al-Sultaniyya*, p. 144; Ibn Sallam, *al-Amwal*, pp. 45-50; Ibn al-Qayyim, *Ahkam Ahl al-Dhimma,* vol. 1, pp. 29-51.

(94)   Ibn Sallam, *al-Amwal*, pp. 51-2.

(95)   Ibid., pp. 49, 191-2, 195-199, 244.

(96)   al-Mawardi, *al-Ahkam al-Sultaniyya*, pp. 144-5

(97)   Ibn al-Qayyim, *Ahkam Ahl al-Dhimma,* vol. 2, pp. 779-788.

(98)   Ibn al-Qayyim, *Ahkam Ahl al-Dhimma,* vol. 2, pp. 764, 766-775; see also the Introduction by Subhi al-Salih, vol. 1, p. 45.

(99)   Ibn al-Qayyim, *Ahkam Ahl al-Dhimma,* vol. 2, pp. 746-8, 755, 759, 763-6; Ibn Jama'a, *Tahrir al-Ahkam*, pp. 259-60.

(100)   See as examples for the emphasis on subjection and humiliation, *saghar* and *idhlal*, and "*kufr*": Ibn al-Qayyim, *Ahkam Ahl al-Dhimma,* vol. 1, pp. 15-6, 23-5, 69, 88-9, 135-8, 208-12, 197, vol. 2, pp. 735-775; also al-Salih, Introduction to Ibn al-Qayyim, *Ahkam Ahl al-Dhimma,* vol. 1, pp. 8, 13, 28-31, 33-5, 71-2; and Kashif, Sayyida, *Misr fi Fajr al-Islam,* pp. 198, 214.

(101)   al-Khirshi, Muhammad ibn Abd Allah (d. 1101 AH/ 1689 CE), Commentary (*Hashiya*) on Mukhtasar Khalil about Maliki jurisprudence, quoted by al-Salih, Introduction to Ibn al-Qayyim, *Ahkam Ahl al-Dhimma,* vol. 1, p. 9.

(102)   al-Shawkani, *Nayl al-Awtar,* commentary on "Muntaqa al-Akhbar" by Abd al-Salam Ibn Taymiyya, vol. 8, pp. 225-6; Ibn al-Qayyim, *Ahkam Ahl al-Dhimma,* vol. 1, pp. 191-200.

(103)   al-Shawkani, *Nayl al-Awtar,* commentary on "Muntaqa al-Akhbar" by Abd al-Salam Ibn Taymiyya, vol. 8, pp. 227-8; Ibn al-Qayyim, *Ahkam Ahl al-Dhimma,* vol. 1, pp. 200-2.

(104)   Ibn al-Qayyim, *Ahkam Ahl al-Dhimma,* vol. 1, pp. 202-6, vol. 2, p. 722.

(105)   al-Qarafi, Ahmad ibn Idris, *al-Furuq,* Beirut: Dar al-Jil, n.d., vol. 3, pp. 14-16.

(106)   Werblowsky, R.J. Zwi & Wigoder, Geoffrey, e.d. "Stranger," *The Oxford Dictionary of the Jewish Religion,* New York & Oxford: Oxford University Press, 1997, p. 657; Smith, William, "Stranger", "Marriage" *Smith's Bible Dictionary,* New York: Family Library, 1973, pp. 664, 377.

As for the "Noahic Laws," *The Oxford Dictionary of the Jewish Religion,* Oxford: 1997 indicates that they were "injunctions traditionally given to Noah, and therefore binding upon Jews and gentiles alike. According to the Talmud, there were seven such laws, or rather categories of laws, derived from the early chapters of Genesis and consisting of: prohibition against blasphemy, idolatry, sexual immorality (including homosexuality), murder (including abortion), robbery, and eating a portion of a living animal, and an injunction concerning the administration of justice" (pp. 504-5).

(107) Mez, *al-Hadara al-Islamiyya*, vol. 1, p. 75.

(108) von Grunebaum, *Medieval Islam*, pp. 184, 180.

(109) See as examples of this contemporary direction to various extents:

- Zaydan, *Ahkam al-Dhimmiyin wa al-Musta'minin fi Dar al-Islam*, Beirut: Mu'assasa al-Risala, doctoral dissertation submitted to the Faculty of Law: Cairo University

- al-Qaradawi, Yusuf, *Ghayr al-Muslimin fi al-Mujtama' al-Islami*, Cairo: Maktaba Wahba, 1977.

- al-Ghannouchi, Rachid, *Huquq al-Muwatana: Huquq Ghayr al-Muslim fi al-Mujtama' al Islami*, Herndon, VA: al-Ma'had al-'Alami li-al-Fikr al-Islami, 1981.

- Huwaydi, Fahmi, *Muwatinun la Dhimmiyun*, Cairo: Dar al-Shuruq, Beirut, 1985.

The author, M. Fathi Osman, published a series of articles, *Hawla Muraja'a al-Ahkam al-Fiqhiyya al-Khasa bi-Wad' Ghayr al-Muslimin*, al-*Aman* Weekly, Beirut, issues no. 18-20, June 1979.

(110) Ibn Sallam, *al-Amwal*, pp. 126-130.

(111) al-Shawkani, *Nayl al-Awtar*, vol. 8, pp. 222-5.

(112) al-Mawardi, *al-Ahkam al-Sultaniyya*, pp. 167-8; al-Shawkani, *Nayl al-Awtar*, vol. 8, pp. 222-5; Ibn al-Qayyim, *Ahkam Ahl al-Dhimma*, vol.1, pp. 175-191.

(113) al-Shaybani, *al-Siyar al-Kabir*, dictated and elaborated on by al-Sarakhsi, vol. 1, pp. 134-5.

(114) Ibn al-Qayyim, *Ahkam Ahl al-Dhimma,* vol. 2, pp. 660-2, 789-810.

(115) al-Salih, Subhi, Introduction to Ibn al-Qayyim, *Ahkam Ahl al-Dhimma*, vol. 1, pp. 39-40.

(116) al-Shaybani, *al-Siyar al-Kabir*, dictated and elaborated on by al-Sarakhsi, vol. 1, pp. 305-7.

(117) al-Mawardi, *al-Ahkam al-Sultaniyya*, p. 146.

(118) Mez, *al-Hadara al-Isamiyya*, vol. 1, p. 75.

IV

The Islamic Concept of "Shura"
in Relation to the Current Concept of Democracy

**As Understood by Muslims
in the Contemporary Muslim World**

Shura in the Quran

Reliance on *shura*, or collective consultation of as many people as possible, is an essential merit of the Muslim community. The Quran sets justice next to the faith in God and keeping up prayers: *"And those who respond to [the call of] their Lord and keep up their prayers, and <u>whose rule [in matters of common concern] is consultation among themselves</u>, and who spend [on others and on common needs] out of what We provide for them as sustenance"* (42:38). Mutual consultation has to be a common Muslim tradition, and so it is required between spouses in conducting family affairs, and between divorced individuals when necessary: "And the [divorced] mothers nurse their children [. . .]; and it is incumbent upon the one to whom the born child is related to provide in a fair manner for their [the mothers'] sustenance and clothing [. . .]; *and both [parents] decide by mutual consent and counsel on the weaning* [of the child. . .] " (2:233).

Shura is a two-way street. As *seeking shura is required from the concerned party, the initiative of presenting a view to others who may need it* is also required. It is an Islamic duty to *advise* anyone who may need advice or benefit from it, whether an individual, a group, an authority, or the general public. The Prophet teaches: "It is the essence of religion to extend advice, as a commitment to God and His Book and the Conveyor of His Message, and to the Muslim leaders and to the Muslim public" [reported by Ibn Hanbal, Muslim, Abu Dawud, al-Tirmidhi, and al-Nisa'i on the authority of the Prophet's Companions Ibn Abbas, Abu Hurayra and Tamim al-Dari, and given the grade of authentic, *sahih*, by al-Suyuti in a*l-Jami' al-Saghir*]. This is also called in Quranic terminology "the enjoining of doing what is right and good,

263

and the forbidding of doing what is wrong and evil (*al-'amr bi-al-ma'ruf wa al-nahy 'an al-munkar*)". It is a merit of the Muslim community, in addition to the belief in God (3:110), the general virtue of all believers in God (3:114), the responsibility of the Muslims who have power (22:41), and the moral values with which younger generations have to be raised (31:17). Negligence of this responsibility towards others is strongly condemned in the Quran (5:78-9).

Prophet Muhammad received revelation, but was a full human being who practiced his personal thinking and judgment in worldly affairs, when no divine revelation was received. In that area of human judgment, the Quran addressed him: "*And take counsel with them in matters of common concern, then when you have reached your decision place your trust in God* [...]" (3:159).

The prominent commentator on the Quran Ibn 'Atiyya (d. 546 AH/ 1151 CE) stated in his commentary on the above verse that "*shura* is one of Shari'a's fundamentals and binding rules, and any who has authority and does not consult those of knowledge and religiosity should be deposed; and there is no controversy about it." He quoted the Prophet's tradition in the battle of Badr when he said to his Companions "Give me your suggestions and advice, O people!" Moreover, he mentioned that Caliph Umar ibn al-Khattab used *shura* when making the decision about who would succeed him in the caliphate after he was stabbed, the most serious emergency that the Muslims had undergone. Al-Qurtubi quoted Ibn 'Atiyya, as well as al-Hasan al-Basri (d. 110 AH/ 728 CE) and al-Dahhaq ibn Muzahim (d. 105 AH/ 1723 CE) who mentioned that God's guidance was that the Prophet let Muslims know the value of *shura* and to follow the Prophet in practicing it. Al-Qurtubi quoted Ibn Khuwayz Mandad Abu Bakr Muhammad ibn Ahmad ibn

'Abd-Allah, a scholar of the late 4ᵗʰ century AH/ late 10ᵗʰ CE, who said that the rulers should take counsel with the *ulama* (scholars of religion) about what they do not know and what may be unclear to them in matters of religion, take counsel with the distinguished military about matters of war, with distinguished people about public interests, and with distinguished administrators, ministers, and provincial governors about the country's welfare and development. Through discussion, *shura* brings out the participants' most polished, sharpened and well-articulated ideas [1].

Tafsir al-Manar comments on the verse in light of its historical circumstances, as it was revealed after the battle of Uhud, during which the opinion of confronting the attacking enemy outside Medina did not lead to winning the battle. Thus, the comment emphasizes the essentiality of *shura* in the matters of this world *under all circumstances, whatever the consequences of the decision based on shura may be.* This is so that Muslims come to practice *shura* instead of blindly following the leader's view even if it is right, since *shura* has its general positive results that exceed any partial negative consequences of *shura* in a certain incident. The comment underscores that *the community is often less errant than the individual,* and the danger that might face the people from delegating full authority to one person is far greater and more serious than any shortcomings of consultation and reaching a collective view. Muhammad Abduh indicates that the divine revelation in the above verse guided the Prophet to set the principle of *shura* through practice [2].

Furthermore, the Quran commands that whatever one is entrusted with should be delivered to those who are entitled to it, and that justice should be strictly followed in judging between people (4:58). Obedience is due first to God and the Conveyor of His message, after which comes the obedience to what the Quran significantly describes as *"those from among you who are entrusted with authority by you/ 'uli al-'amr minkum"* (4:59). This is a clear indication that the people are the source of authority, and they entrust whomever they choose with authority. Hence they have full rights to direct and supervise, a right that may be practiced through some supervising or inspecting body that is different from those chosen for authority. After the death of the Prophet, the first Caliph Abu Bakr spoke to the people: "I have been entrusted with authority and I am not the best of you, if you see me doing well support me, and if not correct me. Obey me as long as I am obeying God, and if I deviate, no obedience for me is due from you." Imam Malik (d.173 AH/ 789 CE) – as reported by al-Suyuti – commented on that text that no imam can have legitimate authority when appointed except on this condition [3]. The juristic heritage, representing various schools of thought and different times and places, stressed that the imamate or caliphate is based on a contract between the people and the ruler [4].

Muhammad Abduh noted that those who understood the verse as a command of absolute obedience to the rulers, *'uli al-'amr*, overlooked the word *"minkum"* which indicates that the rulers are "bound to you." His view is that *'uli al-'amr* are those who are in charge of public betterment or the people's interests, and so they are those known by the juristic term as "the eligible to bind and dissolve/ *ahl al-'aqd wa al-hall.*" Those include the rulers, the *'ulama* (the learned persons of religion), the military leaders and all the public leaders to whom people turn in their common needs and interests. As *Tafsir al-Manar* indicates, two classical commentators on the Quran, al-Fakhr al-Razi (d. 604 AH/ 1207 CE) and al-Nisaburi (d. 850 AH/ 1446 CE) also understood *"'uli al-'amr"* as "the eligible to bind and dissolve/ *ahl al-'aqd wa al-hall.*" Since the *shura* is relevant to the interests of all the people "and those whose rule [in all matters of common concern] is consultation among themselves" (42:38), it may be practiced by representatives in whom the people trust, and whose views they express accurately and effectively [5].

Is the Result of Shura Binding or Simply Informative?

Ibn Atiyya mentioned in his comment on the verse 3:159 that *shura* elicits different views, and the one who seeks the views of others would then choose the correct one [6]. A fundamental question has been continuously raised by jurists past and present: is *shura* decisive and binding especially for the *imam* or public leader, or is it merely informational?

The verse 3:159 follows the command of practicing *shura* by putting one's trust in God, when one decides on or becomes determined to do something following the *shura*. Should that decision or determination be bound by the result of *shura* whether expressed unanimously or by majority, or is it left in the end to the discretion and judgment of the one who seeks the views of others? The question has a very serious effect on the essence of *shura* and the value of its practice, since *shura* can be an empty formality if its results have no binding effect.

The Prophet carried out others' advice in the battles of Badr, Uhud, the Trench or the Confederates (*al-Khandaq/ al-Ahzab*) and on many other occasions [7]. In part based on this, *Tafsir al-Manar* condemns the "personal despotic authority" and criticizes the view that *shura* is an optional virtue [8]. Another scholar of al-Azhar indicates that *the determination mentioned in verse 3:159 has to be based on the result of shura*, and considers the agreement of "*ahl al-shura*" a binding consensus that should be carried out by the government and the people [9].

On the contrary, Abu al-A'la al-Mawdudi, the prominent leader of Jama'at Islami in Pakistan (d. 1979), was of the opinion that the leader may approve of the opinion of the majority or the minority, or carry out his own opinion that is different from both. He elaborated "in all cases he is watched by his people who share together the responsibility of making sure that he is not following personal desires and whims, and they may depose him if he does". However, in his late years, Mawdudi seemed to change his view about democracy in general, and stated that despite acknowledging the many shortcomings of democracy – which multiply when the masses are lacking awareness, as they are poor, illiterate, intellectually confused, and swayed by people who serve personal or factional interests –

"the fact remains that democracy is the only way to avoid the failings of a people and turn them into a grown-up nation. It is a matter of common observation that a person learns to live independently only when he can handle his obligations and responsibilities without external props [...] He receives many kicks and knacks on account of his raw experience. But he does not give up the struggle and continues groping around in the dark of adventure and inexperience. The excitement of enterprise is the justification" [10].

Measuring the Results of Shura:
Reckoning on the Majority

If *shura* is a religious obligation, and is binding, an essential question rises: how can the result of *shura* be measured?

The obvious answer, and maybe the only answer, is counting the supporters of different views and relying on where the majority stands.

However, some Islamic writings have reservations about reckoning on the majority, for the majority is not necessarily always right. A reliance on quantity has been indicated as faulty 25 times in the Quran, and the error of the majority has been mentioned 69 times. The Quran teaches that the evaluation of anything should be based on its qualitative merits, not on the number supporting it (e.g. 5:100). Al-Mawdudi relied on this verse in his reservation about the majority's view, and in stating that the leader may follow the majority or the minority or may even follow his own view, but the people have to watch thoroughly his behavior in conducting public affairs [11]. A change of mind was reflected in al-Mawdudi's late work "Democracy and National Solidarity."

In the life of the Prophet, it seems that his consideration of the results of the *shura* of his Companions was based on the majority, not necessarily accurately counted, but estimated. Caliph Umar entrusted six persons with choosing from among themselves his successor to the Caliphate. He instructed them to reckon on the majority in making their choice, and in case of a tie, he appointed his son Abd Allah merely as a tie-breaker, stressing that he was not himself a candidate [12]. When 'Abd al-Rahman ibn 'Awf gave up his candidacy and volunteered to explore the public's view about their choice, he talked for three full days and nights with the leading persons separately and together, in private and in public, and went further to women within their homes, youngsters in their classes, and to the visitors to Medina and to the bedouins in their possible whereabouts. He discerned a prevalent inclination towards Uthman, except from 'Ammar ibn Yasir and al-Miqdad ibn al-Aswad who stated their preference for Ali ibn Ali Talib to be caliph [13].

Tafsir al-Manar sharply indicates that *the community is often less erroneous than the individual,* and the risk in delegating its common matters to one person is a serious one [14]. In fact, the legal qualification of the relation between the imam or caliph and the people as *a contract* implies that the majority of people should be represented so that the contract is established by genuine consent [15].

Lack of Institutional Mechanisms for Shura in the Muslim Historical Practice

Several modern authors have underscored the historical problem that there has been no effective mechanism by which *shura* developed among Muslim peoples from a moral and intellectual concept into an organizational practical institution [16]. Muhammad Abduh indicated that the Prophet was guided in the Quran to establish *a tradition of shura through practice*. This should be understood in light of the Arab tribal structure, where the clan mentality prevailed over any logical or objective consideration. Muhammad Rashid Rida added that *the Prophet established shura in his time according to the given circumstances in Medina* before reentering Mecca, *as the number of Muslims there was limited* and they often met with him in the mosque.

However, when the number of Muslims increased and came to be spread all over Arabia, a *system for shura became necessary*. Rida believed that such a system *was not created by the Prophet for several reasons*, at the top of which was that such a system *should differ according to the given circumstances of different times and places*. If the Prophet had put certain interim rules for *shura* according to the given circumstances of his time and place, these rules *might have been confused to be permanent* and constitute a rule in the religion, as happened with his sayings in mere worldly matters, in spite of his words: "You are more knowledgeable of your worldly matters" [reported by Muslim], "Whatever is related to your religion has to be referred to me, whatever is related to your worldly matters you know better" [reported by Ibn Hanbal]. According to Rida, it may have been psychologically difficult for the successive generations of believers in different places to change something decided by

272

the Prophet, even with the difference between his historical circumstances and the present circumstances. Moreover, would the Prophet have decided such rules for *shura* through *shura*, or by himself? If he had acted through *shura*, those rulers would definitely have reflected the existing circumstances and shortcomings of the community at that time, and if the Prophet had decided by himself the rules for *shura* he would have been contradicting the principle of *shura* itself.

However, the way of choosing the early Caliphs for their positions and their conduct of state affairs fulfilled the fundamental requirements of *shura*. The Umayyads, followed by the Abbasids, established their hereditary dynasties and their despotic authority. This continued through successive generations, and thus *shura* became unknown among the rulers as well as the ruled [17].

Another modern jurist and historian has articulated the issue in this manner,

"No explicit command was expressed in the Quran about how a successor of the Prophet [as a political leader], would be brought in, except such general commands that are related to the caliphate and else as the principle of *shura* and moral obligations such as honesty in choosing the most capable and righteous. No particular system about electing the caliph was expressed in the Sunna except certain advice for avoiding disputes and splits. It seems as if Shari'a aimed to leave this matter to the Muslims to solve it by their own selves according to their needs and circumstances; otherwise it would have introduced its rules and clarified its ways as had been the case in the prayers and the fasting" [18].

Al-Mawardi in his well known work *Al-Ahkam al-Sultaniyya* dealt with choosing the imam in four pages, in which vague generalities dominate. He spoke of those who are *eligible to choose the imam* (*ahl al-ikhtiyar*) or eligible to bind and dissolve (*ahl al-'aqd wa al-hall*) as the foundation for the whole procedure, and highlighted the requirements for their integrity, knowledge, and wisdom. What are the functional criteria, within these moral and intellectual generalities, to distinguish these eligible people, and how would they carry out their responsibility? How may the candidates for the position of *ahl al-imama* be identified, introduced to the people and evaluated? Al-Mawardi dealt with the matter as if those eligible for the position of *imam* or caliph, and those eligible to choose him, are both very distinctive and widely known beyond question! He simply states that those who are eligible to bind and dissolve have to meet to choose the imam, go through those who are eligible for the imamate, and choose the one who is most virtuous, fulfills the most requirements, and is the most acceptable to the people [19].

As H.A.R. Gibb has rightfully observed,

"The fully developed political theory of the Sunni jurists was not speculatively from the sources of Revelation, but rather *based upon an interpretation of these sources in the light of later political developments, and reinforced by the dogma of the divine guidance of the community and the infallibility of its 'ijma'* [...] Almost every succeeding generation left its mark upon the political doctrine, as fresh precedents were created and the theory was accommodated to them. This close dependence upon historical facts is clearly seen in (and serves to explain) yet another feature of Sunni theory, namely *its refusal to lay down rules for cases which had not*

274

yet arisen in practice, beyond vague generalities and some... deductions [...] Sunni political theory was in fact on the *rationalization of the history of the community"* [20].

Muslims, then, did not develop in the past a system or institutional mechanisms for *shura*. This is in large part because in their history they turned in just a few years from a city state and a tribal society in which practicing *shura* was simple and possible, to an expansive, complex, multi-ethnic and multi-religious universal state. Despotic hereditary monarchies, in which *shura* had no place, ran that extensive state for many successive centuries. In modern times, Europe, followed by the United States, was able to reach unprecedented advancement in various dimensions. A distinctive one was the articulation and the provision of mechanisms for human rights and democracy, which would naturally secure and effectuate the function of *shura* in Islam through certain articulation and institutionalization. Should Muslims ignore such effective and efficient measures because they developed in a different socio-cultural environment, under a non-Islamic, maybe irreligious, if not anti-religion climate? Or should they do so because those measures have not been perfect and have definitely had shortcomings? Would this means that Muslims have to continue waiting indefinitely for their own self-developed measures, no sign of which has yet emerged?

Or do Muslims have no choice but to adapt what is available to their needs and circumstances as much as possible, without contradicting any of the Islamic principles? In this way, they would be following the footsteps of their ancestors in benefiting from the heritage of world civilizations available to them, and then developing their own civilization. They would be following in that way the Prophet's tradition: "The believer is in constant search for wisdom, wherever he

(/she) finds it, he (/she) is the most deserving of it" [reported by al-Tirmidhi, and given the grade of "good"]. The Quran teaches, "Give then this glad tiding to My servants who *listen [closely] to all that is said, and follow the best of it*; it is they whom God has graced with His guidance, and it is they who really use their minds" (39:17-18).

It is sensible therefore to look at the contemporary articulation and institutionalization of human rights and democracy, see how it may or may not be compatible with the principles of Islam, and discuss what reservations may be raised about these issues.

Human and Civil Rights
as the Basis for Public Political Power

Human rights in all their dimensions are essential for the individual and the public, in order to have the basic power and security to practice a genuine democracy with its mechanisms and institutions. In this way, democracy cannot fail to become merely superficial ceremonials, as is the case in some third-world countries. Human rights should be comprehensive: individual and collective, socio-economic and legal, judicial, as well as moral-cultural. Humanity has experienced divine guidance about human dignity through the successive messages, in addition to the contributions of the human mind, God's favor to the *homo sapiens*, as expressed in the human philosophies and thoughts of which the Babylonian, Egyptian, Greco-Roman, Indian, Chinese, and other heritages are examples.

The West has a long history in articulating human rights, from the classical Roman Natural law and the British Principles of Equity to the more recent national documents of the Magna Carta in the year 1215, the Bill of Rights in 1688, and the Declaration of Rights in 1689 in Britain; the Declaration of Independence in 1776, and the Constitution in 1788, with its first 10 amendments known as the Bill of Rights, in the United States; and the Declaration of the Rights of the Human Being and the Citizen in 1789 in France. Intellectual contributions in fields such as philosophy, history, politics, economics, and others have provided a solid and wide base for bringing about public revolutions in different countries and formulating their valuable consequential documents. As examples, one may mention the works of the Briton John Locke (d. 1704) and the Swiss Jean Jacques Rousseau

(d. 1778) on the Social Contract, and the social economic works of the 18th and 19th centuries, with their different approaches from Adam Smith (d. 1790) to Jeremy Bentham (d. 1831), John Stuart Mill (d. 1873), Karl Marx (d. 1803) and others. In Europe, both the Enlightenment movement of the 18th century and the Industrial Revolution later in the same century had a symbiotic relationship that fundamentally affected the conception of human potential and rights, which contributed to the constitutional and democratic movement.

As Robin W. Winks precisely states,

"between 1763 and 1811, it can rightly be seen as a *World Revolution centered in the West* [...] , people who previously thought that they had no right to express themselves politically began a process of transformation not complete to this day. The age of the democratic revolution *grew from the problems and the society that preceded it,* and in this sense marked no sharp break with the past; the processes it so dramatically set in motion, while initially stymied in most societies, *continued as an underground stream* and surfaced again in 1858, in the 1870s, and for Africa and Asia in the 1960s" [21].

During such an age of accelerated qualitative change in the West, Muslim countries were suffering internal stagnation, and external colonial exploitative occupation. When the Muslim countries obtained their independence after a hard struggle, they had to face serious problems in their political, socio-economic and religious cultural development. Looking at their Islamic heritage, they have found perpetual sound, ethical values and general legal principles that provide a solid foundation for justice and progress in the various arenas, including the political one, with certain formal details and articulations as could be related to the given medieval circumstances of time and place. Therefore, what Muslims have desperately needed for their modern development, especially in their political life, have been the institutions and mechanisms that should secure and safeguard the ethical and general legal principles of Islam, and bring about a just and efficient political system and government.

The modern human experience in Europe and the West has been clearly and sharply articulated, and has provided various institutional mechanisms that may be useful in effectuating the ethical and legal precepts of Islam, even though they developed in a non-Islamic, probably non-religious, irreligious, or even anti-religious socio-cultural environment. God's gift of human intellect, as do all His bounties, serves all human beings, regardless of their beliefs. Such human intellectual experiences may be more relevant to the structure and needs of a modern society, even with their recognized shortcomings, than the Muslim heritage in which the human intellect worked under qualitatively different socio-economic circumstances.

Furthermore, the modern national efforts in the field of human and civil rights have been supported and reinforced by international collective efforts, which have broadened the articulation of rights and provided some effective safeguards for them. On 10th December 1948, the Universal Declaration of Human Rights was issued by the General Assembly of the United Nations. On 16th December 1966, the same organization issued the International Covenant on Civil and Political Rights and the International Convention on Economic, Social and Cultural Rights, and both documents became effective on 15th July 1967. In 1950, the European Council met in Rome and issued the European Convention of Human Rights. Later, documents and resolutions about the rights of children and women, and the developmental rights of people in general, followed through successive international conferences held in different cities throughout the world.

- ### *Human Dignity in the Quran*

The Quran strongly states that human dignity has been granted since creation by God the Creator to all human beings, whatever their inborn differences of race, color, and gender, or their acquired differences of language, religion, education, work, and wealth may be. In the verse 17:70, the Quran reads, "We have conferred *dignity on all children of Adam* and have *borne them over land and sea*, and have provided for them sustenance out of the *good things of life,* and favored them far above most of Our Creation".

So, human dignity is the sacred gift of God granted by Him to *all human beings* since Creation, and human authorities have to recognize, secure, safeguard, and sanction this existing human dignity. The authorities do not originate or grant dignity, and they can never deny any person his/her dignity or discriminate in securing the divinely granted dignity for all human beings. Every descendent of Adam – Muslim or non-Muslim, male or female – enjoys dignity. *"Dignity"* encompasses the enjoyment of *rights* and the fulfillment of *responsibilities*; both are inseparably connected in the life of the dignified human being.

Furthermore, the human being is destined by his/ her Creator to be *universal,* and is given the ability and assistance of the Creator through the human mind and the laws of nature to travel the entire world, *over land and sea,* and through *whatever overlying area* the human abilities

280

and natural laws allow the human to reach: "It is God who has made *the sea* subservient to you [through His laws], so that ships might sail through it at His behest, and that you might seek to obtain [what you look for] of His bounty [...] And He has made subservient to you [as benevolence] from Himself all that is *in the heavens and on earth* [...] " (45:12-13).

Human dignity should be also secured through the human being's ability to obtain sustenance out of the *good things of life,* which are healthy and nutritive. This has to be secured by governmental measures, through socio-economic justice and health care.

Worshipping only the One God, and determining the human being's "dignity" by the Creator in His supreme sovereignty and power for all the children of Adam – whatever their inborn or acquired differences may be – are not merely matters of faith or theology They have their fundamental implications with regard to the essentiality of human rights in the human society.. Human dignity is established in Islam by faith, designated through moral values that govern the behavior of the individual, the family, and the society, nurtured by the school, the mosque, and all religious institutions as well as the means of mass communications, and sanctioned by Islamic law, Shari'a, which is implemented and enforced by the state authorities.

The physical and moral sanctity of the individual, his/her home and privacy, and his/her integrity are strongly protected by Shari'a. Freedom of faith is sharply stressed in the Quran which states that "No coercion should ever be in matters of faith" (2:256). Free expression of opinion is a right and an obligation that pertains to the responsibility of bearing witness and of enjoining what is right and good and

281

forbidding what is wrong and evil (*al-'amr bi-al-ma'ruf wa al-nahy 'an al-munkar*) (e.g. 2:143, 282-3; 3:104, 110, 114; 31:17). The rights of assembly and association are secured for all people in order to assure free expression, essential for casual public gatherings and constant civil organizations in order to balance the enormous sweeping power of the modern state, as it has been often emphasized by contemporary constitutional lawyers and political scientists. Rights in socio-economic development, education, and health services are recognized and protected in Islam. Collective national rights of freedom and self-determination are asserted, and a national struggle for this purpose is recognized and has to be universally supported [22]. It is highly required to constitute a special court for the disputes about any violation of the human rights of an individual or a group nationally and internationally, as the Quran has pointed out (49:9). A special court was estabished under the caliphs to hear the complaints about injustice, *mazalim*, and the European community has presented a modern example of this.

Democracy in its various modern forms provides institutional bodies and procedural mechanisms for securing human dignity, and these ought to be benefited from in implementing *shura* (2:233, 3:159, 42:38). A basic rule in Islamic law, Shari'a, is that whatever *means is found necessary for fulfilling an Islamic legal obligation becomes an obligation in itself* [23], if it is naturally permissible and does not contradict another rule of Shari'a. Elections, candidacy, reaching a decision through a majority, and the multi-party system are procedural mechanisms to secure practicing the rights of free opinion and expression, and of assembly and association, and there is no Islamic rejection in principle for any of these mechanisms. Reservations raised by some Muslims about any, some, or all of these methods have no solid ground. Establishing leadership positions,

282

indicating a candidate's capabilities for such a position and relying on the majority in making a decision were all known practices in Muslim history [24].

Let us stress these essential clarifications:
- The sovereignty of the people represented by the state is relative and does not contradict the absolute and supreme sovereignty of God, and the legislative authority of the people's representatives through the legislature does not contradict the faith that God is principally the Lawgiver. God has allowed the community in its collectivity (*al-jama'a*) certain rights and authority, and jurists have called the collective public right "right of God/ *haq Allah*" to underscore its importance and superiority [25].

- The rulers have to be entrusted with authority from among the people by the people themselves, *'uli al-'amr-minkum* (Quran 4:59). They constitute a civil body, and by no means represent a clerical authority.

- Shari'a consists of general legal principles and a certain number of limited particular laws – mainly in the areas of the acts of worship and the family – that the human intellect is required to interpret and implement. *Shari'a allows the human community to practice legislation in the unlimited area of unspecified details in the Quran and Sunna through legitimate ijtihad,* which should not contradict any rule indicated in the revealed sources. The distribution of state powers as executive, legislative, and judicial, the independence of the judiciary, and the efficient distribution of authority with the necessary "checks and balances," secure good governing, comply with the general goals and principles of Shari'a, and do not contradict any of its principles [26].

- The rights of opposition in free opinion, expression, assembly, and association are secured by Shari'a and should be protected by the Muslim authorities. Caliph Ali secured for his opponents *al-Khawarij* assembly in the mosques, the assurance that they would never be met by state forces unless they initiated the use of force, and the guarantee that they would never be denied their financial rights to the public treasury as long as they fulfilled their obligations [27].

Human rights and *shura* are distinctly indicated in the Quran and Sunna, and were mostly interpreted and developed through the successive efforts of Muslim rulers and jurists. Yet contemporary Muslims also benefit from modern thinking and practices in a systematic articulation of concepts, institutionalization of specific bodies and processes, and formulation of legal sanctions. As the prominent jurist Ibn al-Qayyim accurately and eloquently stated, "God has sent the conveyors of His messages and brought down His revealed books to *establish justice in human dealings* [...] Hence, *wherever the signs of rightfulness appear and the evidence of justice rises by whatever way, there is the law and command of God* [...] God only indicates through the ways that He states that His purpose is the establishment of rightfulness and justice" [28].

The Muslim Complex
Towards Western Ideas

The Universal Declaration of Human Rights as well as the principles, institutions and mechanisms of democracy have been developed and crystallized in the West, whereas the Muslims have suffered – and in some cases continue to suffer – the aggression and exploitation of the West in their various forms over the last centuries. Muslims have struggled, and in some cases are still struggling courageously and firmly, against Western military occupation and against Western economic-political-cultural domination. Naturally, many Muslims have lost confidence in any western project or product, be it political, economical, social, or even intellectual or cultural, including whatever advancement has been reached in Western countries. Unfortunately, this formidable loss of confidence has developed, while the West has been persistently progressing in building on modern civilization, and the Muslim societies have been declining in various areas for different reasons, internal and external, material and moral. In short, many Muslims have become apprehensive of any Western product, even ideas, while they have been unable to produce alternatives to respond to their needs.

Many Muslims have been concerned with internal failures and an absence of political and socio-economic rights, as well as with a blemished or distorted national independence. Regarding what may substitute for the existing deficiencies, numerous Muslim hearts and minds may be inclined in one way or another to an aspiration for "*a just despot.*" Jamal al-Din al-Afghani or al-Asadabadi (d. 1314 AH/ 1897 CE) directed his energy towards resisting foreign domination and reforming or changing the rulers, hence expecting reform to come only from above, though via the pressure of the people. There was no real focus on reforming, from below, the people themselves, especially socially and culturally. Following a political independence that was mostly formal and never complete, the political superstructure seemed fully controlled by Western powers and self interests. Accordingly, the so-claimed post-independence democracy never earned the public confidence. Military coups supported by foreign powers frustrated and deceived the masses, and steered public sentiment away from or even against democracy, and at times towards an authoritarianism that boasted vague socialist labels.

In time, many Islamists began to feel, to differing degrees, the essentiality of freedom and democracy, and they set out to express such feelings whenever they were able to do so. However, whether the Islamists' attitude towards democracy was genuine or superficial, tactical or strategic, whenever they are able to participate in parliamentary contests – under the umbrella of other political parties in countries where their organizations are still banned – they always launch in their campaigns the old ambiguous rhetoric: *"Islam is the solution."* Forums such as a debate a few years ago at Kuwait University on *"Shura or Democracy"* imply that the two are mutually exclusive, and that they cannot meet or interact. Such shallow slogans may unfortunately represent, to differing extents, the conception of some or many Islamist groups. Furthermore, many Islamists in different countries have been quite willing to participate in undemocratic regimes with a view to implementing their Islamic agendas from above.

Whatever the Islamists' genuineness in advocating democracy, the rise of Bin Laden's model of violence in the aftermath of the horrific attacks of September 11th, 2001 in

New York and Washington D.C., has exerted its pressure on contemporary Islamic thinking. How should Islamic reform be conducted, peacefully or militantly, from above or from below? After all, it is an urgent Muslim responsibility to transcend such a bitter anti-West complex, and consider the concrete facts and solid realities of our time.

Muslim reform cannot be delayed until Muslims are able to create their own system in their minds or in the real world. Islam does not require that its system should emerge in a vacuum: this is against human nature and against history. Islam allows *ijtihad* as a main principle in the political arena, while it establishes general principles of justice and *shura*. Modern documents of human rights, national and universal, articulate, institutionalize and sanction the human dignity established by God for all human beings. A democratic system provides an articulation and an institutionalization of *shura* that are understandable, approachable, and functional. Islam and Muslims would be better understood and supported globally by a genuine approach towards democracy, through our era of globalization, with its unprecedented and unanticipatable dynamism that would inevitably affect Muslims throughout the world, positively or negatively, according to their efforts for reform.

Notes

(1)   Ibn Atiyya in *al-Muharrar al-Wajiz*, vol. 3, pp. 280-1;
        al-Qurtubi, *al-Jami li-Ahkam al-Quran*, vol. 4, pp.
        249-251.

(2)   Abduh & Rida, *Tafsir al-Manar*, vol. 4, pp. 199-
        200.

(3)   Ibn Kathir, *al-Bidaya wa al-Nihaya,* vol. 6, pp.
        305-6; al-'Azm,, Rafiq, *'Ash-har Mashair al-Islam fi
        al-Harb wa al-Siyasa*, Cairo: Dar al-Fikr al-'Arabia,
        1970, p. 121.

(4)   For the juristic qualification of the relation between
        the imam or caliph and the people as contractual see
        by the author *Min 'Usul al-Fikr al-Siyasi al-Islami,*
        Beirut: Mu'assasa al-Risala, n.d., pp. 390-411.

(5)   Abduh & Rida, *Tafsir al-Manar*, vol. 5, pp. 180-
        188.

(6)   Ibn Atiyya, *al-Muharrar al-Wajiz*, vol. 3, p.281.

(7)   See for example, Ibn Kathir, Isma'il ibn 'Umar,
        Tafsir al-Quran al-Azim, vol. 2, comment on the
        verse 3:159.

(8)   Abduh & Rida, *Tafsir al-Manar*, vol. 4, pp. 204-5.

(9)   al-Zalabani, Rizq, "al-Siyasa al-Dusturiyya al-
        Shar'iyya", *Al-Azhar Journal*, issue 2, vol. 18.

(10)   al-Mawdudi, Abu al-A'la, see respectively:
        "Nazariyya al-Islam al-Siyasiyya" in *Nazariyya
        al-Islam wa Hadyuh fi al-Siyasa wa al-Qanun wa*

al-Dustur, Beirut: Mu'assasa al-Risala, 1969, pp. 58-9, Democracy and National Solidarity, Lahore: Maktaba-E-Mansoorah, n.d., p. 16.

(11)   Ibid., pp. 58-9.

(12)   Hasan, Hasan Ibrahim, *Tarikh al-Islam,* vol. 1, pp. 254-5, quoting al-Tabari in his "*Tarikh*."

(13)   Ibn Kathir, *al-Bidaya wa al-Nihaya,* vol. 7, p. 151.

(14)   Abduh & Rida, *Tafsir al-Manar*, vol. 4, p. 201.

(15)   See the above note no. 4.

(16)   See for example Amin, Ahmad, *Fajr al-Islam*, p. 240.

(17)   al-Mawardi, *al-Ahkam al-Sultaniyya*, pp. 6-9.

(18)   Abduh & Rida, *Tafsir al-Manar*, vol. 4, pp. 199-205, vol. 5, pp. 188-9.

(19)   al-Khudari, Muhammad, *Muhadarat Tarikh al-Umam al Islamiyya,* Cairo: al-Maktaba al-Tijariyya, 6th ed., n.d., vol. 1, pp. 161-2.

(20)   Gibb, Hamilton A.R., "Al-Mawardi's Theory of the Caliphate" in *Studies on the Civilization of Islam*, pp. 154-5.

(21)   Winks, Robin W., *Western Civilization*, Prentice-Hall: Englewood Cliffs, N.J., 1979, p. 253.

(22)   See by the author "Human Rights: An Islamic Perspective," in *Islam in the Contemporary Life,* Los Angeles, and *Huquq al-Insan Bayna Shari'at al-Islam waal-Fikr al-Gharbi*, 1st ed.: Cairo, 2nd ed.: Los Angeles.

(23)   See for example: al-Shatibi, Ibrahim in Musa, *al-Muwafaqat*, commented on by Diraz, Abd Allah, Cairo: al-Maktaba al-Tijariyya, n.d., vol. 4, pp. 194-6; Abu Zahra, Muhammad, *Usul al-Fiqh*, Cairo: Dar al-Fikr al-'Arabi, 1958, pp. 288, 290.

(24)   See for example: for the legitimacy of requesting leading positions, the Quran 12:55, 38:35; also: al-Mawardi, *al-Ahkam al-Sultaniyya*, p. 7; for the legitimacy of presenting the candidate's capability for the position: see the Quran 12:55, noticing that forbidding self-praise is related to praising with piety and God's acceptance [Quran 4:49, 5:18, 53:32]; for relying on the majority in decision making; Ibn Kathir, *al-Bidaya wa al-Nihaya*, vol. 7, pp. 146, 150-2; Abduh & Rida, *Tafsir al-Manar*, vol. 4, p. 199. The Prophet's Companions expressed different attitudes in suggesting a caliph after the death of the Prophet; see e.g. Ibn Kathir, *al-Bidaya wa al-Nihaya*, vol. 6, pp. 305-6; al-Azm, Rafiq, *Ash-har Mashahir al-Islam*, Cairo: Dar al-Fikr al-'Arabi, pp. 972-3, pp. 29-30. Muslim groups such as the Sunnis, the Shi'is, the Khawarij, and later the Mu'tazila expressed their different political views since early Islam, and juristic schools had their differences about the top position of the state, *imama/ khilafa*; see e.g. Hasan, Hasan Ibrahim, *Tarikh al-Islam*, vol. 1, pp. 354-426; Amin, Ahmad, *Fajr al-Islam*, vol. 1, pp. 252-304. See by the author: *Democracy and the Concept of Shura*, Washington D.C.: Center for Muslim Christian Understanding, Georgetown University, 1999.

(25)   Khallaf, *'Ilm 'Usul al-Fiqh*, pp. 210-13.

(26) Abduh & Rida, *Tafsir al-Manar*, vol. 5, pp. 181, 183, 187-190.

(27) al-Mawardi, *al-Ahkam al-Sultaniyya*, p. 58.

(28) Ibn al-Qayyim, *I'lam al-Muwaqqi'in,* vol. 4, pp. 309-10.

V

Secularism:
Irreligiosity,
or a Stand against Religion?
Is Secularism not Varied? Is it not Evolving?

Many Muslims and Islamists believe that there should *never* be any political cooperation with secularists or secularist parties, and a state committed to Islam should not even allow the establishment of a secularist party. Secularism, as a Western product and a post-colonial consequence in Muslim countries, has been loaded with heavy negative connotations according to the historical circumstances through which secularism entered Muslim countries. This requires a serious enquiry into the accurate linguistic and political meaning of "*secularism*" as it has been, and is being, used in its Western home.

Does "*secularism*" negate the state's siding with a particular religion, or work against religiosity and imply an anti-religion attitude?

Does it mean that the state holds an irreligious or even anti-religion attitude, or merely a non-religious bias?

Is it a static or an evolving concept? Is it uniform or varied?

To trace the origin and development of secularism, let us examine its definition in *The New Encyclopaedia Britannica*:

"a movement in society *directed away from other-worldliness to this-worldliness*. In the *medieval* period there was a strong tendency *for religious persons to despise human affairs and meditate on God and afterlife*. As a *reaction* to this medieval tendency, *secularism*, at the time of the *Renaissance*, exhibited itself in the ***development of humanism***, when man began to show more interest in human cultural achievements and the possibilities of his *fulfillment in this world*. The movement towards secularism has been *in progress during the entire course of modern history* and has often been *viewed as being anti-Christian and anti-religious*."

Thus, *"secularism"* has been contextualized as a modern developing human tendency towards *worldliness*, as a *reaction to the medieval tendency* of religious Christians towards other-worldliness and asceticism that focused on a disengagement from this world and its human affairs.

In Islam, this world's life and the eternal life in the world to come are strongly connected. The reward of the eternal world can never be secured except through the human active role and hard work in this transitional or temporal world. It can by no means be achieved through withdrawal from it and an exclusive focus on meditation and worship of God. A Muslim has to observe his/her relation with God through his/her sincere, constructive, and mutual inter-relations with the people in this world's life, and to observe the reward of the eternal life to come through his/her productive hard work in this transitional temporal world. Such hard work in this life is considered worship of God if practiced within this perspective.

The contradiction between the two worlds, and the medieval Christian tendency towards other-worldliness, led to the *reaction* that developed *secularism*, and to conceiving an insoluble contradiction or impossibility of concurrence between commitment to this world's interests as denoted in secularism on the one side, and religion on the other. Hence, the "progress of the movement towards secularism during the entire course of modern history, has often been viewed as being *anti-Christian and anti religious*," as *Encyclopedia Britannica* has put it.

However, the *Encyclopaedia* adds:

"In the latter half of the 20th century, *a number of theologians began advocating 'secular Christianity'*. They suggested

296

that Christianity should be concerned not only with the sacred and the other-worldly, but *rather that man should find in the secular world the opportunity to promote Christian values.* These theologians maintain that the *real meaning of the message of Jesus can be discovered and   fulfilled in the everyday affairs of secular urban living."* [(1)].

Such contemporary Christian theologians may have been thinking along the same lines of the Muslim theologians and jurists, who always looked at Islam in this way.

It may be interesting to follow the development of "secularism" linguistically and ideologically so as to see how initially and basically the adjective *"secular"* has been understood and defined, and how the term *"secularism"* has come to be loaded with historical and ideological connotations from which the original adjective was linguistically free. *Webster's New Collegiate Dictionary* gives this definition for the word *"secular":*

"**1**a: *of or relating to the worldly or temporal*; b: not overtly or specifically religious; c: not ecclesiastical or clerical. **2**: not bound by *monastic vows or rules*; specifically: of, or relating to, or forming clergy not belonging to a religious order or congregation [. . .] ". Then we come to meanings related to time: "occurring once in an age [...]; existing or continuing through ages or centuries [...]", which is not related to our discussion here.

As we reach the ideological formation of the term *"secularism,"* we see this definition in *Webster's New Collegiate Dictionary*:

"Indifference or rejection or exclusion of religion and religious considerations" [(2)].

It is obvious that the word *"secular"* has a clear and straightforward meaning in its origin, while *"secularism"* has been loaded as an ideological term by a specific emerging perception based on a modern humanist reaction against medieval Christian thinking and practice. Thus, the term has reflected a tendency of separating human activities in this world from the traditional religious roots in reaction to the historical experience of the Christian Church in medieval Europe, which was inclined to limit human worldly activities and focus on particular acts of worshipping God with the purpose of receiving salvation in the eternal afterlife.

For a Muslim, secularism can never be loaded with such a historical reaction, since Islam and its history have not provided grounds for what led to this reaction within Christianity. Being secular may be restricted to the origin of the word, denoting conducting affairs of state objectively and neutrally through officials who are only capable of carrying out public responsibilities of their positions without discrimination. Public positions in a Muslim state are by no means clerical religiously or historically, but have always been considered worldly activities that must be run legally and ethically according to the Islamic guidance. This guidance conducts human behavior in this life with a view to reaching the acceptance of God in this present world, and this is the basis for His reward in the eternal life to come.

There is no clergy in Islam, and the Muslim learned persons of religion, *'ulama*, do not claim any theocratic privilege. Each person is evaluated according to individual merits and by no means enjoys a class distinction. The Muslim state in history was never run as a theocracy, so there is no place for "secularism" as an alternative that would focus on human wordly life.

Muslims may be able to contribute to a better conceptual and practical interpretation and representation of the required objectivity, neutrality and fairness in the conduct of state affairs, and to release the term "secularism" from its confusing connotation through constructive engagement with the various trends in contemporary political life. The concept of "secularism" has been evolving during different times and places, as many thinkers all over the world have been underlining the increasing aspects of social ills and moral deterioration even in the most materially developed and strictly secular countries. It varies from Britain, where the Queen is the head of the Anglican Church, to the U.S., where a strict separation between the state and any religious institution has always been observed. When Cyprus obtained its independence, its first president was a priest, and in a referendum about a plan uniting the Greek and Turkish parts of the island after their factual split many years ago, the Greek Church advocated forcefully the rejection of the plan.

William E. Connolly, Professor of Political Science at The John Hopkins University, is described by Barbara Herrnstein Smith, author of *Beliefs and Resistance*, as "one of the subtlest, boldest, and most intellectually fertile political and moral theorists today." She values Connolly's book, *Why I Am Not a Secularist*, as an "incisive *critique of dogmatic rationalism*" and "a valuable analysis of the psycho-social dynamics of *'identity politics'* and a compelling argument for an ethics of *'critical engagement';* as appropriate to *a genuinely pluralistic society*". Connolly argues in his book that secularism, although admirable in its pursuit of freedom and diversity, too often *undercuts these goals through its narrow and intolerant understandings* of public reason. In response, he draws out *a new model of public life* that more accurately reflects the needs of contemporary politics and society. In the Introduction to this book which is given the significant title of "Refashioning the Secular," Connolly refers to Bertrand Russell and his book *Why I Am Not a Christian*, and states,

"I continue to admire Russell's opposition to *bullies on the Christian right*, who first advance profoundly contestable doctrines as the normative ground of life itself, and then pull them above the reach of public debate because of their sacred character. I also accept his judgment that while each metaphysical or religious orientation makes a difference in politics, *no such perspective suffices by itself to determine a political stance.* But over the past few decades, I have increasingly found *secular concepts of language, ethics, discourse, and politics in which Russell participated to be insufficiently alert to the layered density of political thinking and judgment,* as I oppose a religiously centered politics in which the state represents the dictates of *a specific church* of a religious faith as general as Christianity. I am *neither a secularist in my conception of public life, nor the defender of a specific church.* Are there, though, other spaces of possibility [...]? This study is an attempt to engage tensions within myself as well as to advance considerations worthy of the attention of others."

Connolly skillfully puts his finger on the deficiency of secularism that contradicts its claims about its objectives, reasoning, and virtues:

"The historical modus vivendi of secularism, *while seeking to chasten religious dogmatism, embodies unacknowledged elements of immodesty in itself.* The very intensity of the struggle it wages against religious intolerance may induce *blind spots* with respect to itself. I also wonder whether *the time of the secular modus vivendi is drawing to a close.*

We may need to *fashion modifications* in secular practices today, modifications that *both honor debts to it and support more religious and non-religious variety in public life* than many traditional secularists and monotheists tend to appreciate. This is a risky track to pursue. Many believe that the thin blue line of secularism, however frayed and tattered it has become, is still necessary to contain religious enthusiasm and dogmatism. While I harbor a few such anxieties myself, *the strains of dogmatism in secularism* may make a contribution to the effects secularists decry. People say that Communism kept virulent nationalisms alive in Eastern Europe by suppressing public engagement with them. *Maybe secularism in democratic capitalist states has muffled the public ventilation of diverse religious and irreligious perspectives needed to adjust public life to the multidimensional pluralism of today."*

The author strongly believes that *"Refashioning secularism might help to temper or disperse religious intolerance while honoring the desire of a variety of believers and non-believers to represent their faiths in public life.* It might thereby, help to *render public life more pluralistic* in shape, and, particularly, more responsive to what I call 'the politics of becoming.'"* Connolly points out that several variants of secularism

"as they try to seal public life from religious doctrines, they also cast out a set of non-theistic orientations to reverence, ethics and public life that deserve to be heard. These two effects follow from *the secular conceit to provide a single, authoritative basis of public reason* and/or public ethics that governs all reasonable citizens regardless of 'personal' or 'private' faith. To invoke that principle against religious enthusiasts, secularists are also pressed to be *pugnacious against secular, non-theistic perspectives* that call these very

301

assumptions and prerogatives into question." As the author briefly and sharply indicates, "the secular wish to contain religious and irreligious passions within private life helps to engender the immodest conceptions of public life peddled by so many secularists."

The author of *Why I Am Not a Secularist* observantly underscores the limitations in which secularism has been conceived and practiced, which "leave fingerprints all over contemporary life. And yet, ironically, the *precarious, multidimensional pluralization of life* occurring before our eyes may create new conditions of possibility (I do not say probability) to *renegotiate the old modus vivendi of secularism*". In his views, Connolly has crystallized the need of the contemporary life "to cultivate a public ethos of engagement in which a wider variety of perspectives than heretofore acknowledged inform and restrain one another" [3].

Fears and Misgivings about Islam that Resulted from Experiences in the History of the Muslim States

The negative and unfavorable consequences of connecting political authority with or constituting it on a religious basis were gathered from certain human experiences, but they should not justify fears and misgivings about Islam. The basics of the religion and the Muslim historical experience have to be objectively and mindfully considered.

The Principles of Islam

According to the principles of Islam, *the work in this life is the only way to reach the reward in the eternal life of the world to come.* Thus, there is no rejection of working hard to obtain the legitimate material benefits of this world and physical needs for a healthy body, if one does this honestly without exploiting or cheating others, always keeping in mind that he/she will be accountable in the eternal life to come before God about all that he/she has done in this life: "*and seek through what God has granted you [the good of] the [eternal] life to come, without forgetting, withal, your own [rightful] share in this world,* and do good [unto others] as God has done good to you, and seek not to spread mischief on earth, for verily God does not love those who spread mischief" (28:77). Working hard to get the best of the legitimate material benefits in this world within such a perspective would be an act of worship the same as the particular acts of worship, since the human being is entrusted by God to develop himself/herself and develop the earth as well: "He [God] brought you into being out of the earth and *entrusted you with development thereon*" (11:61), "It is He who has made the earth easy to live upon; go about then in all its tracts and *partake of the sustenance which He provides*; but always bear in mind that unto Him you shall be resurrected" (67:15).

The Muslim is commanded to hasten to the prayer as soon as its time comes, but when the prayer is ended the Muslim is commanded to go to work: "*O you have attained to faith! When the call to prayer is sounded on the day of Congregation, al-Jum'a (Friday), hasten to the remembrance of God and leave all worldly commerce, this is for your own good if you but knew it. And when the prayer is ended, disperse freely on earth, and seek to obtain [what you are legitimately able to obtain] of God's bounty; but remember God often [through all your deeds], so that you may attain to successfulness and accomplishment*" (62:9). *The Muslim prays for God's blessings in this world life and the eternal life to come both: "O our Lord! Grant us good in this world life and good in the [eternal] life to come*" (2:201).

Islam stresses in the Muslim mind and heart the human *diversity* and the human *individual differences*. Consequently, the divergence in human views among different individuals and different groups has to always be expected and accepted, even among Muslims themselves who share the same faith and the same divine revelation: "*And among His wonders is the creation of the heavens and the earth, and the diversity of your tongues and colors*" (30:22), "*and We have made you into nations and tribes, so that you might come to know [and recognize and thus complement] one another*" (49:13), "*And had your Lord so willed, He could surely have made all humankind one single community, but [He willed it otherwise, and so] they continue to have divergent views – [all of them]*

304

save those upon whom your Lord has bestowed His grace *[through benefiting from God's guidance in handling their differences]*; *and to this end [of letting them complement one another in their differences and testing them in handling them properly], He has created them* [all]" (11:118), "*And had your Lord so willed, all those who live on earth would surely have attained to faith, all of them; do you, then, think that you could compel people to believe*" (10:99), "*Unto each* [group that follows a certain message of God], *We appointed a* [particular] *law and a way of practice; and if God had so willed, He could surely have made you all one single community, but [He willed it otherwise] in order to test you through what He has brought to you. Vie, then, with one another in doing good works. Unto God you all must return, and then He will make you truly understand all that on which you were used to differ*" (5:48). "*O you who have attained to faith! Obey God, and obey the Conveyor of God's message, and those from among you who are entrusted with authority by you, and if you have a dispute about any matter, refer it unto God and the Conveyor of His message [. . .]* " (4:59).

In such enormous human diversity, and extensive individual differences, rights of free opinion, belief, and expression are secured for all human beings by Islamic law (Shari'a) and the Muslim state authorities: "*No coercion should ever be in matters of faith*" (2:256), "And do not conceal what you see" (2:283), "and neither a scribe nor a witness should suffer harm, and if you do [them harm], behold, it will be a wrongdoing on your part" (2:282).

The moral values that Islam emphasizes are universal. It is significant that the Quran refers to "*the good*" as "*al-ma'ruf*," namely what is recognized and accepted by human nature and common sense, and calls "*the evil*" "*al-munkar*," or what is rejected by human nature and common sense (e.g. 3:104, 110, 114; 7:157; 9:71, 112; 22:41; 31:17). A verse condenses what the Quran commands and forbids as follows: "God enjoins justice, and the doing of good, and giving to [one's] kinsfolk; and He forbids all that is shameful, all that runs counter to common sense, as well as aggression; He exhorts you so that you might bear [this] in mind" (16:90; for more examples see 2:177, 261-274; 3:133-5; 4:36-8, 114, 135, 148; 5:2, 8; 6:151-3; 7:30-33, 157, 199; 16:91-97; 17:22-38; 23:1-11; 49:6, 9-13; 96:1-8; 107:1-7).

Prophet Muhammad, before receiving the divine revelation, attended a tribal covenant that pledged to support any who suffered injustice until he got back his right. As a Prophet, he praised the meeting that he had witnessed when he was young for its virtuous accomplishments, and stated that if he were invited to join a similar covenant in Islam he would do so. That alliance was called deservingly in history "The Alliance of the Nobles" [4].

If "*secular*" originally meant "non-ecclesiastical or clerical," it is highly relevant that there is neither church nor clergy in Islam of the institutional form known in Christianity. The mosque is a place for worship, but any clean spot on earth can be a place for prayer, whether it is a particular building allotted for worship or not, according to the Prophet's tradition [reported by Ibn Hanbal, Abu Dawud, and Ibn Majah]. Those who are learned in religion, *'ulama,* plural of *'alim*, have no theocratic privilege, as individuals or as a group, and any person can ask or argue with any of them if what the 'alim says is not clear or convincing. The *'ulama* usually work as *imams* who lead the prayers at the mosques, deliver the sermons, or teach the masses about religion, as 'teachers' of religion at schools, or as judges at courts.

They have not been dominant in political or administrative positions in the Muslim states throughout history, as was the case in ancient or medieval theocracies around the world.

As Maxime Rodinson observed and lucidly indicated, the *"age of reason"* in Europe with its objectivity and neutrality, which might be the essence that prompted secularism, was what brought a clearer and fairer vision of Islam as a religion and in its historical role:

"People could not view the religious faith which competed with Christianity in an impartial light and even with some sympathy, unconsciously seeking (and obviously finding) *in it the very values of the new rationalist trend of thought* that was opposed to Christianity. In the seventeenth century many authors took up the defense of Islam against medieval prejudices and polemical detractors, and demonstrated the worth and sincerity of Muslim piety. One such author was Richard Simon (d.1712). He was a sincere Catholic, but the soundness of his scholarship made him fight against the dogmatic perversion of objective facts, both in reading the Bible and the study of Eastern Christendom. In his "Histoire Critique des Croyances et des Coutumes des Nations du Levant" (1684), he dealt first with the beliefs and rites of the Eastern Christians, then with those of the Muslims which he expounded clearly and soberly on the basis of a work by a Muslim theologian, without vituperation or disparagement and occasionally with real appreciation and even admiration. When Arnaud (Henri, d.1721) accused him of having been too objective towards Islam, he advised him to ponder on the 'excellent teachings' of Muslim moralists [...].

"The next generation was to go on from objectivity to admiration [...]; following the example set by the Spanish Jews two centuries earlier, the Calvinists of Hungary and

307

Transylvania, the Protestants of Silesia, and the Cossack Old Believers of Russia sought refuge in Turkey [in the Ottoman Empire] or looked to the 'Porte' [the high Ottoman governmental authority] in their flight from Catholic or Orthodox persecution. Islam was looked upon as a *rational* religion, far removed from the Christian dogmas which were so strongly opposed to reason, and containing a minimum of mythical concepts and mysterious rites (the minimum, it was thought, necessary to secure the adherence of the masses). Further it *reconciled the call to a moral life with a reasonable regard for the need of the body, of the senses, and of life in society.* In brief, as a religion it comes very close to the 'Deism' that most of the 'Men of Enlightenment' professed. On the historical level, the *civilizing role played by Islam* was highlighted: civilization had not emerged from the monastery, but had had its origins among the pagan Greeks and Romans and had been *brought from Europe by the Arabs* who were (and so much the better to the mind of the time!) non-Christian" [5].

Islamic Law and the Muslim State

The Muslim state has by no means been a theocracy, for it was never run by persons with expertise in the Islamic faith and Shari'a, but by civil servants. '*Ulama* – as indicated before – working mainly in mosques, religious schools, and courts. The Islamic law that was applied in the courts and throughout the entire state provided details only in family affairs such as marriage, divorce, custody, guardianship, and inheritance – in addition naturally to acts of worship such as prayers (*salat*), fasting (*siyam*), and rendering the purifying social dues (*zakat*). In worldly dealings, *mu'amalat*, the Quran and Sunna often provide general legal and moral principles, which may be parallel to natural law in the history of the Roman law or the Principles of Equity in the history of the British law. Justice *'adl/ qist* was stressed about forty times in the Quran, and a warning against deviation from justice because of love or hostility was strongly emphasized: *"Be ever steadfast in upholding equity, bearing witness to the truth for the sake of God, even though it be against your own-selves or your parents and kinsfolk* [. . .] *Do not, then follow your own desires, lest you swerve from justice* [. . .] *"* (4:135), *"and never let your hatred of people who have barred you from the Inviolable House of Worship [al-Masjid al-Haram] lead you to aggression, and rather help one another in furthering virtue and God-consciousness, but do not help one another in furthering evil and aggression"* (5:2), *"Be ever steadfast in your devotion to God, bearing witness to the truth in all equity, and never let hatred of anyone lead you to deviating from justice; be just, this is closest to being God conscious* [. . .] *"* (5:8).

Impressively, the prominent jurist Ibn Taymiyya (d. 728 AH/ 1327 CE) mentioned that God supports the authority that observes and enforces justice even if it is infidelic, and does not support the unjust authority even if believers are in charge[(6)]. Would theocratic or partisan fears be justified, if such a conception of religious commitment is solidly established and deeply rooted? Being always honest in determining the weight of any matter, material and moral, is frequently stressed in the Quran (about 25 times), and individual responsibility is repeatedly underscored: *"and no bearer of burdens shall be made to bear another's burden"* (17:15; also 6:194; 35:18; 39:7; 53:38).

As examples of Quranic laws, in the field of worldly dealings, *mu'amalat*, we see: *"Do not devour the possession of one another wrongfully not even by way of trade which should be based on mutual agreement, and do not destroy one another"* (4:29), *"and God has made buying and selling lawful and usury unlawful"* (2:275); *"God deprives usurious gains from all blessing, whereas He blesses charitable giving with manifold increase"* (2:276), *"Whenever you give or take a credit for a stated term, set it down in writing, and let a credible scribe write it down for you equitably [...], and call upon two of your men to act as witnesses [...]. And the witness must not refuse [to give evidence] whenever they are called upon. And be not loath to write down every credit, be it small or great, together with the time at which it falls due; this is more equitable in the sight of God, more reliable as evidence, and more likely to prevent you from having doubts [later], but if, however, [the credit] is related to a merchandise which is ready to be transferred directly unto one another, you commit no wrongdoing if you do not write it down; and have witnesses when you trade with one another"* (2:282), *"and neither a scribe nor witness should suffer harm"* (2:282), *"And do not conceal what you have seen [as a witness]"* (2:283).

With regard to *ruler-ruled relations* specifically, the principles in the Quran and Sunna are few and very general, and none of them may allow any claim for theocratic shade. On the contrary, the Quran clearly states that the rulers are those *"from among you who are entrusted with authority by you"* (4:59). The Sunni jurists emphasize that rulership is a *contract* between the ruler and the ruled with *mutual rights and obligations for each party*: the ruler has to serve the people, satisfy their needs, and rule with justice, while the ruled have to support the ruler and obey the laws. Ibn Taymiyya notes that it includes similar aspects to contracts of both guardianship and procuration [7].

Since the divine revelation represented in the Quran and Sunna did not indicate in detail the legal rules about worldly dealings, aside from in family matters, the human mind is authorized by the Prophet to reach a proper judgment whenever a direct rule in the Quran and Sunna cannot be found (tradition reported by Ibn Hanbal, Abu Dawud, al-Tirmidhi, al-Nisa'i and Ibn Majah). Afterall, in all worldly dealings, including family matters, the texts of the Quran and Sunna are limited and the change in worldly dealings is unlimited and unceasing. The human mind is, besides the divine message, the invaluable divine gift to humankind.

The human intellectual effort in reaching the most appropriate judgment to the best of human capability, *ijtihad*, has been the main source for developing Islamic law to meet the ever-changing circumstances at different times and places. Islamic jurisprudence has been rich and dynamic through such intellectual methods of *ijtihad* as: *analogy (qiyas), preference (istihsan)*, and consideration of a *particular public benefit* that may not be specifically and explicitly required or rejected in the texts of the Quran and Sunna (*al-maslaha al-mursala*). Furthermore, a general principle of Shari'a is *that everything is originally considered lawful as long as it is not proven otherwise,* according to the Quranic statement: "It is He who has created for you *all that is on earth*" (2:29, also 45:14). Custom, through its difference from place to place and change from time to time, has its weight in the juristic rulings.

How may a theocracy be claimed with regard to Islamic law or the Muslim state, if there is a place for intellectual sources in Shari'a? Shari'a considers rulership as a contract of mutual rights and obligations between the ruler and the ruled, and stresses the permanent right and responsibility of the people in expressing their opinions

311

about the conduct of state affairs by initially advising the rulers (*nasiha*) (as stated in the Prophet's tradition reported by Muslim, Ibn Hanbal, Abu Dawud, al-Tirmidhi, and al-Nisa'i), or by enjoining the doing of what is right and good and forbidding what is wrong and evil in general, *'al-'amr bi-al-ma'ruf wa al-nahy 'an al-munkar'* (3:104, 110).

Furthermore, Muslims are allowed to adopt any human intellectual or practical experience if it is proven to be wise and helpful and does not contradict any of the teachings of the Quran and Sunna. The Quran urges listening, evaluating, and following whatever is good and constructive: "Give, then, this glad tiding to My servants who *listen* to all that is said, and *then follow the best of it;* it is they whom God has graced with His guidance, and it is they who truly use their minds" (39:17-18). The Prophet teaches, "The believer is an ever searcher for wisdom; wherever he (/she) finds it he (/she) is the most deserving of it" [reported by al-Tirmidhi]. Land-taxation, trade customs, administrative organization (sing. *diwan*, pl. *dawawin*), and currency were adopted from historical administrative precedents that Muslims adapted and applied to their circumstances and needs, then developed and incorporated into Islamic law [8].

The State is Run by Civil Servants, not Clergy

The Muslim state was administered by civil servants who were trained in administrative and financial matters and called "*kuttab*" (scribes, clerks; "*katib*" sing.) [9], and were under the supervision of the state minister, *al-wazir*. None of those were educated as specialists in religion. The distinction between the *katib* and the *'alim* was even apparent in dress. Abbasid caliphs and Muslim monarchs used to chose their ministers from civil servants, not from

312

the *'ulama*, as they considered the former to be the ones qualified to run the state. As a result, some sensitivity or even rivalry developed between the two groups. Adam Mez accurately observed that such a group of *kuttab* represented the most distinction between the Muslim state and Europe during the early Middle Ages, where no one could work in the state departments except those who were related to the religious and clerical culture [10].

Under the Abbasids, a supreme court dealt with cases of serious injustice, especially what might be committed by highly ranked persons in the government or the society. It was presided over by the Abbasid caliph, the minister or a delegate chosen by either; and in regions of the state, the court was presided over by the regional governor. The judge was simply a member of the court among others, such as jurists and scribes. Von Grunebaum described that tribunal as "worldly" [11].

Non-Muslims in the Muslim State

In his time, al-Mawardi indicated many principal positions in the Muslim state that could be occupied by its non-Muslim people, *dhimmi*s. At the top of these was "the executive minister/ *wazir al-tanfidh.*" A *dhimmi* could also be an executive collector of *zakat*, land-tax (*al-kharaj*) or other revenues, an administrator of a certain locality or work, or an employee in the military [12]. These were positions that the jurists allowed for non-Muslims in the Muslim state, during the religion-bound circumstances of the Middle Ages.

In practice, non-Muslims were ministers in Persia, Egypt, and Andalusia. Philip Hitti wrote of the Abbasid society: "Even in cities, Christians and Jews often held

313

important financial, clerical, and professional positions. This led to open jealousy on the part of the Moslem populace [...] ".

Albert Hourani explained that "At a high level, some Jews and Christians held important positions at the court of certain rulers in their administrations. In Egypt of the Fatimids, Ayyubids and Mamluks, Coptic officials were important in the financial service. Non-Muslim officials increased and became so influential in the administration of Muslim states that Muslims might protest and even rebel. They might have their own judges who settled the disputes between parties of the same faith" [13].

Non-Muslim people of the Muslim state shared fairly with the Muslims the public services, such as irrigation, medical treatment, and social assistance for the needy. The jurists stressed that justice in taxation and fair collection should be secured for all tax-payers, whoever they may be. The head-tax paid by the *dhimmi*s, *jizya*, was considered a symbolic participation in the defense charges in return for their exemption from military service, and whenever *dhimmi*s were entrusted with a defense responsibility, they were exempted from playing the head-tax [14]. No discrimination in residence was imposed, for no particular areas were assigned in the cities by the authorities for the residence of any non-Muslim, although naturally a deliberate gathering of some in a certain neighborhood might take place [15].

Non-Muslims might occasionally suffer injustice under a Muslim ruler, but this occurred also to Muslims. As von Grunebaum accurately has elaborated: "Individual rulers might harm the communities or some prominent members – this happened regularly after a period of conspicuous prosperity and political ascendancy – but the Muslims themselves were equally exposed to the arbitrary and unrestrained power of the monarch" [16].

Muslim Civilization: Developed by All, Contributed to by All

Muslims benefited from all the available civilizational heritages around them, and offered their civilizational contribution to all others, including non-Muslim Europe in particular.

- *Muslims actively benefited from the heritages* around them: Greek-Roman-Byzantine, Persian, Indian, and others. As Philip Hitti indicates: "In Syria, in Egypt, in al-Iraq, in Persia [and later I may add India], they [the Muslim Arabs] sat as pupils at the feet of the peoples they subdued. And what *acquisitive pupils* they proved to be". They tried enthusiastically to learn and to develop "that body of knowledge enshrined in books written in the Arabic language by men who flourished chiefly during the caliphate, and were themselves Persians, Syrians, Egyptians, or Arabians; Christians, Jewish or Moslems, and who may have drawn some of their material from Greek, Aramaean, Indo-Persian or other sources" (17).

Majid Fakhry states,

"Not only did the new religion provide the Arabs with a *coherent world view* and enable them to *transcend* the narrow confines of their *tribal existence*, but it thrust them almost forcibly upon the cultural stage of the ancient Near East, setting before them the dazzling treasures of older civilizations [...], Greek philosophy and science, Persian literary and political wisdom, Indian medicine and mathematics [...], the Arabs were able, throughout a period extending from the downfall of the Persian and Byzantine empires in the seventh century to the early Renaissance

316

in the fourteenth, to assimilate almost the whole body of ancient learning, to integrate it into their own culture, and to raise the level of knowledge in the fields of mathematics, medicine, astronomy, and philosophy to unprecedented heights. In fact, they served for almost half a millennium as the sole custodians of Greek and other ancient learning, at a time when Western Europe was plunged in semi darkness [...] ".

In the words of John Badear,

"The distinctive and richly hued civilization that characterized the Muslim world at its height was formed 'in situ' [in the natural position]. It came into being within the new state, giving identity and character to the new order that resulted from the conquests of Islam as it spread among alien peoples. Its major components were at hand within the varied life and traditions of the subjugated people – classical literature, Hellenistic thought, Byzantine institutions, Roman law, Syrian scholarship, Persian art. At first these resources were appropriated directly, with little reshaping. Before long, however, they were more selectively utilized, combined into novel patterns that served as both resource and stimulus to creative Muslim scholarship. The result was not simply a montage of bits and pieces of disparate culture. It was a *new creation* with its own distinctive pattern, infused with a new spirit and expressing a new social order. *This development of a distinctly Islamic culture* reached full stride about the time that the Arab leadership of the empire began to wane [...] Within this new empire *the diverse cultures and societies of the ancient world were shaken out of their regionalism* and forced into *new and fruitful interaction* [...] Before the end of the first Arab dynasty, that of the Umayyads, classical works were being translated into Arabic, impressive buildings inspired by classical designs were being built, and

Arab scholarship in grammar and literature, influenced by Greek patterns, began to flourish. By the time the Arabs lost their preeminence in rule, non-Arab materials had been established in the life and thought of the Islamic community. At the same time, *the diverse subject peoples showed and absorbed one another's culture.* Barriers to *travel* through the Mediterranean and eastern lands were broken down, and subjects flocked from the provinces to the heart of the empire, where they met and mingled in a new relationship" [18].

• *The efforts of Arabs and non-Arabs, of Muslims and non-Muslims combined in building the Muslim civilization* all over the Muslim lands throughout the successive centuries. Its contribution might be material in the various applied economic fields of agriculture, industry, and commerce, or might be intellectual in the various fields of knowledge, whether in hard sciences or humanities. People of different ethnicities and faiths were all partners in developing what became known as "Muslim civilization."

As von Grunebaum accurately stated,

"An ever growing number of the great masters of the Arabic language was recruited from people of non-Arab ancestry. Imperceptibly, *Arabic civilization becomes Muslim civilization, and it is the spontaneous collaboration of the best minds of the Empire's nationalities* that account for the stupendous rise of this civilization in those two hundred years, from 750 to 950, so breathlessly crowded with cultural exploit in the most disparate areas of human accomplishment. It might be suggested [...] that Arab leadership declined just *when the Muslim, and to a certain extent also the non-Muslim, population had successfully assimilated the two great gifts the Arabs had to bestow – their language and their faith.* And it is obvious that under the hands of the

318

Arabicized Muslim both this language and this faith gained such literary and spiritual richness as could never have been evolved in the isolation of the peninsula [...] Greek culture permeated the Roman Empire, but the Greek remained barred from political power. Persian influence on the development of the Islamic world, comparable in many ways to that excercized by the Greeks on the Latin West, was promoted by the leading positions in the government which Persian Muslims attained under the Abbasid dynasty. It was not only the etiquette of the court which became Persianized, or the style of the administration, Iranian thinking habits, Iranian prejudices, Iranian social and economic traditions, even outright Iranian nationalism were introduced in the capital albeit under the cloak of the Arabic language and under careful, if upon occasions somewhat specious, preservation of Islamic orthodoxy" [19].

The abundant and varied material resources of the extensive Muslim lands, their geographic advantages, and the diverse human resources, could not have brought about through their interaction such a flourishing civilization unless *fairness and harmony* dominated through constructive and effective culture and by means of capable, just and indiscriminate civil institutions: governmental and non-governmental. With such enormous potential, as Hourani puts it,

"it was possible there to grow up strong governments, large cities, international trade, and a flourishing countryside, maintaining the conditions of each other's existence [...] Urban demand and the relative ease of communications gave new directions and methods of organization to the long distance trade, [...] From Basra and Siraf, trade with the east was mainly carried on by Iranian, Arab or Jewish merchants, on Arab ships sailing to the ports of western India or even beyond, at one time they went as far as China [...] They went southwards also, to southern and western Arabia and east Africa [...] from Baghdad [goods] could be carried by the Syrian desert routes to Syria and Egypt, or through Anatolia to Constantinople and Trebizond, or by the great route which went from Baghdad to Nisaphur in north eastern Iran, and thence to Central Asia and China [...] along the southern coast [of the Mediterranean, trade was] linking Spain and Maghrib with Egypt and Syria, with Tunisia as the entrepot [...] along [it] many of the merchants [were] Jews [...] Strong governments and large cities could not live without a productive countryside, but the countryside in its turn could not flourish unless there were a strong government and cities to invest in production [...] Landholders who accumulated money in trade or other ways could use it for agricultural production, and with the help of their capital new techniques were brought in [...] By such improvements the agricultural surplus was enlarged and this, together with the growth of manufacture and trade, increased the importance of money in the economy of the Near East and the Mediterranean basin. An internationally recognized monetary system grew up [...] Jews of the Muslim cities also played an important part in long distance trade with the ports of Mediterranean Europe, and until Mamluk time, with those of the Indian Ocean. Among the crafts, those concerned with drugs and with gold and silver tended to be in the hands of Jews or Christians, working for themselves or for Muslims" [20].

Under such a climate of tolerance which Mez considered unique in middle ages, works on comparative religion were compiled, including *al-Fisal* by Ibn Hazm (d. 456 AH/ 1064 CE), *al-Milal wa al-Nihal* by al-Shihristani (d. 548 AH/ 1153 CE) and al-Bayruni's (d. 440 AH/ 1048 CE) work on the religions of India for which he embarked upon a study of the Sanskrit language [21].

- *The Muslim civilization reflected the diversity of its developers within a unity* of the Islamic common basics. Von Grunebaum writes on "Unity in Diversity,"

"the self-identification as a Muslim of a 'nationalistic' Persian of the Samanid period would appear perfectly legitimate, in as much as he would continue to accept the Islamic axioms of monistic theism and prophetism as well as the value judgment which dedicates the life of man to the service of God. It is only within this intellectual – emotional framework, that he strives after the political independence of his people and the revival of the cultural glories of the Iranian past. Under the surface of the Muslim identification, no end of changes may occur, but they will hardly ever affect the identification as such. We can perhaps generalize in societal terms with regard to *the structure of such a super-national civilization* by viewing it, not as one closely knit organism, but rather as a vast number of groups which may almost be described as self-sufficient. Islam superimposes 'a common veneer of general religious culture,' but does not cause those groups 'to lose the peculiar shade of mystical-magical feeling of their own particular life' [...] The cultural area united by the Gemeinfuhl of the followers of the Prophet has always harbored a multitude of local civilizations of greater or lesser completeness and of varying independence with regard to the dominant strain of Islamic civilization; and it cannot be said that this situation has changed significantly in our day."

Such unity and variety in Muslim civilization may be significantly obvious in Muslim *art.* Richard Ettinghausen wrote:

"in spite of the apparent uniform character of Islamic art, everybody who becomes familiar with its various aspects realizes more and more the *tremendous variety in the different regions and even in the changing periods within a single territory*. These differences are so marked that if we take, for instance, pottery, one of the commonest decorated materials, we can date within a century, sometimes within a half or a quarter of a century, any archaeological site where shards have been found, and gain at times also information about influences of trade or of migratory workers. Even in instances where we have not been able to establish specific dates or places of origin for certain objects, we are confident that we will be able to solve these questions once we have become familiar with more material and have discovered documented examples [...] What is actually more intriguing, yet more difficult to establish, than this state of diversity, are the various factors which, through interaction and integration, constantly helped to reinforce the strongly felt *universal aspect* of Muslim art [...] What brings about the great variety in Islam is the *underlying ethnic and cultural diversity of its constituent people* and the fact that the *patrons of the arts were secular,* usually being the members of the ruling dynasties and families. Once the central and universal power of the caliphate was on the wane, rulers of more distant regions who had made themselves independent permitted and even instigated new styles which thus express new political situations, especially secessions" [22].

With regard to religious diversity, von Grunebaum observed that

"The social order of the Islamic world accommodated non-Muslims as well as Muslims. Both groups lived under the same basic conditions, and the eagerness to assert rank

and power affected the Jew and the Christian as it did the Muslim. It would seem that outside the capital the religious groups lived fairly apart, except for their cooperation in official business. But the yardsticks of social success, the mechanisms of social advancement or decline, appear to have been the same everywhere within the dar al-Islam [...] The mores and even the personal law of the religious communities differed to a considerable extent, but the *fundamental social values were held in common*. The three great religious groups evinced the same attitude toward power and the government" [23].

- *The Muslim civilization was open to the world,* and its contributions were evident and manifest for all who might watch or benefit. The prestige of the Muslim civilization or the Byzantine civilization was felt in the territory of each by the other. Von Grunebaum wrote:

"Muslim civilization attracted the non-Muslims far beyond the spell usually cast by ideas and habits of a dominating group or groups of lesser standing and influence. Not only were the contemporaries conscious of the *higher standard of living of the Muslim world and its material superiority* in general, which, incidentally, merely means the perpetuation of the unequal distribution of wealth between East and West in the last centuries of antiquity, but those that did come in *contact with Arab thought and Arab manner* often responded with reluctant admiration and not infrequently found themselves imitating Muslim ways. The splendor of Cordova dazzled the eyes and stirred the imagination of the Latin world [...] The Spanish Christians of the ninth century neglected their classical tradition in favor of Arabic [...] The Franks who settled in the East in the wake of the Crusades accepted a good many customs of their Muslim neighbors" [24].

Latin translations brought Muslim works on medicine first to Europe, in which Gerard of Cremona (d. 1187) and Michael Scot in Toledo, Constantine the Africanus (d. 1087) who was attached to the medical School of Salerno, and Faraj ibn Salim the Sicilian Jew had a distinguished role. Latin translations also brought Muslim works of philosophy to Europe, as well as Greek philosophy that was transmitted to Europe via the Muslim Arabs. Hitti states:

"This influx into Western Europe of a body of new ideas, mainly philosophic, marks the *beginning of the end of the 'Dark Ages'* and the dawn of the scholastic period. Kindled by contact with Arab thought and quickened by fresh acquaintance with ancient Greek lore, the interest of Europeans in scholarship and philosophy let them on to an independent and rapidly developing intellectual life of their own, whose fruits we still enjoy" [25].

Secular as Simply Non-Clerical

Obviously, the Muslim state and the Muslim civilization in the middle ages can not be definitively characterized as theocratic, nor even be considered as opposite to the perception of *"secular" in its essence*, although naturally it could not be described as utterly secular. A balanced equation between religious commitment and religious freedom mostly dominated. Adam Mez rather observed that the greatest difference between the "Muslim empire" and Europe, which was entirely Christian in the Middle Ages, was *the existence of a huge number of the followers of other religions, the dhimmis, among the Muslims*, and their existence initially obstructed – in his view – the formation of a Muslim political unity among Muslim peoples [26]. Such a view may not be completely accurate, but it shows how the non-Muslims enjoyed a particular socio-cultural and even political situation or formed a specific non-integrated entity within the Muslim state.

On the same subject, but in a different vein, von Grunebaum wrote, "It is remarkable how tenaciously these non-Muslim communities maintained themselves throughout and beyond the Middle Ages, and it is equally remarkable to observe how little the Muslim state was really hampered in its operation by the dead weight of those semi-foreign organizations within its structure" [27]. Such observations underscore the distinctive place and at the same time the interaction of the non-Muslims within and with the Muslim people, and the genuine, enduring and tenacious existence and activities of the non-Muslim entities that were accepted and tolerated by the Muslim state itself, whatever reservations and disagreement about certain elements may have existed.

325

I hope that the Islamists and the secularists both would return to the essence and the basics of the secular state as it was initially understood, and the Muslim state as it mostly existed in history, devoid of later accumulations and exaggerations on both sides. It is obvious that *"secularism"* after being an ideology, was exposed to augmentation, and its conception and implementation vary between countries, and even between politicians and scholars within the same country. On the other hand, the *"Muslim state"* or the "Islamic state" as it is sometimes called, is now portrayed by some Islamists as the state established in Medina under the leadership of the Prophet (1-11 AH/ 622-632 CE) and the early caliphate from Abu Bakr to Ali (11-40 AH/ 632-660 CE), ignoring all the qualitative and characteristic changes – whether acceptable or not – that followed through long successive centuries. These are often considered as deviations from the right way drawn by the precedents, Sunna, of the Prophet and the Rightly-guided Caliphs.

But ignoring the long historical developments of the Muslim state, while focusing on the most recent developments of the ideology of secularism, have led to such an extreme widening of the gap between the two sides that it has seemed unbridgeable. Social terms always allow a variance of views and a continuous change in theoretical definition and in practical implementation. Concepts related to human behavior are different from the "truths" that may be established in the experimental material sciences, instead representing the dynamism of human thoughts and actions.

It is my hope that the conception of *"religion,"* *"Islam,"* and the *"Muslim state"* would be better crystallized and clarified in the contemporary Muslim mind, and that the same may happen for the conception of the *"secular state"* with secularalists. Then both can co-exist side by side, interact and cooperate, contributing together to the universal intellectual enrichment, and allowing constructive universal engagement of the spiritual, intellectual dynamics of religion with all human hearts and minds, avoiding any isolation or exclusion of either.

The secular state initially came about to secure religion from the interference of the state, and to prevent the frequent misuse or abuse of religion by state authorities. Islam was not an exception within this general historical phenomenon, dispite the fact that it has no church or clergy as they are understood and established in other religions. If the secular trend remains loyal to its anti-clerical origin, and is freed from developments that were unfavorable towards religion, it may help to meet the essence of justice, fairness, and objectivity of the Muslim state, and avoid any misuse or abuse of religion by the state.

In any case, the *'ulama*, as citizens and as public figures, would naturally maintain their rights in criticizing the authorities. Subsequently, the people and their political institutions may be influenced by this criticism from such people of religious identification. In a similar vein, the Anglican Church and its leader the Archbishop of Canterbury have not rarely expressed their criticism of certain governmental policies; after that, the people may or may not support the criticism of the church leaders, through their political rights and their institutions. The United States often represents – perhaps due to certain historical circumstances – an overstated model of secularism, which sometimes faces criticism from sincere secularists, while undergoing tendencies of moderation or alteration among thinkers and politicians.

Notes

(1)   "Secularism", *The New Encyclopaedia Britannica*, vol. IX, p.18.

(2)   "Secular," "Secularism," *Webster's New Collegiate Dictionary,* Springfield, MA: G. & C. Merriam Co., 1974, pp. 1044, 1045 respectively.

(3)   Connolly, William E., *Why I Am Not a Secularist*, Minneapolis & London: University of Minnesota Press, 1999, pp. 4-7.

        As an example for underscoring contemporary conceptual and moral shortcomings in materially developed countries see *"al-Thaqafa al-Insaniyya wa Falsafa al-Tarbiyya fi al-Sharq wa al-Gharb"*, an international symposium organized by U.N.E.S.C.O., in New Delhi, Arabic translation by Khuri, Antoine, Beirut: Dar al-Nashr lil-Jami'yyin, n.d.

(4)   A Prophet's tradition reported by Ibn Hanbal and al-Hakim in *al-Mustadrak* on the authority of Abd al-Rahman ibn 'Awf; see also Ibn Kathir, Isma'il ibn 'Umar, *al-Bidaya wa al-Nihaya*, vol. 2, pp. 270-2.

(5)   Rodinson, Maxime, "The Western Image and Western Studies of Islam" in Schacht, Joseph & Bosworth, C.E. (ed.), *The Legacy of Islam,* Oxford: Oxford University Press, 1979, pp. 37-8.

(6)   Ibn Taymiyya, Ahmad ibn Abd al-Halim, *al-Hisba*, Kuwait: Maktaba Dar al-Arqam, 1983, pp. 9-10, 91.

(7)   See al-Mawardi, Ali ibn Muhammad ibn Habib, *al-Akham al-Sultaniyya,* pp. 5-9; al-Farra', Abu Ya'la Muhammad ibn al-Husayn, *al-Ahkam al-Sultaniyya,* ed. al-Faqqi, Muhammad Hamid, Surabaya, Indonesia: Maktaba Ahmad ibn Sa'd ibn Nabhan, 1974, pp. 19-20, 23-6; Ibn Taymiyya, Ahmad ibn Abd al-Halim, *al-Siyasa al-Shari'iyya,* p. 13; al-Rayyis, Muhammad Diya' al-Din, *al-Nazariyyat al-Siyasiyya al-Islamiyya,* Cairo: Maktaba Nahdat Misr, 1957, pp. 167-8.

(8)   al-Baladhuri, *Futuh al-Buldan,* pp. 196-7, 241-2, 298, 435-6, 443-4, 451-4; Abu Yusuf, Ya'qub ibn Ibrahim, *al-Kharaj,* pp. 92-93, 145-6; al-Mawardi, *al-Ahkam al-Sultaniyya,* pp. 153-4, 174-5, 199-200, 202-3, 215-6.

(9)   See for a juristic formulation of the responsibilities of the "diwan scribe or clerk" (*katib al-diwan*) al-Mawardi, *al-Ahkam al-Sultaniyya,* pp. 215-218.

(10)   Mez, *al-Hadara al-Islamiyya,* vol. 1, pp 160-1, 321.

(11)   al-Mawardi, *al-Ahkam al-Sultaniyya,* pp. 79-84; von Grunebaum, *Medieval Islam,* p. 164.

(12)   al-Mawardi, *al-Ahkam al-Sultaniyya,* pp. 27, 60, 116, 130, 152, 209.

(13)   Mez, *al-Hadara al-Islamiyya,* vol. 1, pp. 179-180, 93-5, 105-109; Hitti, Philip K., *History of the Arabs,* p. 353, see also p. 537; Hourani, Albert, *A History of the Arab Peoples,* New York: Warner Books, 1991, p. 117.

(14)   al-Baladhuri, *Futuh al-Buldan,* pp. 162, 164, 142, 185-6; Abu Yusuf, *al-Kharaj*, pp. 129-130.

(15)   Abu Yusuf, *al-Kharaj,* pp. 105-106, 115-121, 136, 155-6; Mez, *al-Hadara al-Islamiyya*, vol.1, pp. 92, 93.

(16)   von Grunebaum, *Medieval Islam,* p. 180.

(17)   Hitti, *History of the Arabs,* pp. 240-1.

(18)   Fakhry, Majid, "Philosophy and History," quoted in Badeau, John Stothoff, "The Arab Role in Islamic Culture", in *The Genius of Arab Civilization*, ed. Badeau, John S., Fakhri, Majid et.al., New York: New York University Press, 1975, pp. 55, 6, 9-10.

(19)   von Grunebaum, *Medieval Islam,* pp. 201-202.

(20)   Hourani, *A History of the Muslim Peoples*, pp. 43-46, 117-118.

(21)   Mez, *al-Hadara al-Islamiyya*, vol. 1, pp. 75, 87-8, 384-6, vol. 2, pp. 282, 290.

(22)   Von Grunebaum, Gustave, "The Problem: Unity in Diversity;" Ettinghasuen, Richard, "Interaction and Integration in Islamic Art", in von Grunebaum, Gustave (editor), *Unity and Variety in Muslim Civilization,* Chicago & London: University of Chicago Press, 1955, pp. 19-20, 107-8 respectively.

(23)   von Grunebaum, *Medieval Islam,* p. 173.

(24)   *Ibid.*, pp. 54-58.

(25)   Hitti, *History of the Arabs,* pp. 578-580.

(26)   Mez, *al-Hadara al-Islamiyya,* vol. 1, p. 75.

(27)   von Grunebaum, *Medieval Islam,* p. 184.

Afterword

- Just as the democratic and socialist trends dominated the period from the late 18th to the middle of the 20th century, *"human rights"* have represented the essence and spirit of our times, since the middle of the last century onwards, with all their connotations of peace, democracy, social justice and equal opportunities and pluralism. Following the basic declaration of human rights issued by the General Assembly of the United Nations in December 1948, several world conferences focused in detail on specifications of human rights, such as children's and women's rights. Later, the rights of development were underscored as developing countries felt that an important factor in their deprivation has been the long domination and exploitation of developed countries through the colonial and post-colonial periods. The perpetrators of this domination should be held responsible for it, they felt, and accordingly they should have to pay back for what they did via financial and technological assistance. Globalization brought more attention to these causes, and modern technology has provided universal mass communication and information. On the other hand, globalization has led developing countries to feel more threatened by the fierce domination of developed ones, and "human rights" have begun to include a clear dimension of universal economic justice and cooperative development.

- *Islam*, being based on the faith in and the worship of the One God, spreads constantly liberating waves from absolute submission to any power rather than the Lord Creator, be it cosmic forces, fictitious superstitions, or human individuals or groups: "[...] that we shall worship none but God, and that we shall never consider any human being from among us a god besides Him" (3:69). All human beings are equal, and God only is the Supreme Being: "and none could be compared to Him" (112:4). No human individual is beyond accountability (21:23). Such faith in the One God *liberates*

335

the human mind and heart from the arrogance of the ego as well as from humiliating weakness, since times of power and weakness cycle in human life (3:140). Consequently, the genuine believer in God can often maintain his/her balance and stability, in good times he/she is thankful and grateful to God, in others he/she is patient and firm [a Prophet's tradition reported by Muslim and Ibn Hanbal].

Furthermore, the belief in the One God strengthens and deepens the social equality and cooperation between the haves and have-nots, who all have to work together honestly and fairly in developing their human and material resources with which they are entrusted: "It is He who brought you into being out of earth, and it is He who has *entrusted you with the development there*" (11:61). Accordingly, every human being has to spend from his/her personal and material resources granted to him/her by the Lord Creator to fulfill that responsibility of human and world development. *Human dignity* for all the children of Adam, with its strong connection to other physical, psychological-spiritual, and intellectual merits, is God's appropriation to the entire human species since its creation. In addition, human beings are granted by God abilities for universal movement in every possible way, thus dealing with natural resources through efficient preservation, productive development and fair distribution in order to secure for humankind the good things of life (17:70).

Islam then, as all God's messages, is liberating the human individual and the human society from within: "God enjoins *justice* and [going beyond justice to] doing what is best, and giving one's kinsfolk, and He forbids all that is shameful and all that runs counter to reason and common sense, as well as *transgression*" (16:90), "[...the Prophet...] who enjoins upon them the doing of what is right and good, and forbids them the doing of what is wrong and bad, and makes lawful to them the good things of life and forbids them from the bad things, and lifts from them *their burdens and the shackles* which have been upon them" (7:157). Human dignity, combining both rights and responsibilities, and justice that is preferably exceeded by magnanimity and benevolence, represents the cornerstone of Islam, and the essence of worshipping the One Lord God with His all-grace as reflected in his dealing with His entire creation. The Lord Creator establishes the humans' relation with Him through His messages, so that they would have their positive consequences on human behavior with other humans and with the entire creation.

God's messages settle the human mind and heart on worshipping the One God as the utmost goal in order to secure human rights and dignity, and cannot be considered as merely a theological or epistemological matter. God is in no need of being recognized or denied (51:56-58): "O my servants! If you all, from the first created to the last, agree to follow the most righteous among you, this would add nothing to My dominance, and if you all from the first created to the last agree to follow the most iniquitous among you, this would take off nothing from My dominance [...] It is but your deeds that are counted by Me for you, and I give you back your due in full" (a Prophet's tradition in which God's speech is expressed in the Prophets words, *hadith qudsi*, reported by Muslim).

As reported by al-Tabari (d. 310 AH/ 922 CE) in his *History* within the annals of the Muslim conquest of Persia, a Muslim military leader, Rabi' ibn 'Amer was asked by the Persian military leader Rustum about the Muslims' mission. He answered that the Muslim's goals are "to turn the human beings *from worshipping people to worshipping God, from*

337

the narrowness of the world to its breadth, and from the injustice of rulers to the justice of Islam." Contemporary Muslims have to demonstrate their commitment to securing human rights and dignity throughout the entire world. This would enable them to be a constructive party in contemporary universal thinking and civilization, and to infuse a spiritual moral constituent within it.

• Such an assurance of and a support for human rights and dignity, within Muslim countries and throughout the entire world, has to be within legitimate informative and political means, cooperating with all supporters of human rights all over the world whatever their faith or ideology may be. Muslims should *abandon the idea of imposing Islam from above in Muslim countries, or confronting injustice and violation of human rights with violence through the world. Violence and counter violence, group terrorism and state-terrorism, become associated with and follow one another in a vicious circle.* As a result of the modern technology of mass destruction there is no winner, and it is the innocent civilians who are the everyday victims.

Could Muslims allow "the enjoining of what is right and good, and forbidding what is wrong and bad" and let "jihad" *be an informational and political struggle for securing human dignity and justice* in all their dimensions within Muslim countries and throughout the entire world, cooperating with all who are committed to this noble cause nationally and universally?

• This would require reviewing certain inherited ideas about "the other" throughout Muslim historical practice and intellectual heritage, in light of the genuine guidance of the permanent and binding divine sources, and the contemporary dominant thinking about universal peace, human rights, democracy and even secularism.

As Arnold Toynbee rightfully and concisely pointed out, "All societies exert a *constant reciprocal influence on each other.* The extant representatives of the species are being influenced, in different degrees, *not only by all their contemporaries, but also by the legacies of all societies that have come and gone up to date."* He added:

"The same unprecedented scientific and technological advances that have unified the world by 'annihilating distance', have been put into Mankind's power to annihilate itself with atomic weapons. We are now waking up to the truth that we have unintentionally put ourselves in a new position, in which Mankind may have to choose between the two extreme alternatives of committing genocide and learning to live henceforward as a single family [...]. In a world that has been unified in both space and time, a study of human affairs must be comprehensive if it is to be effective [...] In order to save Mankind, we have to learn to *live together in concord in spite of traditional differences* [...]. In order to live together in concord successfully, we have to *know each other,* and knowing each other includes knowing *each other's past,* since human life, like the rest of the phenomenal Universe, *can be observed by human minds only as it presents itself to them on the move through time."* In another arena, Toynbee underscored that Ibn Khaldun (d. 808 AH/ 1406 CE) was "the most illuminating interpreter of the morphology of history that has appeared anywhere in the world so far. The Muslims' concern for history is not surprising, since Islam [...] is embedded in the history of human affairs [...]. Since curiosity is the generator of intellectual action, an imperative and pertinacious curiosity is the intellectual worker's prime need. If his curiosity is strong enough, it can move mountains" [1].

Earlier, also reviewing the Muslim historical and intellectual heritage in light of contemporary change, the Muslim poet and philosopher of the Indian-Pakistani subcontinent Muhammad Iqbal (d. 1938) stressed that: "The task before the modern Muslim is immense. He has to *rethink the whole system of Islam without completely breaking with the past.* Perhaps the first Muslim who felt the urge of a new spirit in him was Shah Wali Ullah of Delhi (d. 1762)." The author added:

"As a cultural movement, Islam rejects the old static view of the universe, and reaches a dynamic view [...] *The ultimate spiritual basis of all life as conceived by Islam is eternal and reveals itself in variety and change.* A society based on such a conception of reality must reconcile in its life the *categories of permanence and change* [...] But eternal principles when they are understood to exclude all possibilities of change, which – according to the Quran – is one of the greatest 'signs' of God, tend to immobilize what is essentially mobile in its nature [...] What then is the *principle of movement in the structure of Islam?* This is known as '*ijtihad.*' "

To practice a constructive *ijtihad*, Iqbal elaborated:

"we must distinguish traditions of a purely legal import from those which are of a non-legal character. With regard to the former, there arises a very important question *as to how far they embody the pre-Islamic usages of Arabia which were in some cases left intact,* and in others *modified* by the Prophet. It is difficult to make this discovery, for our early writers

340

do not always refer to pre-Islamic usages. Nor it is possible to discover *that the usages, left intact by express or tacit approval of the Prophet, were intended to be universal in their application.* Shah Wali Ullah has a very illuminating discussion on the point. I reproduce here the sustenance of his views. The prophetic method of teaching, according to Shah Wali Ullah, is that generally speaking, *the law revealed by a prophet takes especial notice of the habits, ways and peculiarities of the people to whom he is specifically sent.* The prophet who aims at all-embracing principles, however, can neither reveal different principles for different people, nor leaves them to work out their own rules of conduct. His method is to *train one particular people, and to use them as a nucleus for the building of a universal Shari'at.* In doing so, he *accentuates the principles underlying the social life of all mankind, and applies them to concrete cases in the light of the specific habits of the people* immediately before him. The Shari'at values *'Ahkam'* resulting from this application 'e.g. rules relating to penalties for crimes', *are in a sense specific to that people*; and since their observances is not an end in itself, they cannot be strictly enforced in the case of future generations [...] The fact that Abu Hanifa, who had a keen insight into the universal character of Islam [...] introduced the principle of *'istihsan'*, i.e. juristic preference, which necessitates a careful study of actual conditions in legal thinking, throws further light on the motives which determined his attitude [...] It is, however, impossible to deny the fact that the scholars specialized in the Prophet's traditions, [*'al-muhaddithin'*], *by insisting on the value of the concrete case as against the tendency to abstract thinking in law,* have done the greatest service to the Law of Islam. And a further intelligent study of the literature of traditions, if used as indicative of *the spirit* in which the Prophet himself interpreted his Revelation, may still be of great help in understanding *the life-value of the*

341

legal principles enunciated in the Quran. A complete grasp of *their life-value alone* can equip us in an endeavor to *re-interpret the foundational principles*" (2).

Iqbal quoted the French philosopher Henri Bergson (d. 1941) regarding the continuous change in the human feeling and thinking: "*I change, then, without ceasing*". Iqbal added, "Thus, there is *nothing static in my inner life,* all is a constant mobility, an unceasing flow state, a perpetual flow in which there is no halt or meeting place. *Constant change, however, is unthinkable without time.* On the analogy of our inner experience, then, *conscious existence means life in time*" (3). Iqbal underlined Ibn Khaldun's emphasis of the importance of *time.* He added,

"It is this conception of life and time which is the main point of interest in Ibn Kahldun's view of history, and which justifies Flint's (Timothy, d. 1780) eulogy that 'Plato (d.347 B.C.E.), Aristotle (d.322 B.C.E.), Augustine (d. 430) were not his peers, and all others were unworthy of being even mentioned along with him'. [. . . c] onsidering the direction in which the culture of Islam had unfolded itself, *only a Muslim could have viewed history as a continuous, collective movement, a real inevitable development in time.* The point of interest in this view of history is the way in which Ibn Khaldun conceives *the process of change.* His conception is of infinite importance, because of the implication that history as a continuous movement in time, is a *genuinely creative movement* and not a movement whose path is already determined."

Iqbal stressed, "As a social movement, the aim of Islam was to make the *idea a living factor in the Muslim's daily life,* and thus silently and imperceptibly to carry it towards fuller fruition" (4).

- Muslims believe that the message of Prophet Muhammad was the final divine message to humankind, and thus it was formulated to suit every time and place. To reach this goal, the Quran – God's revealed Book to Prophet Muhammad – was presented in the appropriate flexible way, opening the door for the human mind to understand the text and to apply it according to the changing circumstances of human life in different times and places. The total number of verses in the Quran is 6,236. Of these, 260 verses are related to legal rules about worldly matters, *mu'amalat*, dealing with rulers-ruled relations, peace and war, family matters, civil and commercial affairs, and penal rules, in addition to basic procedural and judicial percepts. The remainder of the verses discuss faith in its various dimensions, the acts of worship, moral values and good manners, and history, especially information about earlier divine messages and how they successively address reform in different human communities, as well as deal with the human nature and societal development.

The Quran is not, then, merely a code of law. The style of the Quranic legal rules may vary from clear obligation or prohibition of a certain action, to the generous rewarding of good deeds, the fair punishing of evil deeds, and the gracious forgiving and rewarding of the wrong-doers who repent. Human understanding may differ about the degree of obligation or prohibition, or about the relation between the several texts related to a certain rule in the Quran and Sunna. That is why the Quranic legal verses may be described according to their formulation as having definite indication, *qat'iyy al-dalala*, or a suggested indication, *zanniyy al-dalala*. Some Quranic legal rules may indicate the reason, *'illa*, for a rule, while others leave such an indication to the human mind that can arrive at it from the general goals and principles of Shari'a, or from thinking about the most possible benefit that would be reached or the most possible harm that would be avoided by that rule in light of the pre-Islamic socio-cultural circumstances of the Arabs whom the message addressed when it was revealed. The legal rules related to worldly matters, *mu'amalat*, are decided merely for the people's benefit and well-being [5].

The Prophet's sayings and deeds, *Sunna*, have presented an interpretation, elaboration and application of the Quranic rules in the given circumstances: "and upon you We have brought down this reminder, in order to make clear to people what has ever been brought down to them, and to let them deeply reflect [over its guidance]" (16:44). The Prophet was a human being, and he used his human intellect and judgment when he met a case on which there had been no directly and explicitly related revelation. He practiced his *ijtihad* in worldly matters, especially within his authority as a leader and as a judge. We have to figure out whether his tradition – verbal or practical – might indicate in its form, content or circumstances God's revelation formulated in the Prophet's words, or whether it expressed merely the Prophet's human judgment. Besides, there were traditions related to the Prophet as a particular person that did not apply to others, such as those discussing his worship or his wives (e.g. 33:28, 30, 50-53) [6].

Because of that general and flexible way in the formulation of the legal rules in the Quran and Sunna, and because Islam was the final message revealed by God to humanity, and thus its definite sources would meet indefinite cases in different given times and places, *"ijtihad" has been the mechanism that secures the dynamism of the Islamic law "Shari'a."* The Prophet himself practiced his discretionary judgment in certain worldly matters when no divine rule had been revealed to him. He repeatedly and clearly indicated this fact: "I am but a human being, and you come to me to make a ruling in your disputes. Some may be more eloquent in voicing his [/her] argument than another, and so I rule for his [/her] benefit according to what I have heard. Whatever I give for any in my ruling which may be the right of another Muslim, it is but a piece of the hell fire, so he [/she] may take it or leave it" [reported by Malik, al-Bukhari, Muslim, Ibn Hanbal, Abu Dawud, al-Tirmidhi, al-Nisa'i, and Ibn Majah], "I am but a human being, if I order you something of your religion you take it, but if I order you something of what I personally see I am but a human being" [reported by Muslim and al-Nisa'i], "I am but a human being like you, and human view may be wrong or right, but whenever I tell you: 'God says', I never lie with regard to God" [reported by Ibn Hanbal and Ibn Majah].

The practice of *ijtihad*, then, is inseparable from the legal function in Islam. A tradition was reported by Mu'adh ibn Jabal when he was sent by the Prophet elsewhere as a judge and was asked by him how he would rule. He answered, "According to the Book of God." The Prophet, who was the most knowledgeable that the Quran might not encompass every detailed issue that might emerge, asked the newly appointed judge, "And if you do not find [the detailed case that you are looking for]?" Mu'adh answered "According the Sunna [of the Prophet]." The Prophet knew that his Sunna might also not encompass every detail that might emerge in any time or place, so he went on asking the future judge, how he would rule if he could not find how to deal with the presented case in the Sunna, and his answer simply was: "I do my best according to my view (*ajtahid ra'yi la 'alu*)". The Prophet agreed and was pleased [reported by Ibn Hanbal]. This tradition has become a significant example of the essentiality and legality of *ijtihad* to meet continuous change and the emergence of new situations. Some criticism was raised that the direct transmitters from Mu'adh were unidentified "companions" of him, but the prominent jurist Ibn al-Qayyim convincingly responded to that criticism [7].

The Prophet's Companions and their Successors, *al-Tabi'in*, practiced *ijtihad* to crystallize legal rules that respond to emerging situations, for which they could not find direct or explicit legal rules in the Quran or Sunna. They sometimes did not find the reason, *'illa*, for the rule indicated in the tradition, and so they tried to figure out the reason so that they could extend the rule to other cases wherever the same reason exists. If they found that the reason indicated in the legal rule did not exist anymore, they felt that the rule could be changed. Thus they would forbid or restrict what was allowed to secure a benefit or avoid a harm, or they might simply do what had not been done at the time of the Prophet because of an emerging common need. For example, the practice of fixing the sale prices of certain commodities – deemed unjust in a Prophet's tradition – was adopted after the Prophet's death in order to observe the interests of both the buyer and seller and respond to a public need [8].

Caliph Umar initiated many such practices. He stopped paying *Zakat* to those "whose hearts are to be won over (*al-mu'alafa qulubuhum*)" (9:60), on the grounds that Islam had been strongly established and therefore such an approach was no longer needed. He also decided that divorcing a wife three times through one pronunciation should make the marriage irrevocable, as was the case in divorcing her through three separate pronunciations, intending that the decision serve as a penalty for such a hasty action. Furthermore, Caliph Umar authorized and protected the passage of a water canal through one person's land to another's, since it would benefit the latter without causing harm to the former who would also be using its water.

In addition, some practices were initiated because they were merely beneficial, with no specific support in the Quran or Sunna, such as the collection of the Quran and the allowed circulation only of the officially accepted version. Caliph Umar did not agree to distribute the conquered lands among the fighters as booty, *ghanima*, and kept them instead in the hands of their indigenous farmers who had to pay the land tax, *kharaj*, to the public treasury, so that the benefit of the land would be secured for successive generations. It is well known that Caliph Umar followed in the annexed lands the precedents of non-Muslim administrations, such as the imposition of land-tax, *kharaj*, and the establishment of financial administration, *al-diwan*.

As the prominent contemporary jurist Muhammad Mustafa Shalabi convincingly put it:

"The Prophet's Companions looked *to Shari'a in its entirety,* observing its general principles and its comprehensiveness at the same time, so they were never stagnant, while others who refused to change the rules according to shifts in what would benefit the people and stuck to the letter, even if its purpose had not been achieved or such a literal adherence brought about pressures and hardships to people – these looked *at each text as a disconnected piece* from others, and considered each piece as eternal unchangeable law."

He strongly appealed to those responsible for executing Shari'a that they would be convinced to follow the Prophet's Companions and their Successors in their way, and thus "rethink what the scholars of *'usul* [fundamentals of Islamic law] wrote in light of the Companions and Successors' way, and devote their efforts to reforming what was written, in order to remove what might have become stuck in some minds that the door of *ijtihad* had been closed, and that Shari'a could not cope with the passing time" [(9)].

The Prophet's Companions in their majority were not textualists and literalists. Rather, they recognized not only the formal generalities of the words, but also the conceptual significance of a certain Quranic statement that applied to other expressions as: " [...] never say [to your old parents] 'ugh'" (17:22), *"Those who unjustly devour the possessions of orphans but fill their bellies with fire"* (4:10), *"And if he [the debtor] is in straitened circumstances, grant him [/her] a delay until a time of ease, and it would be for your own good – if you but knew it – to remit [the debt entirely] as a charity"* (2:280).

Such condensed and swift signals can provide a very enriching source legally and morally *"for those who are endowed with deep thinking and thoughtfulness"* – whom *the Quran cares to address.* Jurisprudence is not merely the knowledge of words and their linguistic general or particular meaning, nor the knowledge of their obvious indication, since this can be reached by any who knows the Arabic language. Jurisprudence is constituted on the understanding of the essence, depth and the wisdom behind the legal form, recognizing the reasons and purposes of laws and the inter-relations of the legal principles and texts in their entirety, so that we may figure out the goals and objectives of the law. These analytical and synthesizing capabilities are what represent the base for the process of *ijtihad* [(10)].

To secure the various people's interests in the given circumstances of time and place, a juristic area was developed called "*al siyasa al-shar'iyya*." This refers to conducting state affairs according to the general principles of Shari'a and through the practice of *ijtihad*, in order to secure the public well-being and respond to the ever-renewing needs of life. Some jurists disapproved of that new area, believing that a literal application of the texts of the Quran and Sunna is the only rightful way for Muslims to solve their developing problems. Ibn al-Qayyim put his finger skillfully and accurately on the root of such rigid and stagnant thinking: it is the "*shortcoming in knowing Shari'a, in knowing the realities of life, and in applying one to the other*." The prominent Hanbali jurist Ibn 'Aqil (d. 513 AH/ 1119 CE) indicated that '*siyasa*' is merely taking actions that let the people be as close as possible to righteousness and virtuousness and far as possible from corruption and viciousness, even if it was not decided by the Prophet nor brought down by God's revelation [11].

In this way, "*al siyasa al-shar'iyya*" represented a development of a specific legal discipline within the practice of *ijtihad*, in conducting the state affairs and responding to the special needs of the daily governmental and administrative life, with its enormous speed of changeability and variety. Later juristic works were frequently devoted specifically to this field in order to provide the rulers with the legal foundation and juristic elaboration for their administrations. Furthermore, the jurists had always been ready to respond to what the Malikis used to call "unforeseeable common exigencies/ *nawazil*," while the Hanafis used to call such emerging situations the common affliction, '*umum al-balwa*.

The juristic works on the fundamentals of jurisprudence, '*usul al-fiqh*, beginning by al-Shafi'i's work *al-Risala*, have crystallized the methods and mechanisms of the practice of *ijtihad*. This, in addition to the rise of the collections of the Prophet's traditions, are what the human effort needs to understand, analyze and synthesize the sources in order to comprehend Shari'a in its entirety, both in its general goals and purposes as well as its specific construction and formulation. Thus can Shari'a's response be secured for all legitimate human needs at different times and places.

However, the dynamism of *ijtihad* was specifically energized by the Maliki elaboration on the goals of Shari'a, *maqasid*, and the common interests of the people, *masalih*. Besides, another juristic method was developed to balance and soothe the technical strictness of analogy, *qiyas*. It was called the preference, *istihsan,* defined as "leaving in a certain case what has been ruled in similar cases for a stronger reason." *Istihsan* is different from *al-maslaha al-mursala*, which cannot be directly and explicitly referred to a specific text in the Quran and Sunna. In addition to the Malikis who were strong advocates of *al-maslaha*, it was accepted to different extents as legitimate reasoning by Hanafis and Hanbalis, and even implicitly to some degree by al-Shafi'i.

Imam Abu Hanifa was outstanding in practicing *istihsan*. Muhammad ibn al-Hasan al-Shaybani, the prominent Hanafi jurist, reported that Abu Hanifa used to debate with his companions about cases of analogy on which different views emerged, but whenever he resorted to *istihsan*, no one could match him. The Maliki prominent jurist Ibn al-Qasim quoted Malik as saying, "*Al-Istihsan* represents nine tenths of [juristic] knowledge." Its complexity stemmed in part from the fact that it was built on the consideration of a variety of factors such as an analogy with a less than obvious reason, the necessity of the circumstances, the common interest of

350

the people, the avoidance of harm and removal of hardship, and the prevailing custom [(12)].

As has been frequently pointed out, the early divine law as represented in the Quran and Sunna has significant characteristic basics: it is *gradual, and limited to a response to the needs and interests of the people through a conceptual integration of the comprehensive general principles and the particular detailed specifics. Meanwhile, the general rule in Shari'a is that all things are in principle allowed until any is proven forbidden* through definitely authentic and indicative evidence. The Prophet taught: "God has commanded obligations: do not then neglect them, and He has made determined bounds: do not then transgress them, and He has prohibited things: do not then breach them, and He has not mentioned things as a grace not because of oblivion: do not then search for them" [(13)]

In many cases, the Quran states general principles in human worldly affairs, leaving the details to each society according to its given circumstances of time and place. Examples include: "God enjoins justice, and the doing of good, and giving one's kinsfolk; and He forbids all that is shameful and that runs counter to reason and common sense, as well as transgression" (16:90); "God bids you to deliver all that you have been entrusted with to those who are entitled to it, and whenever you judge between people to judge with justice [...] Pay heed to God and the Conveyor of His message and to those who have been entrusted by you with authority; and if you have a dispute over any matter, refer it to God and the Conveyor of His message [...] " (4:58-9); "[...] and whose rule in their [common] matters is consultation among themselves; and who spend [on others or for a common cause] out of what We provide for them as sustenance" (42:38); "Do not devour one another's possessions in violation of what is right, and when you have trade, it should be based on mutual agreement" (4:29); "and neither a scribe nor a witness should suffer harm" (2:28); "And if [the debtor] is in straitened circumstances [grant him/her] a delay until a time of ease; and it would be for your own good – if you but knew it – to remit [the debt entirely] as a charity" (2:280); "[. . .] and to forgo what is due to you is more in accord with God consciousness" (2:237); "Repel the evil with something that is better" (23:96).

Moreover, the Islamic law in the Quran and Sunna has assured that its goal is to put people at ease and not to burden them: "God wills that you shall have ease, and does not will you to suffer hardship" (2:185), "God does not want to impose any hardship on you, but wants to make you pure and to bestow upon you the full measure of His favors and blessings" (5:6), "but if one is driven by necessity, neither coveting it nor exceeding his [/her] immediate need – no wrong doing shall be upon him [/her]" (2:173), "and He has so clearly spelled out to you what He has forbidden you, unless you are compelled [to do it]" (6:119). Throughout all of Shari'a, it is clear that the basic goal is to secure the people's needs and common interests [14].

Since *ijtihad* is fundamental in a law whose revealed sources represented the final message of God to humanity, intellectual approaches to practicing *ijtihad* have been elaborated upon by the jurists. Differences in conclusions of *ijtihad* have always existed according to the different circumstances of given times and places, in addition to the individual difference of merits and approaches. Such a difference might be between the various juristic schools, or within the one juristic school, through different individuals, times and places.

Sometimes even one jurist might hold more than one opinion on the same issue. Imam al-Shafi'i had juristic views about certain issues when he lived in Iraq, and had different ones about the same issues after he moved to Egypt. As a prominent contemporary jurist, the former Shaykh of al-Azhar Dr. Abd al-Rahman Taj, accurately pointed out: "the change of the jurist's view and his departure from his earlier *ijtihad* is not caused in all cases by realizing what is right after being mistaken, nor by the appearance of strong evidence that was not known to him before, *but is frequently caused by the travels of the mujtahid through the countries and his acquaintance of difference of customs and usage in different countries,* and so he observes in his rulings and views that difference. Thus, both of the jurist's different views are right and to be considered, for it is a difference that was elicited by the difference of circumstances and customs" [15]. In addition, the human mind is dynamic and always works as long as the human being is alive, and its practice may lead to different conclusions at different times.

The interaction, then, between the *human mind* and the *divine sources* through the ever-changing circumstances is an unceasing one. The divine sources as well as the human mind are *both favors and blessings from God, and so they have to interact together* and not be split from or contradict one another. It is natural, then, that contemporary Muslims would be influenced by the dominant world concepts of their time about peace and human rights in all dimensions, including women's and children's rights, democracy, equal opportunity and social justice, economic development, and pluralism. Even secularism has to be considered in its present reality and concrete relations. Coping with the dominant principles in the world is a part of human nature. Such interactions may be accepted by Shari'a as well, as long as their principles do not contradict God's teachings, but instead bring about benefits for Muslim peoples by providing articulated rules that actualize and fulfill the goals and principles of Shari'a for human dignity, justice, and magnanimity in their various dimensions. Such interaction between the Muslims and the dominant principles in the world would let Islam become more conceivable to more people rather than just the Muslims. A Prophet's tradition teaches: "Wisdom is always searched for by the believer, wherever he(/she) may find it, he(/she) is the most deserving of it" [reported by al-Tirmidhi].

The historical Muslim civilization successfully assimilated the available heritages of eminent world civilizations: the Greek-Roman-Byzantine, the Persian and the Indian, as well as other traditions from Egypt, North Africa, South Spain, and Central, South, Southeast and East Asia. It selected aspects of these cultures, according to its value system. Then, the historical Muslim characteristic civilization was developed through its creativity and productivity in various fields such as science and applied sciences, architecture, philosophy, religion, history, geography, literature, and art. A symbol of such universal interaction is obvious in Ibn Rushd's book (d. 595 AH/ 1198 CE) significantly titled *Determining Words on the Correlation between Shari'a and Philosophy* (*Fasl al-Maqal fima bayna al-Shari'a wa al-Hikma mina al-Ittisal*), and al-Bayruni's book (d. shortly after 442 AH/ 1050 CE) impressively titled *Verification of the Lore Related to India: Whether Accepted or Rejected by the Mind* (*Tahqiq ma li-al-Hind min Maqula: Maqbula fi al-'Aql aw Mardhula*). Such works displayed the enriching diversity and variety of the extensive range of that civilization in place and time, as numerous historians and scholars have pointed out [16].

What is mostly needed by contemporary Muslims is the practice of a *"comprehensive ijtihad."* Such a practice considers *Shari'a as an entire consolidated and unsplittable system or legal body.* Through such a vision we see the entire Shari'a in a new light, free from the fractioning seen in the juristic heritage. We recognize the inter-relation between one rule and another, see their interaction with the entire legal body, and conceive of Shari'a in its entirety as general goals and principles, or particular details in the light of contemporary universal wisdom. In this way, the miraculous and the challenging merits of the Quran will always be evident as indicated in the Prophet's tradition: "its wonders will never come to an end, and it will never be worn out by the repeated readings and reflections on it" [reported by al-Hakim].

Notes

(1) Toynbee, Arnold, *A Study of History*, one-volume edition, London: Thames and Hudson, 1979, pp. 45, 46-7, 489-490.

(2) Iqbal, Mohammad, *The Reconstruction of Religious Thought in Islam*, New Delhi: Kitab Bhaven, 1984, pp. 97, 146, 147-8, 171-3.

(3) *Ibid.*, pp. 46-7.

(4) *Ibid.*, p. 141.

(5) Khallaf, Abd al-Wahhab, *Khulasat Tarikh al-Tashri' al-Islami,* Kuwait: Dar al-Qalam, 1986, pp. 24-9; *'Ilm 'Usul al-Fiqh,* Kuwait; Dar al-Qalam, 1978, pp. 32-6.

(6) Khallaf, *'Ilm 'Usul al-Fiqh,* pp. 43-44; see also al-Qarafi, Ahmad ibn Idris, *al-Ihkam fi Tamyiz al-Fatawa 'an al-Ahkam*, ed. Abu Ghudda, Abd al-Fattah, Aleppo, Syria: Maktab al-Matbu'at al-Islamiyya, 1967, esp. pp. 86-109.

(7) Ibn Qayyim al-Jawziyya, Muhammad ibn Abi Bakr, *I'lam al-Muwaqqi'in,* Cairo: Idara al-Tiba'a al-Muniriyya, n.d., vol. 1, pp. 175-6. Some criticism was raised that the direct transmitters from Mu'adh were unidentified "Companions" by him, but the prominent jurist Ibn al-Qayyim convincingly refuted that criticism.

(8)   Shalabi, Muhammad Mustafa, *Ta'lil al-Ahkam,* Cairo: Matba'a al-Azhar, 1943, pp. 35-66, 72-90, esp. pp. 35-8, 43-4, 49-59, 64, 78.

(9)   *Ibid.,* pp. 71, 93.

(10)   Taj, Abd al-Rahman, *al-Siyasa al-Shar'iyya wa al-Fiqh al-Islami,* Cairo: Matba'a Dar al-Ta'lif, 1953, pp. 55-7, 59.

(11)   Ibn Qayyim al-Jawziyya, *I'lam al-Muwaqqi'in,* vol. 4, pp. 309-313; cf. *al-Turuq al-Hukmiyya* by the same author.

(12)   Taj, *al-Siyasa al-Shar'iyya wa al-Fiqh al-Islami,* pp. 100, 103, 120-1, 126, 129-130.

(13)   A prophet's tradition quoted by Ibn Kathir, *Tafsir,* commentary on the Quran verse 5:101, vol. 2, p. 109, and graded as authentic.

(14)   Khallaf, *Khulasa Tarikh al-Tashri' al-Islami,* pp. 18-23. More Quranic verses about general principles for worldly affairs are mentioned within this "Afterword."

(15)   Taj, *al-Siyasa al-Shar'iyya wa al-Fiqh al-Islami,* p. 60.

(16)   See for example: von Grunebaum, Gustave ed. *Unity and Variety in Muslim Civilization.*